The System 7 Book

"I could give you 7 reasons to buy this book,
but one will do—it will help you
get the most out of System 7."

Steve Goldberg
Product Manager, System 7
Apple Computer, Inc.

The System 7 Book

Getting the most from your new macintosh operating system

By Craig Danuloff

VENTANA
PRESS

The System 7 Book

Library of Congress Cataloging-in-Publication Data

Danuloff, Craig

    The System 7 book : getting the most from your new Macintosh operating system / Craig Danuloff — 1st ed..
             p.   cm.
    Includes bibliographical references and index.
    ISBN 0-940087-58-8 : $22.95
    1. Operating systems (Computers).   2. System 7.   3. Macintosh (Computer)—Programming. I. Title.
    QA76.76.063D348 1991
    005.4'469—dc20   91-13837
                                             CIP

Book design: Craig Danuloff
Typography: Olav Martin Kvern, from an unoriginal idea by Craig Danuloff
Cover design: Nancy Frame, Durham, NC
Cover illustration: Katherine Mahoney, Belmont, MA
Editor: Marion Laird
Editorial staff: Jeff Qualls, Pam Richardson
Production staff: Rhonda Angel, Karen Wysocki
Production and illustrations: Craig Danuloff and Loren Imes
Technical reviewers: Joel E. Battiste, J. Christian Russ, Jon K. Ward, Microcom, Inc., Durham, NC (Developers of Virex software); Chris Potter, Southern Media Design and Production, Chapel Hill, NC

First Edition, Sixth Printing
Printed in the United States of America

Ventana Press, Inc., P.O. Box 2468, Chapel Hill, NC 27515
919/942-0220   FAX 919/942-1140

Dedication

Charles and Lillian Danuloff

Louis and Lillian Reisman

Acknowledgments

This book has been in development since the System 7 announcement
in May, 1989. At that time, it wasn't easy to convince anyone that a
book about Macintosh System Software would be necessary. The
earliest believers were Bill Gladstone at Waterside Productions,
and Joe Woodman at Ventana Press.

Everyone at Ventana Press made the writing and production
of this book a pleasure. Many thanks to all of them for their
enthusiasm, professionalism, and total lack of corporate bureaucracy.
Definitely a "Macintosh Way" company, even if this is their first Mac book.

At Apple Computer, thanks go to Steve Goldberg and Martha Steffen,
plus Jim Stoneham, Ken Feehan, and Dan Torres.

And finally, this may be System 7, but it's number 20 for the
gentlemen of PRI, Inc.: R.D., J.G., S.R., J.G., A.E., and D.M.

Colophon

This book was created in various pre-release versions of System 7. It was written in Microsoft Word 3.0, and produced in Aldus PageMaker 4.01. Screen shots were taken with Capture and Image Grabber, and edited using DeskPaint. Adobe PhotoShop and Aldus FreeHand were also used for illustration.

Type is set in ITC Garamond Condensed from Adobe Systems Inc.

Trademarks

Other Books by Craig Danuloff

Encyclopedia Macintosh☆

Encyclopedia Macintosh Instant Software Reference☆

Up & Running with PageMaker on the Macintosh

The PageMaker Companion☆

Mastering Aldus FreeHand☆

Expert Advisor: Harvard Graphics

Desktop Publishing Type & Graphics☆

☆Co-Author Deke McClelland

Table of Contents

Chapter 1: System Software Basics   *1*

Chapter 2: Finder 7   *27*

Chapter 3: Managing Your Hard Drive 79

Chapter 4: The System Folder 121

Chapter 5: System 7 and Your Software 145

Chapter 6: Working With Multiple Applications 175

Chapter 9: Introduction to File Sharing 263

Chapter 10: Working on a Network 307

Chapter 11: Memory Management   *325*

Appendix A: Installing System 7   *349*

Foreword

Welcome to System 7! After almost two years of rumors and speculation, this major Macintosh operating system upgrade has finally arrived. Although the development of Apple's System Software 7 has not been a well-kept secret, specific details about its features have been scarce. And we could only guess how System 7 would affect the way we use the Macintosh.

As you'll discover, the excitement surrounding this new release is more than justified. System 7 improves and expands existing Macintosh features and introduces powerful new capabilities that exceed even the most optimistic expectations.

In this book, you'll learn how to use all these features and how they can help you save time and effort by making your hardware and software work more efficiently.

Who Should Read This Book?

Quite simply, everyone who uses a Macintosh. This may sound like a hopeful author's delusions of grandeur, but it's probably true. System 7 is the future of the Macintosh, and whether you intend to take advantage of it right away or wait a few months before installing it on your Mac, eventually every Macintosh user will learn to use System 7.

System 7 is compatible with all Macintosh models; it will quickly become the standard Macintosh operating environment. New Macintosh software and all upgrades of existing software will be designed for System 7 compatibility. Apple will pre-install System 7 on the hard drives of all new Macintoshes. Some current users may wait for the dust to settle, just to be sure everything works as advertised, but ultimately every Macintosh will be running System 7.

This book was written with three types of users in mind:

- Those who have not yet upgraded to System 7.

- Those who have recently upgraded to System 7.

- Those who are new to Macintosh and are learning System 7 as their first Macintosh operating system.

Regardless of which category you fit into, *The System 7 Book* will tell you what you need to know in order to take advantage of System 7's features.

If you're a Macintosh user who has not yet upgraded to System 7, this book will

- Explain all the new System 7 features, in a way you can understand even without hands-on System 7 experience.

- Give you a clear picture of System 7's benefits. And you'll also look at a few drawbacks. You'll be able to make an informed decision about whether you should upgrade now.

- Clarify System 7's hardware requirements. A few System 7 features are supported only by specific Macintosh hardware configurations. I'll identify those that may require you to upgrade your hardware.

- Wait patiently on your bookshelf for the day you do upgrade. At that time, *The System 7 Book* will provide all the details you need in order to quickly set up and operate your Mac using System 7.

If you've recently upgraded to System 7, or are a new Macintosh user getting started with System 7, this book will

- Describe each new feature in System 7, so you won't have to play the trial-and-error guessing game in order to fully understand the System Software upgrade.

- Provide specific tips on using System 7. We'll go beyond the basics and look at ways you can take advantage of the new System 7 abilities to improve your productivity and enhance your computing power.

- Explain ways that System 7 will alter the way you use the Mac. There are a number of areas where System 7's new abilities will alter the way you do things. To help you make the most of these changes, I'll give you real-world situations that show the results of these features in your work.

What's New in System 7?

Any great product improvement keeps the existing product's solid familiar features, adds exciting new breakthrough features and throws in subtle enhancements for good measure. System 7 is no exception. As a result, booting up with System 7 will give even the most sophisticated Macintosh user a renewed sense of power and possibility.

Broadly speaking, the new System 7 features fall into three categories:

- **Enhanced ease-of-use.** The basic metaphors that make the Mac so friendly, such as point-and-click operation of mouse and icons, have been extended, so that even more complex tasks—such as moving fonts and changing control panels— are now more intuitive. The result is a Macintosh environment that everyone will find easier to use and customize.

- **Support for recent hardware advances.** Almost every aspect of Macintosh hardware and peripherals has evolved and improved by several orders of magnitude since the January 1984 introduction of the 128K Macintosh; but until now, the System Software has never received the overhaul it needed to fully support this equipment. System 7 is a completely new System Software, designed for the technology of the Nineties.

- **Inter-application communication**. The Macintosh has always allowed data to be shared between separate software applications, using the Clipboard or the Scrapbook. In System 7, the interaction between applications moves forward several light years, not only improving data-sharing between programs, but also making it possible for applications to communicate with and control one another.

It would take a whole book to describe everything new in System 7 (hey, there's an idea), but just to whet your appetite, here's a brief listing of specific new ways System 7 improves the Macintosh:

- Allows file sharing between AppleTalk-connected Macs.

- Displays hierarchical outline-format views of nested files and folders.

- Eliminates the Control Panel.

- Eliminates the Font/DA Mover.

- Enhances MultiFinder and Background Printing functions.

- Expands application launching options.

- Expands file-finding capabilities.

- Improves font display and typographic support with TrueType.

- Introduces the ability to store files in more than one place.

- Introduces live copy-and-paste of data between applications.

- Provides additional file information in Finder windows.

- Supports full-color icons.

- Supports virtual memory for increased RAM availability.

System 7 continues in the Macintosh tradition of providing intuitive features. But despite the range and depth of these improvements, a deliberate effort has been made to retain the Macintosh spirit, in commands and design elements. You may not even notice the improvements when you first use System 7—everything seems like the familiar Macintosh environment you're used to. But closer inspection will show you signs of change almost everywhere. This is not your father's System Software!

Other Things You Should Know

With the exception of *Chapter 1, System Software Basics*, this book primarily focuses on the new System 7 features. If you've been using a Macintosh running System Software 5.0 or later, you're ready to begin.

If you're completely new to the Macintosh, be sure to read Chapter 1 carefully; the basic information presented there will help you understand System 7-specific issues introduced in later chapters. You could also consult other resources focused more on introductory topics, including the reference manuals that came with your Macintosh and *The Little Mac Book*, by Robin Williams (published by Peachpit Press).

There are many other sources of Macintosh information you may want to use as well:

- **Other books.** For the widest possible range of Mac tips, tricks and information for intermediate to advanced users, *Encyclopedia Macintosh*, by Craig Danuloff and Deke McClelland (published by Sybex), is selfishly recommended.

- **Magazines**. Popular informative periodicals, such as *MacWorld, MacUser* and *MacWEEK*, provide the latest news on Macintosh hardware and software, including issues that relate to using System 7 on your Mac.

- **User groups**. It's a great idea to visit your local Macintosh user group. User groups provide local support on virtually every Macintosh topic. The introduction of System 7 will undoubtedly be the topic of many user group meetings. You can find a group near you by calling the Apple User Group Connection at 800-538-9696, extension 500.

- **Bulletin board systems**. If you have a modem, check out the many Macintosh-related areas on the CompuServe Information Service. CompuServe provides you and your Mac direct access to thousands of other Mac users and to many software and hardware developers. Spending a little time on-line is often the best way to get a Macintosh-related question answered; you can also browse through detailed information on almost any Macintosh topic and even download useful software utilities or upgrades.

What's Inside?

The System 7 Book is made up of 11 chapters, one appendix, plus the usual glossary and index.

Chapter 1: System Software Basics

In order to provide a context for discussing System 7's enhancements and additions, Chapter 1 summarizes System Software's basic concepts, and the ways they function on the Macintosh. This information can be used as a review for those who need it and an introduction for first-time Macintosh users.

Chapter 2: Finder 7

The Finder gives you tools for organizing and manipulating your disks and files. System 7's Finder greatly expands these capabilities with new menu commands, more ways to view and manipulate files in Finder windows, additional on-screen help, improved Get Info dialog boxes and more.

Chapter 3: Managing Your Hard Drive

Several new System 7 features can help you organize your hard drive more efficiently and access your stored data quicker and more conveniently. These features include "aliases," the new Find command, the Label Menu and improved support for comments. This chapter shows you how all these features help you control your hard drive and other storage media.

Chapter 4: The System Folder

The System folder remains a unique and important part of your Macintosh in System 7, but many changes have been made to the way you use the System folder and its files. You'll learn about the new System folder organization and many of the files and folders found there. You'll also learn how to modify and customize the System file.

Chapter 5: System 7 and Your Software

The introduction of System 7 will have a direct impact on every software application you use on your Macintosh; this chapter shows you how and why. First, the important issue of System 7 compatibility and the requirements for the new "System 7-Friendly" status are discussed. Then we look at some new features System 7 provides to all applications, including ways to launch applications, using Stationery Pads, the Desktop level and the new status of desk accessories.

Chapter 6: Working With Multiple Applications

System 7 allows you to open and use as many different programs as your Macintosh's available memory can accommodate. This chapter introduces the concepts and capabilities of multitasking, providing examples of how multitasking helps you work more efficiently. Included are discussions of the background, the Hiding commands and the memory implications of using multiple applications.

Chapter 7: The Edition Manager and IAC

The Edition Manager and Inter-Application Communication (IAC) are two brand-new System 7 features that make a significant contribution to data-sharing between applications. The Edition Manager provides the much-talked-about "live copy and paste" that makes it possible to share data between applications and update that shared data at any time. Inter-Application Communication provides a framework that software developers will use to facilitate automatic data-sharing and communication between programs.

Chapter 8: Fonts in System 7

One of the most eagerly awaited System 7 additions is Apple's collection of TrueType fonts, developed with outline font technology. The new TrueType fonts supplement the Mac's existing bit-mapped fonts and compete favorably with PostScript fonts. This chapter provides a detailed look at these font technologies, and the effects of these font types on the documents you create and print on your Macintosh.

Chapter 9: Introduction to File Sharing

When you're running System 7, you can share any folder or volume from your hard drive with any other computer on your Macintosh network. This chapter looks at the many advantages of the File Sharing feature, including granting others access to your shared files, controlling access privileges to those files and folders and monitoring the use of your shared data by other network users.

Chapter 10: Working on a Network

This chapter looks at the other side of the File Sharing coin—ways you can access data from other Macintoshes on your network. Included is information on using AppleShare file servers and logging onto your own Mac hard drive from another network computer. The IAC feature of Program Linking is reviewed, and issues involved in working on a network that includes Macintoshes still using System Software 6.0x are also covered.

Chapter 11: Memory Management

Additional System Software features, together with today's more sophisticated Macintosh hardware and software, put more demands than ever
on your Macintosh's memory. This chapter documents two new System
7 features that expand the amount of memory you can make available
to your Mac, and focuses on overall concepts of memory management
that relate to System 7's built-in multitasking.

Appendix: Installing System 7

Unless you were fortunate enough to have Apple or your computer
dealer install System 7 on your hard drive, the first thing you must do
to get running is use the System 7 Installer. This chapter explains how
to use Apple's Compatibility Checker utility, and helps you understand
the options and intricacies of the System 7 Installer. Also included is
information on using the installer on an AppleTalk network to install
System 7 from a remote Macintosh.

Updates: *The System 7 News*

System 7 is the last word in Macintosh System Software—for now. And
The System 7 Book is the last word in System 7 information—for now.

In the coming months, Apple may introduce updates to System 7, and
new information and tips about using System 7 will be discovered as
users accumulate more experience. To keep you informed of these
developments, your purchase of *The System 7 Book* includes a two-
copy subscription to *The System 7 News*, a newsletter that will provide
up-to-date information about the features and use of System 7.

To get your copies of *The System 7 News,* all you have to do is return the Registration Card you'll find in the back of this book. The first copy of *The System 7 News* is scheduled for release in the fourth quarter of 1991, to be followed by semi-annual updates.

Comments, Ideas, Suggestions?

We would like to hear what you think of *The System 7 Book*, and what you think of System 7 in general. Are there any aspects of System 7 you wish were covered more completely? Do you think our explanations and examples are clear? Did you find a typo? Please let us know!

Also, we'd love to hear any tips on additional ways to use specific System 7 features that you've discovered. We'll pass them on to our other readers in *The System 7 News*. And any questions you have about System 7 features are always welcome; we'll also try to address them in *The System 7 News*.

You can send us your messages electronically or by letter at the addresses below. Thanks in advance for your comments and assistance.

Craig Danuloff
CompuServe: 76566,1722
AppleLink: PubRes
Fax: (206)524-4935

Ventana Press
P.O. Box 2468
Chapel Hill, NC 27515
(919)942-0220
Fax: (919) 942-1140

Chapter 1: System Software Basics

There are some things about the Macintosh that almost everyone knows: it has a friendly graphical user interface; all its software applications use similar menus and commands; and its hardware and peripherals are easy to configure and use. What some people may not know is that all these helpful features are provided by the basic software that operates the Mac—*System Software*.

Many Macintosh users, even those who've been using the Mac for a long time, have never given much thought to the System Software or understood its role in the Mac's operation. But System 7 has focused a lot of attention on the System Software. To help you better understand the features of System 7, this chapter begins by introducing and defining Macintosh System Software functions.

We'll also take a quick tour of the basics of using a Macintosh and the more common commands and features the System Software provides. This introduction is designed for those who're using a Macintosh for the first time, and people who'd like a little review before jumping into System 7 features.

If you're comfortable using your Macintosh, you can skip the "Basic Macintosh Operations" section of this chapter and jump ahead to *Chapter 2, Finder 7*, after reading the System Software introduction.

What Is System Software?

In order to start and use your Mac, a System folder containing the System file, Finder and several other files must be present on your startup disk. Other specific files are required in order to print (LaserWriter or ImageWriter drivers), set control panel options (General, Mouse, Monitors, etc.), use fonts (screen fonts, printer fonts) and perform other basic tasks.

Collectively, this group of required files is known as the *Macintosh System Software*. Together with some additional software that exists on the Macintosh ROM chips (which are inside every Macintosh), the System Software serves as the Macintosh operating system, providing a link between your hardware, your software and you. (For the purposes of this discussion, we'll use the terms System Software and operating system synonymously.)

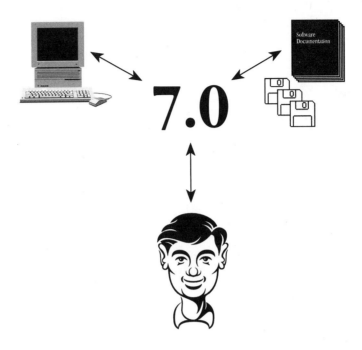

*Figure 1.1: System Software provides the link between you,
your Macintosh and your software.*

System Software performs three main tasks: it controls your Macintosh
hardware and peripherals, it provides common elements and features
to your software applications, and it lets you manage your disks and
files.

- **Hardware control**. The operation of each component of your
  Macintosh hardware, including RAM memory, disk drives,
  video monitors, keyboards, the mouse and printer and scan-
  ner peripherals, is controlled by software applications via the
  System Software. This includes saving files on disk, drawing
  images on the screen and printing.

- **Common software elements**. Every Macintosh software application has common elements: menus, dialog boxes, support for fonts, etc. These common elements are delivered to software applications from a "software toolbox" in the System Software. By centrally providing these elements, consistency among applications is assured, and software developers are spared the difficult task of programming these elements.

- **Disk and file management**. The Finder, which is a part of the System Software, provides the ability to format disks, copy, move, rename and delete files, and display icon and text-based information about disks and files. The Finder also allows you to launch other software applications. How useful would the Macintosh be if you couldn't arrange files on disks and other storage devices?

Without System Software, each application would have to provide its own self-contained operating features for running the hardware and managing your disks and files. There would be no continuity from one application to the next, and software programs would be far more complex, as well as time-consuming and costly to develop.

Fortunately, Apple's System Software performs all these tasks well, allowing application developers to focus on unique and sophisticated programs, and leaving the rest to Apple.

Parts of the System Software

The most prominent files that make up the Macintosh System Software are the System file and the Finder, but printer and network drivers, control panel devices, extensions and resources (fonts, DA's, sounds, Fkeys) are also part of the System Software. The list below summarizes the functions of these components:

- **System file**. The System file is involved in the most important and most frequently used aspects of the System Software. It also acts as a framework that other parts of the System Software can connect to. The System file helps the Mac start up, and provides many of the dialog boxes and menu bars, commonly used icons and code that help applications manage memory and other hardware resources.

- **Finder**. The Finder is a program designed to help you control your disks, drives and files. It provides many utility features such as formatting disks, printing disk catalogs and deleting files; it's also a "home base" to launch other application programs from.

- **ROM**. Portions of the Macintosh operating system are stored in Read-Only Memory (ROM) chips on the computer's logic board. These are not considered part of the System Software, but they're vital to its operation. ROM-based software handles initial computer startup and many basic aspects of Macintosh hardware control.

- **Printer drivers**. Printer drivers are small conversion programs that change data from its original format into a format the printer can digest and output. Printer drivers are selected in the Chooser and "run" with the PRINT command.

Apple provides printer drivers for most Macintosh printers and output devices, but other vendors offer printer drivers that allow the Macintosh to be used with output devices that Apple drivers don't support.

■ **Network drivers**. Network drivers are also accessed using the Chooser control panel. They help your Macintosh communicate with network file servers, print service, remote modems and other network devices. Apple provides network drivers for AppleTalk, Ethernet and Token Ring network communications. Many other network drivers are provided along with third-party Macintosh network hardware.

■ **Extensions (inits)**. Because Macintosh System Software is modular, it can be enhanced, modified or extended by small files that temporarily become part of the System Software when loaded at startup. These files are called extensions. (They were called inits in previous versions of the System Software.)

Several extensions are provided with the System Software, but most are created independently by third parties. Most extensions add some new feature or capabilities to the System Software. Examples include SuperClock!, which displays the current time on your menu bar; Disk Doubler, which lets you compress your files in order to save hard drive space; and Suitcase II, which makes using fonts, sounds and Fkeys more convenient.

■ **Resources**. Resources files also add capabilities to the Macintosh. Resources, including fonts and sounds, can exist as stand-alone files, or can be placed into the System file itself.

■ **Control panels**. These are mini-applications that provide preference or general control over some aspect of the System Software, an extension utility or a hardware peripheral. Control panels, provided along with the System Software, control your Mac's memory, its internal clock, colors, File Sharing and many other system attributes.

■ **Desk accessories**. These are also independent files, and in System 7 they operate just like normal applications. (In previous versions of the System Software, DA's were special files accessed only from the Apple Menu.) Desk accessories provide utility functions not built into the System Software. DA's provided as part of the System Software include the Chooser, Alarm clock, Calculator and Key Caps.

Using System Software

System Software is used almost constantly from the moment you turn your Macintosh on. To fully understand its important role, lets take a look at a few of the tasks it controls or assists:

■ **Startup**. From just a moment after the power is turned on, your Macintosh's System Software controls the startup process, running any available inits, verifying that your hardware is functioning properly and loading the Finder.

■ **File management**. When you work on the Finder desktop, manipulating windows and icons, your actions are translated from the on-screen graphic display into actual changes to the files on disk. But files aren't stored on disk as cute little icons; they're simply strings of magnetic 1's and 0's. It's the System Software that turns them into meaningful text and graphics.

- **Application launching**. When you run a software program, the System Software starts up the computer and sees to it that the correct portions of the file are read from disk, that the available memory is properly managed and allocated and that data files (and sometimes temporary work files) are created and maintained on disk.

- **Font usage**. Every time a font is used on the Macintosh, whether it's a bit-mapped, PostScript or TrueType font, character information, including the way it should look in any particular size and style, is provided by the System Software.

- **Dialog boxes**. System Software provides the basic format of almost every dialog box used on the Macintosh. For Open and Save As dialogs, the scrolling file listing and support for reading files from disk or writing them to disk are also provided.

- **Printing**. An application must pass its data through one of the System Software's printer drivers so it can be converted into a format the printer can understand. After this, the System Software communicates the file to the printer, and in some cases receives feedback from the printer during output.

- **Screen display**. System Software is responsible for producing the display that appears on your Macintosh screen. Applications communicate the display information to the System Software in a format called QuickDraw; then the ROM-based portions of the System Software convert this information and use it to draw the screen.

- **Networking.** Nearly every aspect of communication between computers and sharing peripheral devices is controlled by the System Software. This includes data transfer from the disk to the AppleTalk port; cabling, the timing of operating network communications while other software is being run on-screen; and two-way communications with sophisticated printers, modems and storage drives.

So as you can see, almost any task you perform on your Macintosh—from the smallest mouse click to the largest data transfer—relies on the System Software. Fortunately, you don't need to understand the technical intricacies of how System Software does its tasks in order to use your Macintosh. But it is useful to have an appreciation for the range and depth of the System Software's functions.

Basic Macintosh Operations

From the technical descriptions of the System Software provided above, we'll now turn to the easiest and most fundamental aspects of using the Macintosh. This section looks at the things you do need to know in order to use the Macintosh efficiently. It also defines terms you'll encounter throughout the book.

This information is intended primarily for those who are using System 7 in their first experience on the Macintosh. If you've been working with the Macintosh under System Software 6.0x, you'll probably want to skip this section and move ahead to *Chapter 2, Finder 7*.

The Graphical User Interface

The first and most fundamental requirement for using the Mac is understanding its graphical user interface. Instead of communicating your commands in words, you select pictures, or icons, that represent words. These icons, along with windows and menus, represent Macintosh hardware and software functions and features. And you use the mouse cursor to communicate with the Macintosh. (Yes, you'll use the keyboard too, but we'll assume you've already mastered that device.)

Let's look at each of these elements individually:

- **Icons**. These are small graphics (drawings) of things that appear on the Macintosh screen and represent items such as disks and folders (the icon actually looks like a disk or folder, as shown in Figure 1.2).

Figure 1.2: Disk and folder icons.

Various versions of icons are used to represent files stored on your disks. The particular version of file icon tells you what kind of file it is. The standard application file icon and the standard document file icon are shown in Figure 1.3. But many application and document files use custom icons. A collection of custom application and document file icons appears in Figure 1.4.

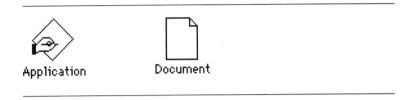

Figure 1.3: Standard application and document file icons.

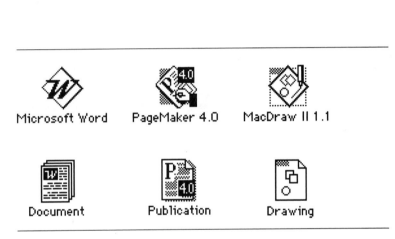

Figure 1.4: Custom application and document file icons.

- **Windows**. When a Macintosh file is opened, its contents are displayed in a window. The most common type of window looks like the one shown in Figure 1.5: it includes a *title bar* at the top and scroll bars on its right and bottom edges. You can move a window around (by dragging its title bar), close a window (by clicking the close box in its upper left corner), and change the size of a window (by dragging the size box in its lower right corner).

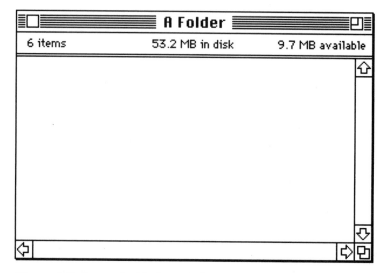

Figure 1.5: A sample Finder window.

However, there are other types of windows, including *dialog boxes*. A sample dialog box is shown in Figure 1.6. These small specialized windows usually present a set of options that allow you to customize a command or activity.

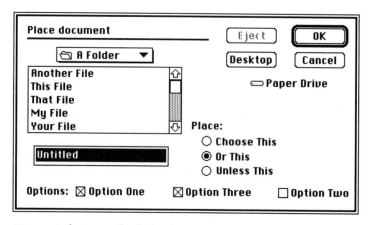

Figure 1.6: A sample dialog box.

There are four common kinds of dialog box options. Small round buttons, known as *radio buttons*, present a set of mutually exclusive choices. Small square buttons, known as *check boxes*, present a set of choices you can select in any combination. An *option box* is a small area where you type in your choice. Some options provide a set of alternatives in a *pop-up menu*; you can click on the one you want with the mouse.

Some dialog boxes don't present options but simply provide information. Usually this information is feedback concerning a command or action you're engaged in, or a message from one of your hardware devices. These are called Alert dialogs; a sample is displayed in Figure 1.7.

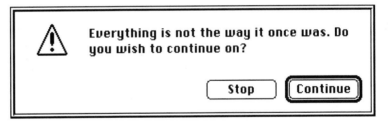

Figure 1.7: An Alert dialog box.

Another type of window, used in some software applications, is called a palette. A palette is a small "floating" window, so called because you can move it around easily. A palette presents a set of icons that represent tools you can work with; or sometimes they present a text list of commands or options you can choose from.

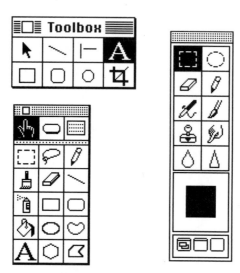

Figure 1.8: Sample palettes.

- **Menus**. Most commands in Macintosh applications are presented in menus displayed along the menu bar at the top of the screen. Commands are usually grouped logically, with logical names that provide clues about what they're used for.

  Menus drop down when the mouse is clicked on the menu name; they remain visible for as long as the mouse button is pressed. As you drag the mouse down, each command highlights as it's selected. Releasing the mouse while the command is selected executes that command. (More about using the mouse in the next section of this chapter.)

  There are four basic types of menu commands. Some commands execute as soon as they're selected. Others toggle the status of some features, such as the display of rulers, on and off. Command names that end with an ellipsis (...) bring up a dialog box of related options.

And the fourth type presents a hierarchical display of
subcommands. Holding the mouse button down lets you select
one of these normal, toggling or ellipsis subcommands.
Examples of all four command types are shown in Figure 1.9.

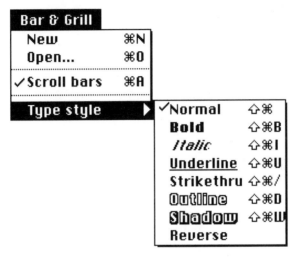

Figure 1.9: Four command types.

All these graphic elements interact with your Macintosh via mouse
manipulation. Operating the mouse is simple enough: you move the
mouse on your desk and the mouse cursor moves on-screen. The type
of cursor that appears at any given time depends on the item being
pointed to, the software being used, the commands chosen and the
keys pressed on the keyboard. When working at the Finder desktop,
the mouse cursor will be the arrow.

Arrow cursors appear whenever you're pointing to the menu bar,
regardless of the application being used. Macintosh applications also
use the arrow cursor to select and manipulate objects. Other common
cursors are shown in Figure 1.10.

Figure 1.10: Common cursors.

There are five common actions you can make with the cursor. These actions manipulate icons, invoke Macintosh commands and control application tools:

- **Pointing.** Positioning the cursor over a particular icon or other object or window element. If the cursor is an arrow, the arrow's tip marks the specific point. Other cursors have their own "hot spots."

- **Clicking.** Quickly pressing and releasing the mouse button. In most cases, the click executes when the button is fully released, not while it's depressed. Mouse clicks select objects, including icons, buttons and dialog box options.

- **Double-clicking.** Pressing and releasing the mouse button twice in rapid succession. Most beginners don't double-click fast enough to prevent the Macintosh from interpreting them as two single clicks instead of one double-click. Double-clicking controls many Macintosh actions; one example is opening icons to display their windows.

- **Pressing.** Holding down the mouse button while a command or action is completed. For example, the mouse button must be held down for menus—they're visible on-screen only while the mouse button is down.

- **Dragging**. Moving the mouse, and therefore the cursor, while the mouse button is pressed (held down). This action usually moves an item or causes the current cursor tool to be used while the mouse button is down (such as in the case of drawing a line with a pencil tool).

Files and Folders

Once you understand icons and windows, and you're comfortable working your mouse, you're ready to put all that knowledge and skill to work. One of the most important tasks will be manipulating files at the Finder desktop.

There are many different types of files—including applications, data documents, System Software files, utilities, fonts and dictionaries. To keep all these files organized, you'll put them into *folders*. You can create new folders to hold any type of file whenever you like, using the File Menu's NEW FOLDER command. You can also create folders inside other folders, establishing a hierarchical arrangement of files and folders, as shown in Figure 1.11.

To reposition files or folders, adding them to a folder, or copying them to another disk or hard drive: point to the icon of the file or folder you want to manipulate, click and hold the mouse button, drag the file onto the destination icon and release the mouse button. If you drag files to a different folder on the same disk, the files are *moved* (they now appear only in the new location, not in the old location). If you drag files to a different disk, or to a folder on a different disk, they're *copied* (they appear in their new location and the old location).

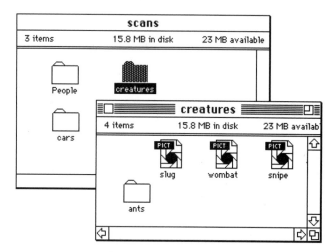

Figure 1.11: In this example, the "ants" folder is inside the "creatures" folder which is inside the "scans" folder.

Floppy Disks

Two types of floppy disk are supported by the Macintosh: 800K floppies, (sometimes known as "regular" or "double-density") and 1.44-megabyte floppies (sometimes called "High-Density.") Most Macs can use either disk type, but some (Mac Plus, Mac II and older Macintosh SE's) can use 800k disks only.

Before using a floppy disk for the first time, it must be formatted. This erases the disk and prepares it for use. (If the disk has been used before, formatting erases whatever is on it.) When you insert a new floppy disk, the Macintosh can tell that the disk has never been used, and asks you if you want to format it. You can reformat a disk at any time, deleting all its files, by inserting the disk, selecting its icon and choosing the ERASE DISK command from the Special Menu.

Macintosh Utilities

There are several utilities you use frequently when you're working on the Macintosh:

- **The Chooser.** This desk accessory is an electronic switchbox that lets you select from printers, networks, and file servers your Macintosh is connected to. The Chooser appears, as shown in Figure 1.12, when its name is chosen from the Apple Menu. On the left side of the Chooser are icons of the devices that may be available. Selecting an icon brings up a list, in the right side of the dialog box, of available devices. Selecting the name of the device you want connects your Macintosh.

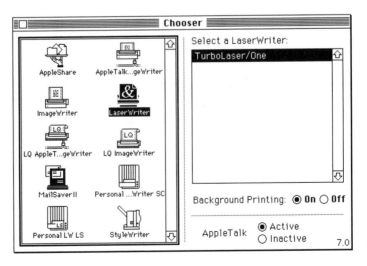

Figure 1.12: The Chooser.

■ **Control Panels.** Several of the control panels in the Control Panels folder, accessed in the Apple Menu, are used to specify basic settings and preferences for your Macintosh.

The General control panel is used to set the color and pattern that appears on the Finder desktop, as well as the date and time kept by your Macintosh. The General control panel is shown in Figure 1.13.

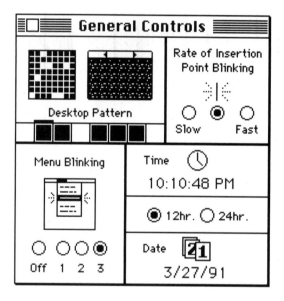

Figure 1.13: The General control panel.

The Monitors control panel is used to define your monitor's display of colors or gray values, and the relative position of each monitor, if you have more than one connected to your Macintosh. The Monitors control panel is shown in Figure 1.14.

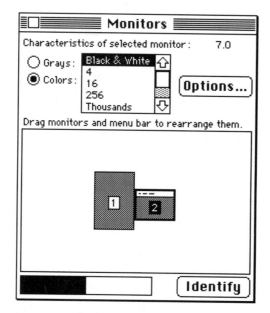

Figure 1.14: The Monitors control panel.

The Mouse control panel is used to define the speed of your
on-screen cursor relative to the speed with which you
actually move the mouse, and the amount of delay between
clicks which will be interpreted as two mouse clicks instead
of one double-click. The Mouse control panel is shown in
Figure 1.15.

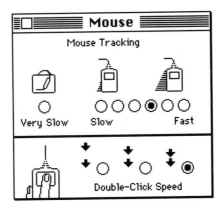

Figure 1.15: The Mouse control panel.

The Sound control panel lets you specify the volume and type of sound used as the System beep. Several sound options are provided, and many more are available from bulletin boards and user groups. The Sound control panel is shown in Figure 1.16.

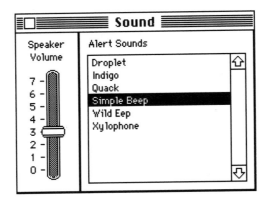

Figure 1.16: The Sound control panel.

The Clipboard and the Scrapbook

The Macintosh System Software provides a simple built-in method for transferring text and graphic elements from one location to another—the Clipboard. You can use the Clipboard to move items within a document or from one document to another—even if the documents were created by different software applications.

You never access the Clipboard directly; instead, you manipulate the contents of the Clipboard, using the Cut, Copy and Paste commands.

- The Cut command removes the objects selected from their current location, and places them on the Clipboard, replacing the previous Clipboard contents. (The Clipboard can contain only the result of the last Cut or Copy command.)

- The Copy places the selected objects on the Clipboard, but leaves them in their current location as well. The objects that are copied replace the previous contents of the Clipboard.

- The Paste command places a copy of the objects currently on the Clipboard into the current document at the cursor location. Using the Paste command does not remove items from the Clipboard; you can paste the same item repeatedly.

There are many ways to use the Clipboard. The most common is to move an element—like a paragraph or graphic item—from one place to another in the same document. To do this you select the element, choose the Cut command, position the cursor at the new location, and choose the Paste command.

The Clipboard is also frequently used to move elements between applications. For example, to move a chart from your spreadsheet into your word processor,

- Open the spreadsheet and choose the chart. Use the COPY command, since you want to leave the chart in the spreadsheet even after it has been moved to the word processor.

- Open the word processor, or switch to it if it's already open. Open the document that will receive the copied chart. You can quit the spreadsheet, but it's not necessary. (Details on opening and switching between several applications are presented in *Chapter 6, Working With Multiple Applications*.)

- Position the cursor where you want the chart placed. Choose the PASTE command.

Another related Macintosh tool is the Scrapbook, a desk accessory that can hold a catalog of text and graphic elements you use frequently or need to move from one document to another. Elements are moved into or out of the Scrapbook via the Clipboard and the CUT, COPY, and PASTE commands previously described. A Scrapbook, with a single element, is shown in Figure 1.17.

Figure 1.17: The Scrapbook.

For example, if you needed to use a set of icons throughout a maga-
zine layout you were creating, you could transfer them all into the
Scrapbook and access them from there as needed. To do this, you
would:

- Open the file containing the icons. Select one icon, and
  choose the COPY command to move it to the Clipboard.

- Open the Scrapbook, and choose the PASTE command to move
  the icon on the Clipboard into the Scrapbook. The Scrapbook
  automatically creates a new page each time you paste in a
  new element.

- Go back to the file containing the icons, select another icon,
  and again use the COPY command to move it to the Clipboard.
  Access the Scrapbook again, and paste in the new icon. Repeat
  this process until the Scrapbook contains all the needed icons.

■ Open your page layout program, and as each icon is needed, open the Scrapbook, locate the icon, and use the Copy command to transfer it from the Scrapbook onto the Clipboard. Set the cursor at the location where the icon is needed, and choose the Paste command to transfer the icon from the clipboard into your layout. Repeat this procedure until all icons are in place.

Moving On...

System Software is the core of what we think of as the Macintosh. System Software makes it possible for the computer to interact with other software programs, and these programs with help in controlling Mac hardware and peripherals. System Software standardizes the Macintosh, and allows software developers to produce high-quality applications.

Some of the features System Software provides to the user are

■ Icons, Windows and Dialog Boxes

■ Mouse controls and Menus

■ Windows and pallettes

■ The Clipboard and Scrapbook

In Chapter 2 we'll examine another important aspect of System Software, the Finder, which provides tools that help you to control the disks and files you use on the Macintosh.

Chapter 2: Finder 7

After the friendly Welcome to Macintosh dialog box, the most comforting sight to most Macintosh users is the Finder desktop. The Finder, with its familiar menu bar, disk and folder icons and Trash Can, is a haven where most Macintosh users feel safe and in control.

System 7 introduces many enhancements to the Finder although, as you'll discover, its basic nature is unchanged. This chapter starts by defining the Finder, then examines the changes and additions System 7 makes to the Finder, including menu commands, the way files are displayed and manipulated in Finder windows, Help Balloons, the Trash Can and the Get Info dialog box.

Because the Finder is such a fundamental part of the Macintosh, it affects almost every aspect of using the Mac. As a result, many Finder features introduced in this chapter are more thoroughly covered in

later chapters. For example, aliasing, the FIND command and the Label
Menu are the subjects of *Chapter 3, Managing Your Hard Drive,* and
the ABOUT THIS MACINTOSH... command is described in detail in *Chapter
11, Memory Management.*

What Is the Finder?

The Finder is an application you're not supposed to notice. It bridges
the gap between the Macintosh hardware and the user, and does so in
an elegant, intuitive and friendly way. When you're using the Finder,
you are supposed to think you're *using the Macintosh itself.*

The Finder has been largely successful in this role. In fact, many of the
most common elements people think of when considering the Macintosh are really attributes that are entirely, or at least primarily, Finder
attributes:

- Icons that represent disks, files and folders.

- Resizable windows that display disk, file or folder contents.

- The Trash Can.

- Pull-down menus and the Finder menu-bar commands.

- Direct manipulation of on-screen objects with the mouse.

But like all other software applications, the Finder does have a specific
job. Put simply, the Finder is a software application that helps you
manage the disks and files you use on your Macintosh: you use it to
copy and delete files, organize and manipulate the data on your drives

and launch software applications. Of course, the Finder also serves as a "home base," running automatically on startup and when any other application is quit.

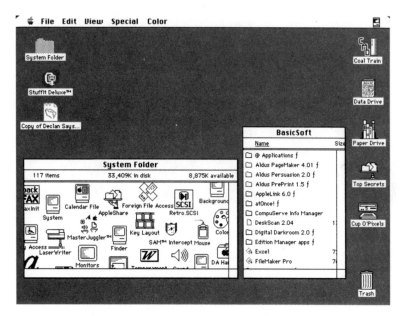

Figure 2.1: The Finder desktop in System Software 6.0.x.

New in System 7

In System 7, the Finder's disk and file management tools have been updated, enhanced and expanded, providing more information about your disks and files, more consistency in commands and features and additional customizing capabilities. Fortunately, these benefits come without a change in the Finder's familiar interface—if you're comfortable working in Finder 6.0. you'll have no problem adjusting to the new Finder and taking advantage of its expanded capabilities.

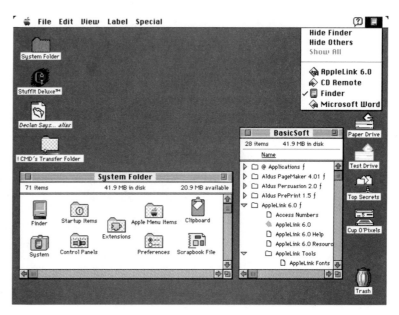

Figure 2.2: The Finder desktop in System Software 7.

New Finder Menus

A good way to become familiar with any new or upgraded application is by taking a quick tour through its menu bar and menu commands. We'll use this approach to start learning about System 7's Finder.

Figure 2.3 shows the Finder menus and commands as they appear on most Macintosh systems when System 7 is first installed. Your menus may vary slightly, depending on your hardware configuration and option settings.

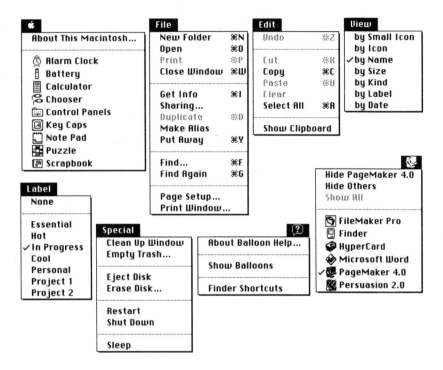

Figure 2.3: The default Finder menus in System 7.

More than half the Finder commands are unchanged in name or position from previous versions, and most work the same today as they did previously. To save space (and avoid boring you), this section discusses only commands new to Finder 7 or previous ones that have been improved or upgraded.

The new commands are listed on the following pages in the order they appear in the menus, from left to right on the menu bar.

- ABOUT THIS MACINTOSH (Apple Menu). This command now displays more information about your Macintosh, such as available memory, and open applications. (More information about this dialog box is in *Chapter 11, Memory Management*.)

- SHARING **Command** (File Menu). This command controls access privileges you grant other users on your AppleTalk network. You can allow or disallow sharing of your Macintosh files, and determine which users can read and write particular folders and volumes of shared files.

  The SHARING command does not appear unless File Sharing has been installed; it remains dimmed until File Sharing is turned on. (Complete discussion of File Sharing and other System 7 networking features is in *Chapter 9, Introduction to File Sharing*.)

- MAKE ALIAS **Command** (File Menu). MAKE ALIAS, found in the File Menu, creates a duplicate icon for a file or folder without duplicating the file or folder itself. This duplicate icon, called an alias, can be freely positioned on any volume or folder and used as if it were the original file or folder. The benefit of creating and using an alias rather than a copy is that an alias takes up no space on your hard drive, the alias remains linked to the original file and any changes made to the alias are reflected in the original and vice versa.

  The MAKE ALIAS command lets you store a file or folders in two places at once—in fact, in any number of places at once, since you can create many aliases for a single file or folder. (More about aliasing is in *Chapter 3, Managing Your Hard Drive*.)

- FIND **and** FIND AGAIN (File Menu). The FIND command, located in the File Menu, replaces the Find File desk accessory of previous System Software versions. This new FIND command can search for files by file name, size, creation date, label,

etc., and when files matching your search criteria are located,
the Finder opens the window containing the file and selects
the file's icon. Using the Find Again command, (Command-G)
you can repeat the last search, locating and displaying the
next file matching the current search criteria. (A complete
discussion of Find and Find Again commands is in *Chapter 3,
Managing Your Hard Drive*.)

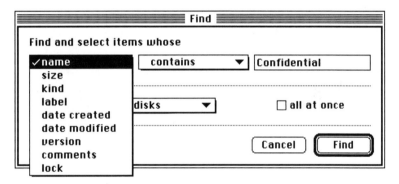

Figure 2.4: The Find items dialog box.

■ **Label Menu**. The new Label Menu is in some ways similar to
the Colors Menu used in System Software 6.0x: it allows you
to specify colors for file and folder icons. A few important
improvements have been added to this colorization process:
you can now color-code your files by specifying a classification title for each color (see Figure 2.5). In addition, color
labels are supported by the View Menu and Find command, so
you can use label categorizations as part of your hard-disk
organization and management strategy. (More on the Label
Menu is in *Chapter 3, Managing Your Hard Drive*.)

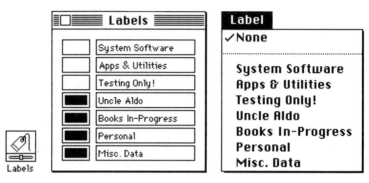

Figure 2.5: The Label control panel icon (left), Label control panel (center) and customized Label Menu (right).

- **Clean Up Command** (Special Menu). The new Clean Up command is an enhanced version of the old Clean Up command used to rearrange icons on the desktop or in Finder windows. (More information on this command is presented later in this chapter.)

- **Empty Trash Command** (Special Menu). This is an improved version of the Empty Trash command from previous versions. In Finder 7, files and folders remain in the trash until the Empty Trash command is selected; they're not deleted when applications are run, when your Macintosh is shut down or at any other time. (More information on this command is presented later in this chapter.)

- **Help Menu**. Near the right edge of the menu bar, under the question-mark icon, System 7 provides a new Help Menu, which is available at all times, not just when you're using the Finder.

The most important command in this menu is Show Balloons, which turns on context-sensitive Help Balloons that pop up as you point to menu commands, dialog box options, icons and other Macintosh screen elements. In some cases, additional commands, like Finder Shortcuts, also appear in this menu. (More on the Help Menu is presented later in this chapter.)

- **Applications Menu**. This is the last addition to the menu bar; it's located in the upper-right corner. This new feature lets System 7 open multiple applications simultaneously, so you can quickly switch from one open application to another. It's available at all times, not just when you're using the Finder.

  The name of every open application will automatically appear in this menu. To switch from one application to another, select the name you want from the Applications Menu, and that application and its windows immediately appear.

Figure 2.6: The Applications Menu.

The Applications Menu also lets you temporarily hide all
windows from the current application or all windows except
those of the current application, thus reducing the on-screen
clutter that can result from running multiple applications at
once. (See *Chapter 5, System 7 and Your Software*.)

Finder Windows

As a disk and file management tool, the Finder's menu commands
play only a small part. Most of the time, you move, copy, delete,
arrange and open files by using the mouse to directly manipulate
icons on the Finder desktop and in Finder windows. In Finder 7, your
ability to see and manipulate files and folders in these windows has
been dramatically improved.

The basic attributes of Finder windows, however, have not changed:

- Windows are created each time a volume or folder is opened.

- Each window has a title bar, zoom box and close box.

- Windows can be freely positioned by dragging their title bars.

- Windows can be resized by dragging on the resize box.

- Windows display the files and folders contained in the volume
  or folder.

- The window display is controlled via the View Menu.

Like many other aspects of System 7, the improvements to Finder windows give you more control over your environment, a more consistent user interface and a wider range of working options:

- More customization of fonts, icon size and information displayed in each Finder window.

- Keyboard commands that let you navigate windows and select files without using the mouse.

- The ability to display the contents of any folder or subfolder in hierarchical format in any window.

- Smart zooming that opens windows only enough to display their content.

- File and folder manipulation at different hierarchical levels at one time.

These and other new features and improvements to the operation of Finder windows are discussed below.

The Views Control Panel

In previous Finder versions, the presentation of text and icons in Finder windows was preset and could not be modified. Text was always listed in Geneva 9 point, and icons appeared in preset sizes in each icon view. In System 7, the new Views control panel provides a variety of options that let you control the information and the way it's displayed in Finder windows.

It should be noted here that control panels are the System 7 evolution of the cdevs (control devices) that used to appear in the System 6.0x Control Panel desk accessory. In System 7, a control panel is a small independent application launched by double-clicking on its icon, just like other applications. The only distinction between a control panel and a regular application is that the control panel is implemented in a single window and provides no menus. Control panels are stored in the Control Panels folder, which in turn is stored inside the System folder.

To access the Views control panel, you can either open the System folder and the Control Panels folder, or you can select the CONTROL PANEL command from the Apple Menu. (Although the CONTROL PANEL command initially appears in the Apple Menu, it may not appear there if your system has been customized.) Once the Control Panels folder is open, double-click on the Views icon to open the Views control panel (shown in Figure 2.7).

Changes in Finder windows register instantly as you modify the options in the Views control panel. You don't need to close the Views dialog box to see the effect of your selections. When you're satisfied, close the Views control panel by clicking the close box in the upper-left corner of its title bar.

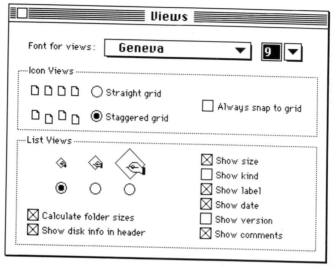

Figure 2.7: The Views control panel.

The Views control panel options are grouped in three sets. The first is
"Font for views," a typeface and type size option that control the display of text in all Finder windows. The "Font Name" pop-up menu
presents the names of all fonts installed in your System file; you may
select the ones you want for all Finder windows. Use the "Size" pop-up
menu to select the point size for the text display. If you want to use a
point size not available in the pop-up menu, type the size you want
directly into the Size option box.

A word of warning: Although it's appealing to be able to choose from
such a wide range of fonts and sizes, you may find that the default,
Geneva 9-point, provides the most legible text display. Geneva is optimized for on-screen display, and while it doesn't look very good in
print, it remains an excellent font for display purposes.

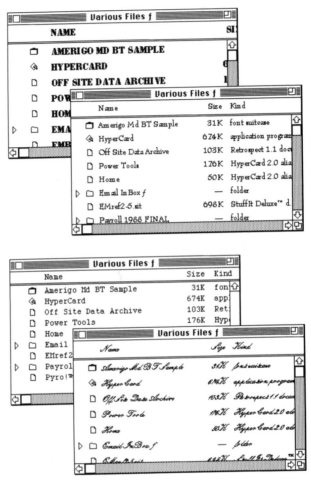

Figure 2.8: Finder windows in various fonts.

The second set of Views dialog box options are grouped in a box titled "Icon Views." These options affect the way icons are positioned while the BY ICON or BY SMALL ICON commands from the View Menu are selected. The "Straight grid" and "Staggered grid" options determine whether icons are arranged on a common or an irregular baseline. All versions before System 7 have arranged icons on a straight grid, which can sometimes force file names to overlap, leaving them illegible, as shown in Figure 2.9. The "Staggered grid" option positions icons so their names cannot overlap.

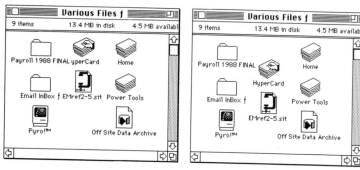

Figure 2.9: Examples of Finder windows using the "Straight grid" and "Staggered grid" options.

The "Always snap to grid" option forces any repositioned icons to automatically snap to the nearest point on an invisible grid. This is the same invisible grid used by the CLEAN UP command, and will result in either normal or staggered baseline alignment, depending on whether the "Straight grid" or the "Staggered grid" option is chosen. The concept of keeping files always grid-aligned in this way may sound appealing, but it can be disconcerting when the Finder grabs and relocates files while you're trying to position them. In most cases, it's probably better to leave this option off and use the CLEAN UP command to correct any icon alignment problems in Finder windows.

"List Views" is the final set of Views dialog box options. These options apply to the display for all windows except those using the BY ICON or BY SMALL ICON commands from the View Menu (e.g., BY NAME, BY DATE, etc.). This set of options includes three groups: one specifying icon size, one offering additional information in Finder windows and the last controlling the actual window columns and View Menu commands.

The icon display size is determined by choosing among the three different icon size radio buttons. The result of each option is shown in Figure 2.10. As with the "Font for views" option discussed earlier, icon sizes are probably best left unchanged.

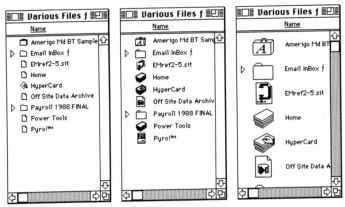

Figure 2.10: Finder windows using the small, medium and large icons corresponding to the Views control panel options.

Below the icon size radio buttons are two check-box options: "Calculate folder sizes" and "Show disk info in header." These options add additional information to that already provided in Finder windows.

- **Calculate folder sizes.** It would be difficult to determine the "one little thing" that most bothered users in previous Finder versions, but the fact that folder sizes were not displayed in Finder windows was high on many users' pet-peeves list. The "Calculate folder Sizes" option lets you add the size of a folder's contents to all text view displays.

This option, unfortunately, causes a perceptible slowdown in the display of some windows, particularly when the windows contain numerous large folders. You'll have to decide whether the slower display speed is a fair price to pay for the additional information, and turn this option off or on accordingly. When it's turned off, an alternate way to determine the size of a folder is by selecting the folder and choosing the GET INFO command.

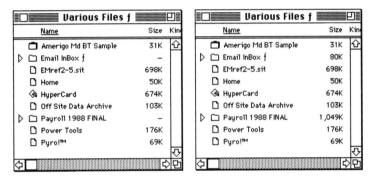

Figure 2.11: The same Finder window with and without folder sizes displayed.

- **Show disk info in header.** Selecting this option adds three pieces of information to the upper section of each window: the number of items contained, the total space consumed by files on the disk, and the amount of free space on the current volume. This helpful information fits discreetly in the window header, as shown in Figure 2.12.

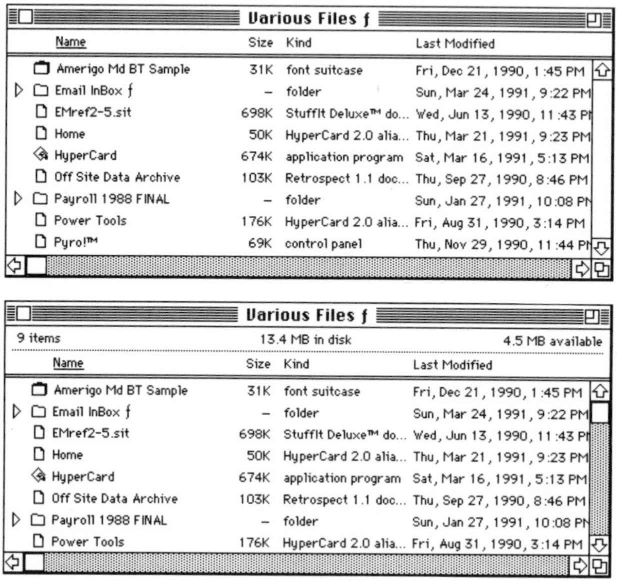

Figure 2.12: A Finder window including the information added by the "Show disk info in header" option.

The last set of options, listed on the right side of the List Views box, toggles the display of commands in the Finder's View Menu and the display of columns in Finder windows. If you deselect the "Show date" option, for example, the BY DATE command is removed from the View Menu, and the Date column is removed from all Finder windows.

These commands can customize your Finder windows to suit the way you work with files and organize your hard drive, eliminating the display of information you don't find useful and reducing the on-screen clutter of windows with too much information. For example, if you're not using the Label Menu to apply meaningful labels to your files, then the "Show Label" option should be deselected. Similarly, if you won't be entering extensive comments into the Get Info dialog boxes of your files, the "Show Comments" option can be deselected.

(The Get Info dialog box and comments are discussed more thoroughly later in this chapter.)

Figures 2.13 and 2.14 show the Finder window resulting from two different option settings.

	Name	Size	Label	Comments
	⬛ Amerigo Md BT Sample	31K	–	
▷ ☐	Email InBox ƒ	80K	Personal	Danuloff's Email Recieved Jan-Ju...
☐	EMref2-5.sit	698K	Books In-...	Encyclopedia Macintosh Quick Ref...
☐	Home	50K	Apps & U...	Craig's custom Home stack
◈	HyperCard	674K	Apps & U...	
☐	Off Site Data Archive	103K	Misc. Data	Archive file for syquest kept in s...
▷ ☐	Payroll 1988 FINAL	1,049K	Uncle Aldo	Final Payroll datasheets, with ta...
☐	Power Tools	176K	Testing O...	Came with HC 2.02
☐	Pyro!™	69K	System S...	Screen Saver utility from Steve ...

Various Files ƒ

Figure 2.13: A Finder window as it appears when the "Show kind," "Show date" and "Show version" options are deselected in the Views control panel.

	Name	Size	Kind	Last Modified
	⬛ Amerigo Md BT Sample	31K	font suitcase	Fri, Dec 21, 1990, 1:45 PM
▷ ☐	Email InBox ƒ	80K	folder	Sun, Mar 24, 1991, 9:22 PM
☐	EMref2-5.sit	698K	StuffIt Deluxe™ do...	Wed, Jun 13, 1990, 11:43 PM
☐	Home	50K	HyperCard 2.0 alia...	Thu, Mar 21, 1991, 9:23 PM
◈	HyperCard	674K	application program	Sat, Mar 16, 1991, 5:13 PM
☐	Off Site Data Archive	103K	Retrospect 1.1 doc...	Thu, Sep 27, 1990, 8:46 PM
▷ ☐	Payroll 1988 FINAL	1,049K	folder	Sun, Jan 27, 1991, 10:08 PM
☐	Power Tools	176K	HyperCard 2.0 alia...	Fri, Aug 31, 1990, 3:14 PM
☐	Pyro!™	69K	control panel	Thu, Nov 29, 1990, 11:44 PM

Various Files ƒ

Figure 2.14: A Finder window without label, version or comments.

The View Menu

The Finder 7's View Menu, like View Menus in past Finder versions, determines how information is displayed in the current active window. Previous versions of the View Menu let you display files and folders by icon, small icon, name, date, size, kind and color. In Finder 7, the View Menu provides all these view methods except for color, but adds view by label, version and comment.

Each time you apply a View Menu command to a particular window, that window's display is arranged according to the selected format (by icon, by small icon, etc.) and it retains that view format until a different View Menu command is applied to it. When a window is closed and later reopened, it always appears in the same display view as before it was closed. There's no way, unfortunately, to change the view option for all open or closed windows, since the View Menu controls each window independently.

Choosing the By Icon or By Small Icon commands cause only the file icon and file name to be displayed. The other view commands display a small icon, the file name, and additional columns of data as specified in the Views control panel described above. The particular view command that's selected determines the order in which files in the window are sorted:

- By Size. This command sorts files in descending size order. If you've selected the "Show folder sizes" option in the Views control panel, folders are also sorted in this list according to their size. Otherwise, folders are grouped alphabetically at the end of the list.

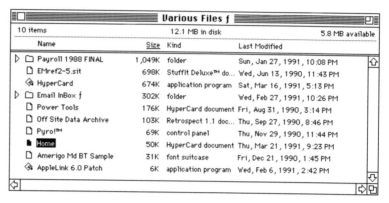

Figure 2.15: A Finder window viewed by size.

Commonly, the By SIZE command is used to find files known
to be either very large or very small, or to locate large files
that could be deleted to free up disk space.

- By KIND. This command sorts files alphabetically by a short
  description based on the file type, a four-letter code assigned
  by the developer or application creator. Document files associated with a particular application program include the name
  of their application, using "Word 4.0 document" or "Hyper-
  Card 2.0 document," for example, as the kind.

  Common file kinds include Alias, Application Program,
  Chooser Extension, Database Extension, Desk Accessory,
  Document file, Folder and System Extension. Viewing files by
  kind is useful if you know the kind of file you're looking for
  and if the window containing that file has many different files
  in it. Figure 2.16 shows a System folder using the By KIND view.

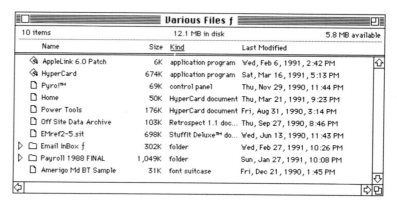

Figure 2.16: A Finder window as it appears using the View Menu's
By Kind command.

- **By Label**. This command sorts by the label name given to the
  file with the Label command. Labels, as discussed in *Chap-*
  ter 3, Managing Your Hard Drive, group files according to
  some user-defined scheme. For example, you might have a
  group of files that all relate to personal (non-business) issues,
  a group relating to one project you're working on, etc.

  In any case, this command lets you sort the files in the current window according to labels previously applied. Files are
  arranged in order as they appear in the Label Menu.
  Unlabeled files appear at the bottom of the listing.

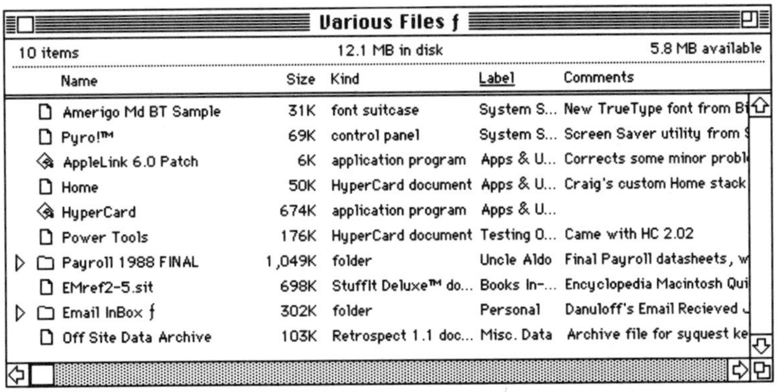

Figure 2.17: A Finder window as it appears using the View Menu's
BY LABEL command.

■ **BY DATE.** This command sorts files by the date they were
modified, with the most recently updated files at the top of the
list. This view is useful when you're looking for files that are
much older or much newer than most of the other files in a
certain folder.

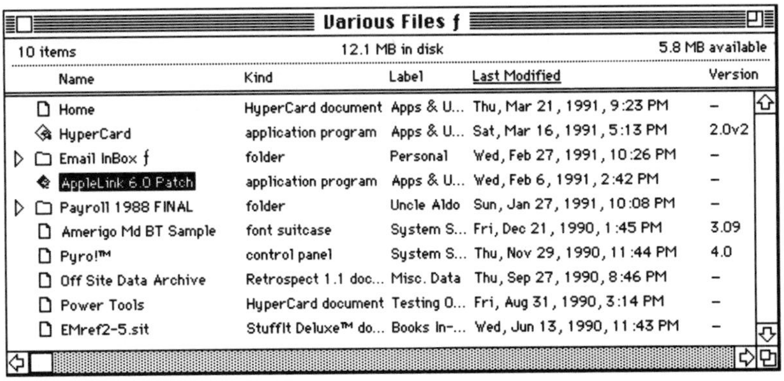

Figure 2.18: A Finder window as it appears using the View Menu's
BY DATE command.

■ **BY VERSION.** Useful only for application files, this command sorts by the software developer's assigned version number. Ancillary application files (e.g., dictionaries and references) and data files you create do not have this type of version number.

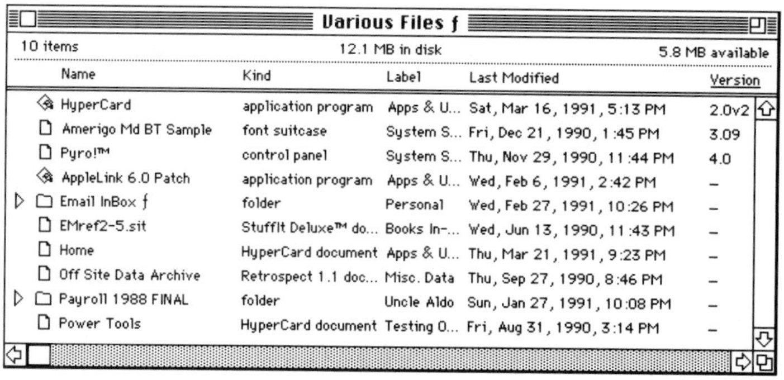

Name	Kind	Label	Last Modified	Version
⬟ HyperCard	application program	Apps & U...	Sat, Mar 16, 1991, 5:13 PM	2.0v2
▢ Amerigo Md BT Sample	font suitcase	System S...	Fri, Dec 21, 1990, 1:45 PM	3.09
▢ Pyro!™	control panel	System S...	Thu, Nov 29, 1990, 11:44 PM	4.0
⬟ AppleLink 6.0 Patch	application program	Apps & U...	Wed, Feb 6, 1991, 2:42 PM	–
▷ ▢ Email InBox ƒ	folder	Personal	Wed, Feb 27, 1991, 10:26 PM	–
▢ EMref2-5.sit	StuffIt Deluxe™ do...	Books In-...	Wed, Jun 13, 1990, 11:43 PM	–
▢ Home	HyperCard document	Apps & U...	Thu, Mar 21, 1991, 9:23 PM	–
▢ Off Site Data Archive	Retrospect 1.1 doc...	Misc. Data	Thu, Sep 27, 1990, 8:46 PM	–
▷ ▢ Payroll 1988 FINAL	folder	Uncle Aldo	Sun, Jan 27, 1991, 10:08 PM	–
▢ Power Tools	HyperCard document	Testing O...	Fri, Aug 31, 1990, 3:14 PM	–

Various Files ƒ — 10 items — 12.1 MB in disk — 5.8 MB available

Figure 2.19: A Finder window as it appears using the View Menu's BY VERSION command.

■ **BY COMMENT.** This command sorts files alphabetically by the text contained in their Get Info dialog box comment fields. Displaying comment text in Finder windows is a major new file management feature, but it's useful only if the first characters of the comment are significant, or if you just want to separate all files that have comments from those that don't. Files without comments are placed at the bottom of any windows using the View Menu's BY COMMENT command.

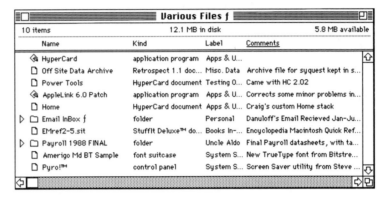

Figure 2.20: A Finder window viewed by using the By Comment command.

Hierarchical Views

This important new Finder 7 feature displays the contents of any folder without opening a new folder window. In previous versions, the only way to view and manipulate folder contents was to open the folder, thereby creating a new window. In Finder 7, you can display any folder contents by clicking on the small triangle that appears to the left of the folder icon. The contents then appear, indented slightly under the folder icon, as shown in Figure 2.21.

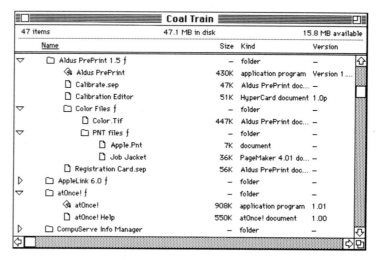

Figure: 2.21: A Finder window with hierarchical display.

This display is a hierarchical view because it allows you to see the contents of several levels of nested folders (folders inside of folders) at one time simply by clicking on the triangle next to the appropriate folder. (Alias folder icons, which you'll examine in Chapter 3, appear without a triangle and cannot be displayed hierarchically.) Figure 2.22 displays a window with the contents of several nested folders displayed.

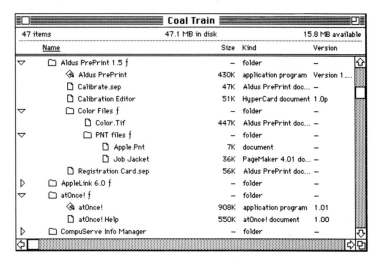

Figure 2.22: Finder window with hierarchical folders open.

You can drag hierarchically displayed files and folders from one location to another just as if they appeared in separate windows. In the example above, you could move the file "Job Jacket" to the "AppleLink 6.0 ƒ" folder by dragging its file icon into that folder. You can also drag files or folders to other volumes (copying the files); to other open Finder windows (moving the files); to the desktop; or to the Trash Can. In short, you can take advantage of the new hierarchical view to do everything you need to.

The primary benefit of hierarchical views is the elimination of desktop clutter, since there's no need to open a new Finder window for every folder you want to open. In addition, hierarchical views allow you to select and manipulate files and folders from different hierarchical levels at the same time, which was not possible in previous Finder versions because each time you clicked the mouse in a new window the selection in the previous window was released.

Figure 2.23 displays this ability, showing four different files and a folder, each on a different hierarchical level. The files and folder in this selection can now be copied, moved, trashed or manipulated just like any single file. To select files and folders at multiple levels of the hierarchy at the same time, hold down the shift key while selecting the file names.

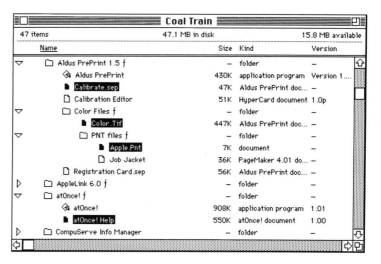

Figure 2.23: Finder window with multiple open nested folders with four files selected.

To collapse a folder's hierarchical display, click the downward pointing triangle next to the folder icon again; the enclosed files and folder listing disappear. When you close a window, the hierarchical display settings are remembered and will reappear the next time the window is opened.

Of course, you can still open a new window for any folder, rather than display its contents hierarchically. Simply double click on the folder

icon rather than on the triangle. Or select the folder icon, then the
OPEN command from the File Menu.

Navigating From the Keyboard

Even though the Macintosh relies primarily on its graphic interface
and the mouse, there are many times when you need keyboard control.
In Finder 7, a variety of keyboard shortcuts let you select files, move
between file windows and manipulate desktop icons. The keyboard
commands that follow are available in all Finder windows and on the
Finder desktop:

- **Jump to file name.** Typing the first few letters in a file name
  selects that file. For example, if you want to select a file
  named "Budget," when you type "B," the first file name
  starting with a "B" is selected. When the "u" is typed, the
  selection will be the first file name starting with "Bu," etc.
  You must not pause between letters or the Mac will interpret
  each additional letter as the first letter of a new search.

  If you don't know an exact file name, type an "A" to cause
  the display to scroll to the top of the list, an "L" to scroll to
  the middle or a "Z" to scroll to the end.

- **Select next alphabetical file name.** This is done by pressing
  the tab key. All files visible in the current window, including
  those displayed in hierarchically open folders, are included in
  this selection.

■ **Select previous alphabetical file name**. Press Shift-Tab. This is useful when you press the tab key one time too many and need to back up one step in reverse alphabetical order.

■ **Select next file**. Down, Left and Right Arrow keys select the next file or folder icon in the respective direction.

■ **Open selected file or folder**. Command-Down Arrow opens the selected file or folder, unless the selected file or folder is already open, in which case this key combination brings its window to the front.

■ **Open selected file or folder, close current window**. Press Command-Option-Down Arrow. If the selected file or folder is already open, this key combination brings its window to the front and closes the current folder or volume window.

■ **Open parent folder window**. Press Command-Up Arrow. If the selected file or folder is already open, this key combination brings its window to the front.

■ **Open parent folder window, close current window**. Pressing Command-Option-Up Arrow closes the current window.

■ **Edit file name**. Press enter or return. (File names can also be opened for editing by clicking the cursor on the text of the file name.) You can tell the name has been selected for editing when its display changes from inverted to selected and a box is drawn around the file name.

Once open for editing, the backspace key deletes characters, the Right and Left Arrow keys position the cursor. To complete the renaming, pressing enter or return again saves the file-name changes and returns the name to an inverted display.

- **Make desktop active**. Command-Shift-Up Arrow makes the current window inactive and the Finder desktop active.

The following keyboard commands are available only when working in Finder windows using text views (By NAME, By SIZE, By KIND, By VERSION, By LABEL or By COMMENT):

- **Expand hierarchical display**. Command-Right Arrow hierarchically displays the folder contents.

- **Expand all hierarchical display**. Command-Option-Right Arrow hierarchically displays the contents of the current folder and all enclosed folders.

- **Collapse hierarchical display**. Command-Left Arrow collapses the hierarchical display of the current folder.

- **Collapse all hierarchical display**. Command-Option-Left Arrow collapses the hierarchical display of the current folder and all enclosed folders.

Dragging Files Between Windows

Another Finder 7 feature lets you select and move a file from an inactive window. In previous Finder versions, as soon as an icon was selected, the window containing that icon became the active window and brought the window forward. This created a problem when that window overlapped and obscured other folder icons. In Finder 7, any visible icon in any window can be selected and dragged to a new location without the source-file window becoming active.

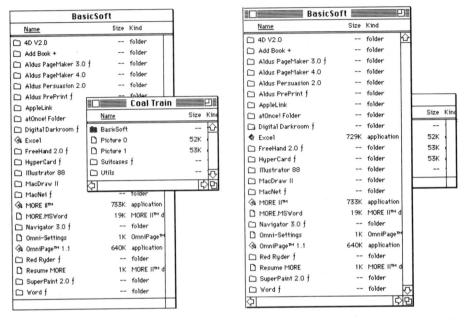

Figure 2.24: Dragging files between overlapping windows is made possible in Finder 7.

This is more clearly described by an example. Suppose we want to drag a file or folder from the "BasicSoft" window into a folder on the "Coal Train" drive. This would be impossible in previous Finder versions without repositioning the Coal Train window; as soon as the BasicSoft file was selected the BasicSoft window covered the Coal Train window, as shown at the right of Figure 2.24.

In Finder 7, however, we can simply point the mouse to the item to be moved from the BasicSoft window and hold the mouse button down while dragging the icon into the Coal Train window. As long as the mouse button is not released, the BasicSoft window won't be selected and therefore won't overlap the Coal Train window.

However, this method cannot be used to move more than one file. To move multiple files from BasicSoft to Coal Train, the Coal Train window would have to be repositioned. To move a Finder window without making it active, hold down the Command key while dragging the inactive window's title bar.

Working With Multiple Files

To perform any operation on one or more files, first select that file or group of files. Most aspects of selecting files in Finder 7 is the same as in System 6.x, but there are some changes and new features:

- **Immediate marque selection**. The marque (selection rectangle), created by clicking the mouse button and dragging with the button pressed, now selects files as soon as any part of the file name or icon is inside the selection rectangle. In previous versions, files were not selected until the mouse button was released, and only files completely contained in the selection rectangle were selected.

- **Marque selection in text views**. Previously, the marque could be used only in By Icon or By Small Icon views or on the desktop. In System 7, the selection rectangle is supported in all Finder windows; you can drag select in the By Name or By Date views, for example.

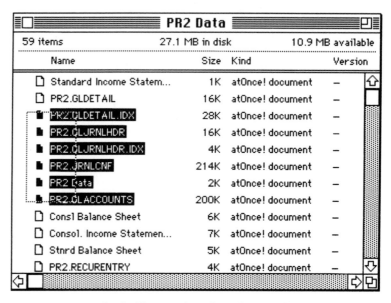

Figure 2.25: Multiple files can be selected using the marque even when files are listed by name.

- **Shift select.** Using the shift key, the marque can select discontiguous sections of any Finder window.

- **File dragging.** It's no longer possible to drag files by clicking on their names; you must specifically click on the file icon, since clicking on a file name now opens the name for editing.

- **Finder scrolling.** When dragging with a marque, the Finder window scrolls automatically as soon as the cursor hits one of its edges, as shown in Figure 2.26. This is very useful when selecting in Finder windows displaying icons.

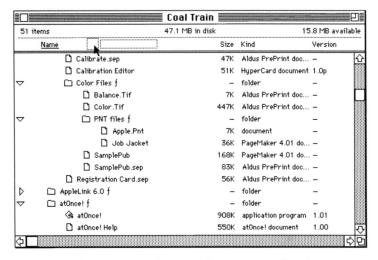

Figure 2.26: Finder windows scroll automatically when items are dragged past their edges.

Title Bar Pop-Up Menu

While hierarchical window views make it easy to move down the folder hierarchy, there's also a new way to move up the folder hierarchy—via a pop-up menu that appears in the title bar of any window when you hold down the command key and click on the folder's name.

Figure 2.27 shows the pop-up menu for a folder named "System 7 Letters ƒ", which is inside the "Technology Topics ƒ" folder, which is inside the "Email Inbox ƒ" folder, on the "Data Drive" disk. This pop-up displays the current folder's parent folder names and the volume on which the current folder is located. (In this case, since the "System 7 Letters ƒ" folder is inside the "Technology Topics ƒ," "Technology Topics ƒ" is the parent folder and "System 7 Letters ƒ" is the child.)

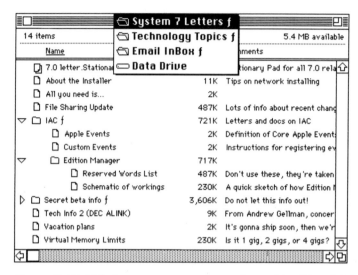

Figure 2.27: Title bar pop-up menu, and graphic of hard drive arrangement producing this menu.

Selecting a folder or volume name from this pop-up menu opens a new Finder window that displays the folder or volume contents. If a window for the selected folder or volume was already open, that window is brought forward and made active. This feature is a real time-saver when hunting files down in the Finder.

Holding down the command and option keys while selecting a folder or volume name from the Title bar pop-up menu causes the current window to be closed as the new folder or volume is opened, helping you to avoid a cluttered Finder desktop by automating the process of closing windows that aren't being used.

Holding down the option key also closes windows in several other situations:

- **Folders**. While opening a folder by double-clicking on its icon at the Finder, the current folder will close as the new one is opened.

- **Windows**. While clicking the close box in any Finder window, all Finder windows close.

- **Applications**. While launching an application, the window in which the application appears closes.

Improved Zooming

To resize an open window, you can either drag the size box in the lower-right corner or click in the zoom box in the upper-right corner of the window title bar. The zoom box operation is improved in System 7: it now expands the window size just enough to display the complete file list or all file icons; it no longer opens the window to the full size of the current monitor unless that size is necessary.

Cleaning Up Windows and Icons

The Finder's new versions of the CLEAN UP command rearrange icons in Finder windows or on the desktop to make them more orderly and visible. Finder 7 introduces several new alternative versions of this command, designed to help arrange icons in specific situations, or to create custom arrangements. The alternative versions that appear in place of the standard Clean Up command depend on the current selection and whether you're using the shift, option or command key:

- **Clean Up Desktop.** When you're working with icons on the desktop (not in a Finder window), the Clean Up command normally reads Clean Up Desktop, and will align icons to the nearest grid position.

- **Clean Up All.** Holding down the option key, however, changes the command to Clean Up All, which returns all disks, folders and volume icons to neat rows at the right edge of your primary monitor. (Again, this command is available only on the desktop, not in Finder windows.)

- **Clean Up Window.** When you're working in a Finder window, the Clean Up command is dimmed when the View command is set to anything other than By Icon or By Small Icon. When By Icon or By Small Icon is selected, the Clean Up Window command appears and arranges all icons in the current window into either aligned or staggered rows, depending on the settings in the Views control panel (discussed elsewhere in this chapter).

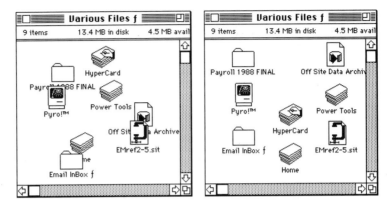

Figure 2.28: A Finder window before and after using CLEAN UP WINDOW.

■ CLEAN UP BY NAME (BY SIZE, etc.). Holding down the option key while selecting a Finder window lets you arrange icons by file name, size, date, comment, label or version. The specific option presented is the one selected in the View Menu before the BY ICON or BY SMALL ICON command was chosen.

To arrange icons by size, select the respective windows for the icons you want to affect, choose BY SIZE from the View Menu, choose BY ICON (or BY SMALL ICON) from the View Menu, then hold down the option key while choosing CLEAN UP BY SIZE.

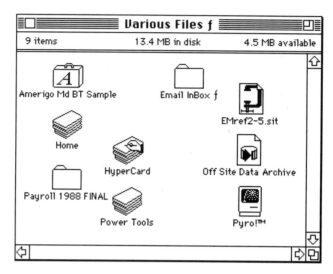

Figure 2.29: A Finder window with icons arranged alphabetically.

- CLEAN UP SELECTION. While a specific file or group of files is selected, holding down the shift key presents CLEAN UP SELECTION, which will reposition only the selected files.

The Help Menu and Help Balloons

One of the most interesting additions to System 7 is the Help Menu and Help Balloons. These give all Macintosh software applications, including the Finder, the ability to provide on-screen context-sensitive help.

Help Balloons are turned on by selecting the SHOW BALLOONS command, then positioning the arrow cursor over any menu command, window element, dialog box option or icon. A HELP BALLOON will appear with a brief description of that command, element or icon function.

Then the SHOW BALLOONS command changes to HIDE BALLOONS which turns off the Help Balloons display.

Using Help Balloons

Help Balloons make it easier to learn new applications and refresh your memory when accessing infrequently used commands or dialog box options. Their only limitation is that they can appear only in applications that have been written or upgraded specifically for System 7—so it will take some time to extend their availability.

The System 7 Finder and control panels supply extensive Help Balloons, some of which are shown in Figure 2.30.

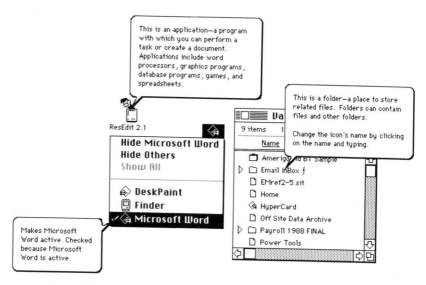

Figure 2.30: A sampling of the Finder's Help Balloons.

Additional Help

Optionally, some applications may add additional commands to the Help Menu, usually to provide access to more in-depth on-line Help systems. The Finder provides an example of this additional help with the FINDER SHORTCUTS command and dialog box. This dialog box is shown in Figure 2.31. In each application you use, check the Help Menu for additional commands and on-line Help systems.

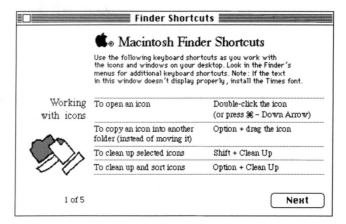

Figure 2.31: The Finder Shortcuts dialog box.

Trash Can and Empty Trash

The big news in System 7 trash is that the garbage collector no longer comes without being invited—the Trash Can is emptied only when the EMPTY TRASH command is chosen from the Special Menu. In previous versions of the System Software, the trash was automatically

emptied when any application was launched, or when the Macintosh
RESTART or SHUT DOWN commands were selected. Now items remain in
the Trash Can until EMPTY TRASH is selected, even if the Mac is shut
down.

*Figure 2.32: The Trash Can window displays files currently in
the trash.*

When the EMPTY TRASH command is accessed, a dialog box appears
asking you to confirm that you want to delete the current Trash Can
files. This dialog box appears regardless of what files the Trash Can
contains, and informs you how much disk space will be freed by
emptying the trash.

Figure 2.33: The Empty Trash? dialog box.

Trash Can Tips

While the basic use of Trash Can is straightforward, there are several less-obvious aspects you'll want to know about:

- **Avoid trash warnings.** If you hold down the option key while choosing EMPTY TRASH, the confirmation dialog box will not appear and the Trash Can will be emptied immediately.

- **Disable trash warnings.** You can also disable the warning dialog by selecting the Trash Can, choosing the GET INFO command and deselecting the "Warn before emptying" option. Of course, this will make it easier to delete application and system software files accidentally, so this option should be deselected with caution.

Figure 2.34: The Trash Can Get Info dialog box.

- **Retrieving Trashed Items.** Anytime before the EMPTY TRASH command is chosen, items inside the Trash Can may be recovered and saved from deletion. This is done by double-clicking on the Trash Can icon and dragging the file icons you want to recover out of the trash window and back onto the desktop, or onto any volume or folder icon.

■ **Freeing disk space**. Only when the trash has been emptied and this command is chosen is disk space released. In previous systems, dragging items to the Trash Can alone was sufficient to cause disk space to be freed—although not always immediately.

■ **Repositioning the Trash Can**. In System 7, you can reposition the Trash Can on your desktop and it will stay there even if you reboot. It's no longer automatically returned to the lower right desktop corner each time you reboot. This is helpful if you use a large monitor or multiple monitors.

The Get Info Dialog Box

As in previous Finder versions, selecting any file, folder or drive icon and choosing the GET INFO command from the File Menu brings up an Info dialog box (usually called a Get Info dialog box) that displays basic information and related options. The Finder 7 basic Get Info dialog box, as shown in Figure 2.35, is only slightly different from those in previous Finder versions.

Figure 2.35: The Get Info dialog box for files.

There are now five different versions of the Get Info dialog box—one each for files, folders, applications, volumes and alias icons. Options may differ among versions, but the basic information each provides is the same:

- **File name.** The exact file name that appears on the desktop, which cannot be changed from within this dialog box.

- **Icon.** This appears to the left of the file name, providing a visual reference for the file.

  Interestingly, you can customize the icon of any data file, application, or volume by pasting a new icon on top of the existing icon here in the Get Info dialog box. To change an icon, copy any MacPaint or PICT graphic onto the Clipboard, select the icon in the Get Info dialog box (a box will appear around the icon indicating its selection) and choose the PASTE command from the Edit Menu. Close the Get Info dialog box and the new icon will appear in the Finder window or on the desktop.

- **Kind**. Provides a brief description of the selected file. For data files, this usually includes the name of the application that created the file.

- **Size**. The amount of disk space that the file consumes.

- **Where**. The location of the selected file, including all folders enclosing it and the volume it's on.

- **Created**. The date and time when the file was created. This date is reset when a file is copied from one volume to another or if a new copy is created by holding down the option key while moving a file into a new folder.

- **Modified**. The date and time the contents of the file last changed.

- **Version**. Lists the software application's version number. No information on data files, folders or volumes is provided.

- **Comments**. Although it isn't obvious here, System 7 vastly improves its support for adding comments to this Get Info dialog box field. This is possible because comments can be displayed in Finder windows and you can use the new FIND command to locate files by the comment text. A complete discussion of comments is provided in *Chapter 3, Managing Your Hard Drive*.

Several other options appear in some Get Info dialog boxes:

- **Locked**. Makes it impossible to change or delete the selected file. The Locked option appears for data files, applications and aliases. Locking ensures that unwanted changes are not accidentally made to data files that should not be altered. Locked data files can be opened, in most applications; but changes cannot be saved unless you use the Save As command to create a new file.

  Locked files are also spared accidental deletion, since they must be unlocked before they can be emptied from the Trash Can. If you try to delete a locked file, the dialog box shown in Figure 2.36 appears.

Figure 2.36: The warning that appears when locked items are in the Trash Can.

- **Memory**. These options appear only for application files and include Suggested Memory Size and Current Memory Size. Suggested Memory Size specifies the application developer's recommendations for the amount of memory to be allocated to the program when it's opened. The Current Memory Size option specifies how much memory will actually be allocated to the program when it's opened. (A discussion of these options is presented in *Chapter 11, Memory Management*.)

- **Stationery Pad**. Available for data files only, this turns the selected document into a template. (A template is a master document on which new documents are based.) With this option, each time the selected document is opened, a copy of the file is created, and any changes or customizations are made to this copy, leaving the original Stationery Pad document available as a master at all times. (A complete discussion of Stationery Pads is provided in *Chapter 5, System 7 and Your Software*.)

Get Info for the Trash Can

The Trash Can's Get Info dialog box, shown in Figure 2.37, contains two important pieces of information and one useful option. The dialog box lists the number of files and the amount of disk space they consume, which lets you know how much space will be freed by the EMPTY TRASH command. It also lists the date when the most recent item was placed in the Trash Can.

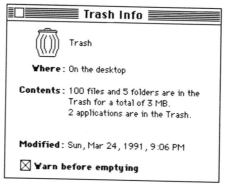

Figure 2.37: The Trash Can's Get Info dialog box.

The "Warn before emptying" option, which is a default, causes the dialog box to display when the EMPTY TRASH command is selected (shown in Figure 2.38). If you don't want the dialog box to display each time the EMPTY TRASH command is chosen, deselect the "Warn before emptying" option. However, without this warning dialog box, you increase the risk of permanently deleting files you may want later.

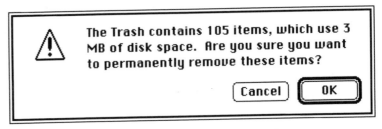

Figure 2.38: The Empty Trash confirmation dialog.

Get Info for Alias Icons

The Get Info dialog box for alias icons is different in several ways from the one used by standard files. First, the Version information normally displayed beneath the dates is replaced with the path and file name of the original file.

Figure 2.39: The Get Info dialog box for an alias icon.

Also, the Get Info dialog box includes the FIND ORIGINAL button that locates the disk or folder containing the original file (from which the alias was made). It can open the disk or folder window and select the original file icon. If the disk or volume containing the original file is not available, a dialog asks you to insert the disk containing the original file, or in the case of a network volume, the volume will be mounted.

Comments and Locked are available for aliases, behaving exactly as they do for any other files. The "Stationery Pad" option, however, is not available for alias icons.

Moving On...

The Finder is the most visible part of the Macintosh System Software; as we've seen in this chapter it gives you powerful and intuitive tools to manage the disks and files you're using with your Macintosh:

- The new Finder menus.

- The many ways you can see and manipulate data in Finder windows.

- The Help Menu and Help Balloons.

- The Trash Can and EMPTY TRASH command.

- The Get Info dialog box, in its many forms.

From general disk and file management tools, we move into *Chapter 3, Managing Your Hard Drive*, where four new System 7 features will be documented in detail. Aliasing, the FIND command, labels and comments—all used at the Finder—are vital to control and productivity on your Macintosh.

Chapter 3: Managing Your Hard Drive

As we've seen already, Finder 7 provides a comprehensive set of commands and features that help you manage disks and files. The new
Finder does not, however, require you to organize your electronic files
in any particular way; it's still up to you to decide the best way to
arrange your files.

File management is an interesting challenge; you must balance your
available storage space with the quantity and size of files you need to
keep available, and you must design a logical arrangement that will
allow you to quickly locate the files you need.

Fortunately, System 7 provides several file-management tools, including the MAKE ALIAS command, the FIND command and the Label Menu.
These commands will affect the way you store files on your hard disk,
and on floppy disks, removable cartridges, network file servers or any

other storage devices. In this chapter, you'll take a look at these new features and how they can help you organize your hard drive.

Aliasing

Wouldn't it be nice to be in several places at one time? Imagine, for example, that while you were hard at work earning your paycheck, you could also be lying on a beach enjoying the sun. And if being in two places at once sounds appealing, how would you like to be in any number of places at one time. For example, you could be at work earning a living, at the beach getting a tan, at the library reading a book and on a plane bound for an exotic destination, all at the same time.

System 7 extends this convenience to your electronic files through a feature called aliasing. Aliasing is perhaps the most significant improvement System 7 offers the average Macintosh user, because it removes the single largest constraint—space limitation—from the task of organizing files and thereby makes it easier to take full advantage of your software applications and data files.

Basic Aliasing Concepts
(or "How I came home from work with a tan")

In simple terms, an alias is a copy of a file, folder or volume, but a very special kind of copy—different from copies created with the DUPLICATE command or other traditional methods. An alias is not a copy of the file, folder or volume, but rather it's a copy of the file, folder or volume *icon*.

To understand this distinction, think of a file icon as a door; the file that the icon represents is the room behind the door. As you would expect, each room normally has just one door (each file has one icon), and opening that door (the icon) is the only way to enter the room.

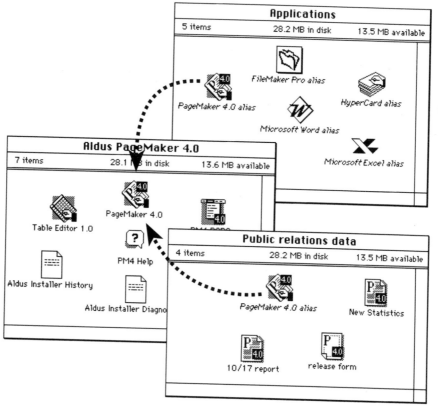

Figure 3.1: Each alias points to the original file that was used to create it.

Creating an alias is like adding an additional door to a room; it presents another entrance, usually in a location different from the existing entrance. Just as you wouldn't have two doors to the same room right next to each other, you won't usually have two icons for the same file (the original and an alias) in the same location. This is the first important feature of an alias: it can be moved to any folder on any volume without affecting the relationship between the alias and its original file. In fact, the link between an alias and its original file is maintained even if both files are moved.

Another key feature of an alias is that it requires only 1K or 2K of disk space, regardless of the size of the original file. That's because the alias is a copy of the icon, not a copy of the file itself. The alias's small size is an important attribute, since it consumes very little storage space.

Details about these and other aspects of aliases are provided later in this chapter, but before getting too far into the technical aspects, lets take a quick look at a few practical ways to use aliases:

- **Aliases make applications easier to launch**. Since double-clicking on an application's alias launches that application, aliases make applications easily accessible.

  For example, you can keep one alias of your word processor on the desktop, another in a folder full of word processing data files and yet another alias in the Apple Menu folder. You could then launch this application using the icon that's most convenient at the moment.

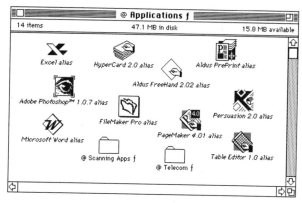

Figure 3.2: Aliasing an application makes it more convenient to launch.

- **To organize data files more logically.** Alias copies of data files allow you to keep them in as many folders as they logically belong in.

  A spreadsheet file with information used on your income taxes, for example, might normally be kept in a folder along with all your spreadsheets created during that year. You could also keep an alias copy of that same spreadsheet in a personal-finances folder, in another tax-file folder and in a general-accounting folder.

  Storing alias copies in multiple locations has several benefits. First, it lets you quickly locate the file you're looking for, because there are several places to find it. It's also easier to find files because they can be stored along with other files they're logically connected with. Finally, archival storage lets you move the originals off the hard drive, saving disk space while still allowing access to the file via aliases.

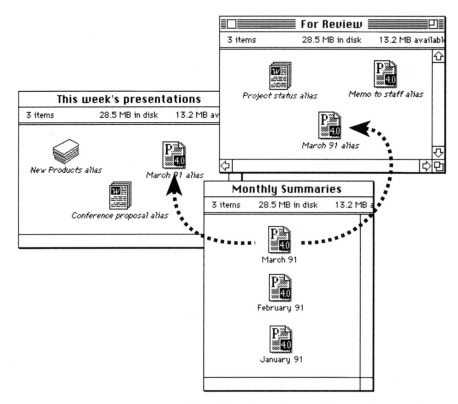

Figure 3.3: Aliasing data files allows them to be stored in multiple logical locations.

■ **To simplify access to files stored on removable media.**
  Keeping aliases from floppy disks, removable hard drives, CD-ROMs and other removable storage media on your local hard drive lets you locate those files quickly and easily.

  When an alias of a file stored on removable media is opened, the Macintosh prompts you to insert the disk (or cartridge) that contains the original file.

- **To simplify access to files stored on network servers.**
  Placing aliases of files from network file servers on your local
  hard drive is another way to quickly and easily locate the files
  no matter where they're stored.

  When an alias of a file stored on the network server is opened,
  the Macintosh automatically connects to the server, prompting
  you for necessary passwords.

Creating and Using Aliases

To create an alias, select the file, folder or volume icon and choose the
MAKE ALIAS command from the File Menu. An alias icon will then
appear, with the same name and icon as the original, followed by the
word "alias," as shown in Figure 3.4.

/DTP Forum   /DTP Forum alias

Figure 3.4: An original file and an alias of that file.

For the most part, alias icons look and act just like other files, folders
or volumes. You can change the file name of an alias at any time;
changing the file name doesn't break the link between the alias and its
original file. Changing a file name is like changing the sign on a door;
it doesn't change the contents of the room behind the door.

/DTP Forum   *Navigator June Session*

Figure 3.5: An original file and an alias of the file that's been renamed.

You've probably noticed that alias file names appear in italic. This is always true, even when they're listed in dialog boxes, *except* when aliases are listed under the Apple Menu. The italic helps you distinguish Alias files from original files.

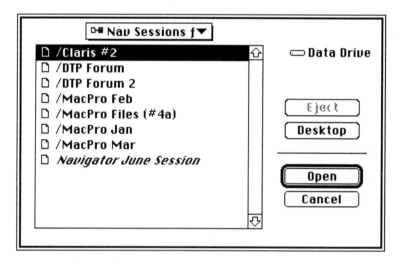

Figure 3.6: Alias file names appear in italics in dialog boxes.

As mentioned earlier, alias icons can be moved to any available folder or volume without losing the link they maintain to the original file. This is the magic of aliases and the key to their utility. No matter how files are moved, the links are maintained.

Original files can also be moved, as long as they remain on the same volume; and they can be renamed without breaking the link with their aliases. When the alias icon is opened, the Macintosh finds and opens the original file.

To illustrate how this automatic linkage is maintained, assume you have a file called "1991 Commission Schedule," which is stored in a folder named "Corporate Spreadsheets." You created an alias of this file, copied the alias into a folder called "1991 Personal Accounting" and renamed the alias "1991 Commissions" (see Figure 3.7).

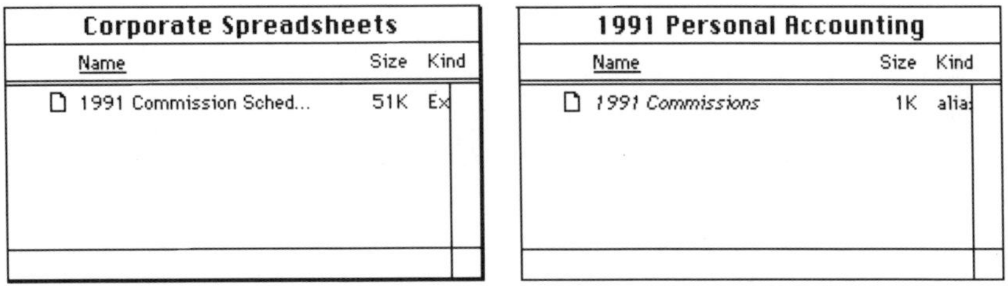

Corporate Spreadsheets				1991 Personal Accounting		
Name	Size	Kind		Name	Size	Kind
🗋 1991 Commission Sched...	51K	Ex		🗋 *1991 Commissions*	1K	alia

Figure 3.7: Files and aliases as originally named and positioned.

Later, you decide that this file will contain only data for the first six months of 1991, so you rename the original file "1991 Pt1 Comm. Sched," and put it in a new folder inside the "Corporate Spreadsheets" folder named "Jan-June Stuff" (see Figure 3.8).

Even though both the original file and the alias have been moved and renamed since they were created, double-clicking on the "1991 Commissions" file (the alias) will open the "1991 Pt1 Comm. Sched" file.

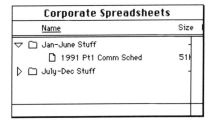

Figure 3.8: Files and aliases after being moved and renamed.

Advanced Aliasing Concepts

Once you understand the basic concepts of aliases and begin using them, you may have questions, such as: How many aliases can one file have? Is it possible to alias an alias? What happens when an alias's original file is deleted? The answers to these and other questions follow.

- **Multiple aliases**. There's no limit to the number of aliases you can create from a single file, folder or volume.

    When creating multiple aliases, alias names are designated by numbers, to distinguish them from existing alias names. (The first alias of a file named "Rejection Letter" is named "Rejection Letter Alias"; the second, "Rejection Letter Alias 1"; and the third, "Rejection Letter Alias 2," and so on until the earlier aliases are renamed or moved to different locations. (These alias numbers have no significance beyond serving to avoid file-name duplication.)

- **Aliasing aliases**. You can create an alias of an alias, but this causes a chain of pointing references: the second alias points to the first, which points to the original. In most cases, it's better to create an alias directly from the original file.

If you do create a chain and any one of the aliases in the chain is deleted, all subsequent aliases will no longer be linked to the original file. To illustrate this problem, assume an alias named "New Specs Alias" was created from an original file named "New Specs," then "New Specs Alias 2" was created from "New Specs Alias" (see Figure 3.9).

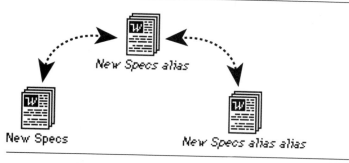

Figure 3.9: Creating an alias of an alias causes a chain which can be broken if one alias is deleted.

At that point, each of these files can be repositioned and renamed and the alias links will be automatically maintained. However, if the "New Specs Alias" file is deleted, "New Specs Alias 2" will no longer be linked to "New Specs." There's no way to re-establish the link should a break occur.

■ **Deleting aliases**. Deleting an alias has no effect on the original file, folder or volume. It simply means that in order to access the item that the alias represented, you'll have to access the original item or another alias.

You can delete aliases in any of the ways you delete normal files: drag the alias to the Trash Can, then choose the Empty Trash command; select the alias and choose the Cut command; select the alias and choose the Clear command; select the alias and press the backspace or delete key; or delete the alias using some other file deletion utility.

■ **Moving original files**. The link between an alias and its original file is maintained regardless of how the original is moved on one volume; but links are not maintained when you copy the original file to a new volume then delete the original file. In other words, there's no way to transfer the alias link from an original file to a copy of that original file.

If you're going to move a file from which aliases have been created from one volume to another, and you must delete the original file, all existing aliases will be unlinked and therefore useless. You could create new aliases from the original file in its new location and replace the existing aliases with the new ones, but you'd have to perform this process manually.

■ **Deleting original files**. Deleting a file from which aliases have been made has no immediate effect; no warning is posted when the file is deleted. But when an attempt is made to open an alias of a file that's been deleted, a dialog box appears informing you that the original file cannot be found.

There's no way to salvage a deleted file to relink with this alias, so in most cases you'll want to delete the orphaned alias.

The exception to this rule is when the original file is still in the Trash Can. In this case, if you try to open an alias, a dialog box will inform you that the file cannot be opened because it's in the Trash Can. If you drag the original file out of the trash, it's again available to the alias.

■ **Finding original files**. Although an alias is in many ways a perfect proxy for a file, there are times when you'll need to locate the alias's original file—for example, if you want to delete the original file or copy the original file onto a floppy disk or other portable medium.

To locate the original file for any alias icon, simply select the alias icon and choose the GET INFO command (Command-I) from the Finder's File Menu. This brings up a special Get Info dialog box (shown in Figure 3.10) that displays basic information about the alias icon, the path information for the original file, and the FIND ORIGINAL button.

When the FIND ORIGINAL button is clicked, the original file, folder or volume is selected and displayed on the Finder desktop. If the original file is located on a removable volume that's not currently available, a dialog box appears prompting you to insert the disk or cartridge containing that file. If the original file is located on a network file server, the Macintosh attempts to log onto the server to locate the file, prompting for any required passwords.

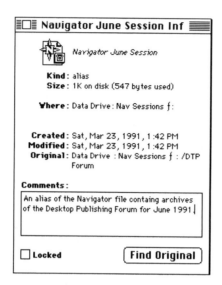

Figure 3.10: The Get Info dialog box for an alias.

If the current alias is an alias of an alias, clicking the FIND ORIGINAL button will find the original file, not the alias used to create the current alias. If the alias file has been accessed via File Sharing, the FIND ORIGINAL button will usually be unable to locate the original file, although its location is accurately documented in the original text of the Get Info dialog box.

■ **Replacing alias icons.** As introduced in *Chapter 2, Finder 7,* new icons can be pasted into the Get Info dialog box for any file. This is also true of alias icons. Replacing the icon of any alias has no effect on the icon of the original file.

Aliasing Folders or Volumes

So far, most of this section has focused on aliasing in relation to application and data files. But almost without exception, aliasing works the same way for folders and volumes. Folder aliases are created, renamed, repositioned, deleted and linked to their originals in exactly the same way as the file aliases previously described:

- Aliasing a folder creates a new folder icon with the same name as the original, plus the word alias.

- The name of an alias folder appears in italics, on the desktop or in dialog box listings.

- Folder aliases can be renamed at any time. Of course, an alias cannot have the same name as an original or another alias while in the same location.

- Folder aliases can be moved inside any other folder or folder alias or to any volume.

- When an alias folder is opened, the window of the original folder is opened. Aliasing a folder does not alias the folder's content. For this reason, the original folder must be available anytime the folder alias is opened. If the original folder is on a volume that's not currently mounted, you'll be prompted to insert the volume or the Macintosh will attempt to mount the volume if it's on the network.

- Deleting a folder alias does not delete the original folder or any of its contents.

But there are some unique aspects of folder aliases.

- When a folder alias is displayed hierarchically in a Finder window, it cannot be opened hierarchically (no triangle appears to its left) because the folder alias has no contents, strictly speaking. You can open the folder alias by clicking on it to open a new Finder window.

- Folder aliases appear in standard file dialog boxes, and the contents of the original folder can be revealed from within these dialog boxes.

- Anything put into a folder alias is actually placed into the original folder, including files, folders and other aliases. The folder alias has no real contents; it's just another "door" to the original folder.

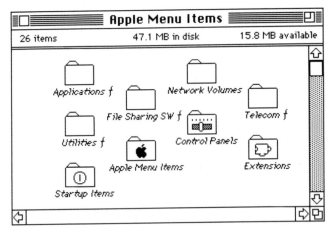

Figure 3.11: Alias folders are commonly used in the Apple Menu.

Volume aliases are similar to file aliases, but have some of the same characteristics as folder aliases.

- Opening a volume alias mounts the original volume if it's not already available. If the original volume is not currently mounted, you'll be prompted to insert the volume, or the Macintosh will attempt to mount the volume if it's on the network.

- Opening a volume alias displays the Finder window of the actual volume and the contents of this window.

- Aliasing a volume does not alias the volume contents, just the icon of the volume itself.

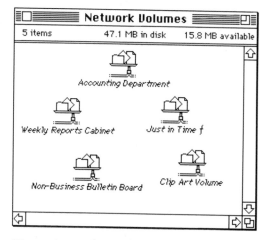

Figure 3.12: Alias volumes, stored in a folder.

Using Aliases

Aliases can be used in many ways in many different situations. Following are some of the more interesting possibilities:

- **Alias applications.** The easiest way to launch an application is to double-click on its icon. But many of today's applications are stored in folders containing a morass of ancillary files — dictionaries, color palettes, Help files, printer descriptions, etc. Amid all this clutter, it's hard to locate the application icon in order to launch it. Aliasing allows easier access.

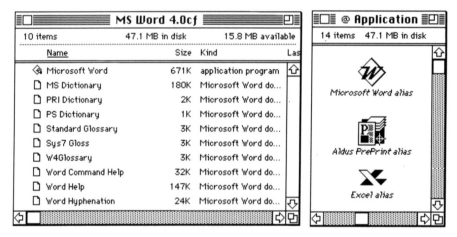

Figure 3.13: Microsoft Word along with its ancillary files (left), and an alias of Word in a folder with other application aliases (right).

The most straightforward way to simplify application launching is to alias each of your applications and place these aliases in the Apple Menu folder of your System folder. You can then launch the applications by simply choosing their names from the Apple Menu.

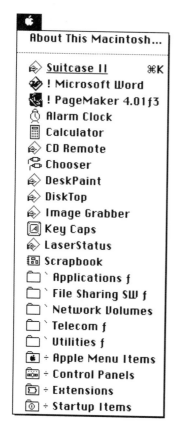

Figure 3.14: An Apple Menu customized with folders and applications.

Or instead, you might group your application aliases into folders, then alias these folders and place them in the Apple Menu. Doing it this way takes two steps instead of one, but this method leaves room in your Apple Menu for other folder, volume and file aliases. Of course, you could leave a few applications that you use extensively directly in the Apple Menu.

Figure 3.14 shows an Apple Menu configured with application-group folders. Note that an accent grave (`) has been added to the start of each folder name. This not only makes it easy to identify folders from other elements in the Apple Menu, but more importantly it groups them all together near the top of the Apple Menu listing. (See *Chapter 4, The System Folder,* for more tips on working with the Apple Menu.)

You can also put application aliases, along with groups of documents created with the application, on your Finder desktop. But since double-clicking on any document will launch the application anyway, this is not really very useful.

- **Multiple data-file aliases.** To avoid having to remember all the places where a frequently used file is stored every time you want to use it, you can use aliases to store each data file in as many places as it logically fits—anywhere you might look for the file when you need it later.

Suppose, for example, that you write a letter to your boss about a new idea for serving your company's big client, Clampdown Inc. Depending on your personal scheme, you might store this letter, along with other general business correspondence, in a folder pertaining to Clampdown Inc., or you might even have a file where you keep everything that has to do with your boss. Using aliases, you can store the file in all these locations and in a folder of all work you've done in the current week.

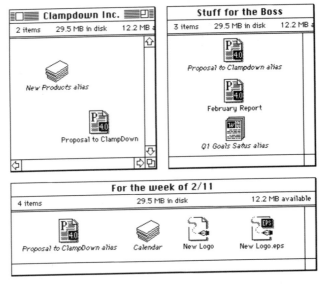

Figure 3.15: Aliasing a file into multiple locations.

■ **Aliases of data files from remote or removable volumes**. You can store hundreds of megabytes worth of files on your hard drive, regardless of how big it is, by using aliases. Keeping aliases of all the files you normally store on removable disks or drives and all the files from network file servers that you occasionally need to utilize lets you locate and open the files by simply searching your hard drive (at the Finder, in dialog boxes or using a search utility) without the cost of hard-drive space.

This is perfect for storing libraries of clip-art files, down-loadable fonts, corporate templates or other infrequently used file groups. Storing these aliased files on your hard drive lets you browse through them whenever necessary. The hard drive will automatically mount the required volumes or prompt you for them when they're needed.

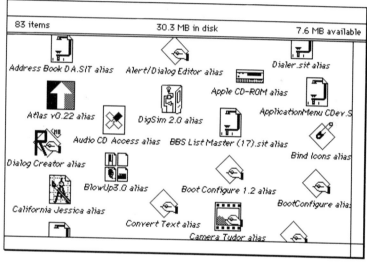

Figure 3.16: A folder full of aliased utility files stored on a removable volume.

- **Trash Can alias.** You can alias the Finder's Trash Can and store copies of the trash in any folder. Dragging folder files to the Trash Can alias is the same as dragging them to the actual Trash Can. Files trashed in this way will not be removed until the EMPTY TRASH command is used, and can be retrieved by simply opening the Trash Can or a Trash Can alias and dragging the file back onto a volume or folder.

- **Removable cartridge maps**. Create a folder for each removable cartridge, drive or floppy disk. Alias the entire contents of these volumes and store the aliases in the volume's folder. Then you can "browse" these volumes without mounting them. You may also want to keep other aliases of files from these volumes in other locations on your drive.

- **Network file-server volume maps**. Create a folder called "Network" and place an alias of each remote volume inside that folder. You can then log onto any remote volume by simply double-clicking on the volume alias. This eliminates the need to access the Chooser, locate the file server, then locate the volume every time you want to use the volume. Of course, you'll be prompted for any required passwords.

- **Hard-drive alias**. If you work on a large AppleTalk network, put an alias icon of your hard drive on a floppy disk and carry it with you. If you need to access your hard drive from another location, all you have to do is insert the floppy disk containing your hard drive alias into any Macintosh on the network, double-click on the alias icon and your hard drive will be mounted via AppleTalk.

Aliasing Summary

- You can alias any file, folder, volume icon or the Trash Can.

- To create an alias, select the desired icon and choose the MAKE ALIAS command.

- An alias initially takes the same name as its original file with the word alias appended.

- Alias names always appear in italics, except in the Apple Menu.

- Aliases can be renamed at any time. The standard Macintosh 32-character name limit applies.

- Aliases can be moved to any location on the current volume or any other volume.

- An alias is initially given the same icon as its original. The icon can be changed in the Get Info dialog box.

- Alias icons require only 1K or 2K of storage space.

- The link between an alias and its original file is maintained even when the files are renamed or repositioned.

- Deleting an alias icon has no effect on its original file, folder or volume.

- Copying an alias to a new location on the current drive (hold down option key while dragging) is the same as creating a new alias of the original file—it does not create an alias of an alias.

- Use the GET INFO command to locate an alias's original file.

- Opening a folder alias opens the window of the original folder.

- Opening a volume alias opens the window of the original volume.

The Find Command

Regardless of how well organized your electronic filing system is, it's impossible to always remember where specific files are located.

To solve this problem in the past, Apple provided the Find File desk accessory to let you search for files, by file name, on any currently mounted volume. Find File locates the files and lists them in a section of its window. Once a file is found, selecting the file name reveals the path of the located file, along with other basic file information, as shown in Figure 3.17. Using this information, you can then quit the Find File DA and locate the file yourself, or Find File can move the file to the Finder desktop where it's easy to access.

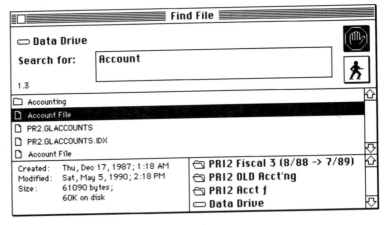

Figure 3.17: The Find File desk accessory.

Beyond Find File, other file-finding utilities have also been available. Most of them let you search for files not only by file name but also by creation date, file type, creator, date modified, file size and other file attributes and combinations of attributes. Like Find File, most of these utilities locate matching files, display the path information, and let you return to the Finder and use or modify the file as required. The Find feature in DiskTop 4.0, a very popular desk accessory, also allows you to direct copy, move, rename and even launch located files.

In System 7, a new FIND command has been added to the Finder. This command and its companion, FIND AGAIN, significantly improve on the Find File desk accessory. Because these new commands are built into the Finder itself, they offer important advantages over other available file-finding utilities.

Using the FIND Command

The new FIND command is located in the Finder's File Menu, while desk accessory-based utilities put it in the Apple Menu. Having the FIND command in the Finder is not really a disadvantage, since the Finder is always available in System 7. (To access the FIND command while using another application, you use the Applications Menu in the upper right corner of the menu bar to bring the Finder to the foreground. After using the FIND command, you use the Applications Menu again to return to your software application.)

When the FIND command (Command-F) is selected, the Find dialog box appears. This dialog box, shown in Figure 3.18, can search files only by name, much like Find File. Additional search criteria are

accessed by clicking the MORE CHOICES button, which brings up the Find
Item dialog box (shown in Figure 3.19).

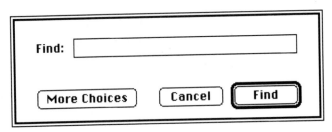

Figure 3.18: The FIND dialog box.

Let's start with the simple Find dialog box; later in this section, you'll
look at the other options available with the Find Item dialog box. In
both sections, you'll evaluate the FIND command's capabilities in
finding files, but it should be noted that the FIND command will also
locate folders matching the selected search criteria.

The Find Dialog Box

Using the basic Find dialog box to locate files by name, you can enter
the complete file name or only the first portion of the file name.

- **Enter a complete file name.** If you know the complete file
  name you're looking for, enter it into the "Find" option box.
  In most cases, only the correct file will be found, but if you
  make even a slight error in spelling the file name, the correct
  file will not be found. This is not the most efficient way to
  execute a file search.

- **Enter only the first portion of a file name.** Entering the first few characters of the file name is the most commonly used and usually the most efficient file-name search method. This locates all file names that begin with the characters you've specified. The exact number of characters you should enter will depend on the circumstances; the goal is to enter enough characters to narrow the search down but not so many that you risk a spelling mistake and therefore a chance of missing the file.

  As an example, if the file you wanted to locate was Archeology Report, specifying only the letter 'A' would yield a huge number of files to sort through. On the other hand, entering six or seven characters could allow files with spelling errors, such as "Archio" or "Archae," to escape the search. Decide on the number of characters according to how common the first few characters are among your files and how well you remember the file name. In this example, searching for files starting with "Arc" would probably be the best strategy.

After specifying the search criteria, click the FIND button to start the search. The search starts at the startup drive and proceeds to all mounted volumes. If the search will take more than a few seconds, a Progress dialog box appears. When a file matching the search criteria is located, a window is opened, and the file is displayed.

At this point, you can use or modify the file as required. If the selected file is not the one you wanted, or if after modifying the selected file you want to continue searching for the next file that matches the search criteria, choose the FIND AGAIN command from the File Menu or press Command-G. As each matching file is located, you can use or modify it, then repeat the process to proceed to the next matching file.

The Find Item Dialog Box

Clicking the MORE CHOICES button in the Find dialog box brings up the Find Item dialog box (shown in Figure 3.19), which has several advantages over the standard Find dialog box:

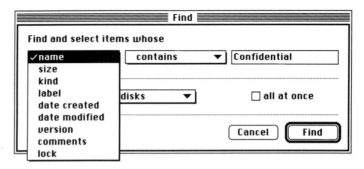

Figure 3.19: The FIND ITEM dialog box.

- **More search criteria.** While the basic Find dialog can search only for file names, the Find Item dialog can search with the additional criteria shown in Figure 3.19. You can also limit your search location to specific volumes or selections.

- **More range control.** For each search parameter, the Find Item dialog lists specific search constraints (see Figure 3.20).

- **More result control.** The "All At Once" option lets you look at a group of files matching the specified criteria all together.

Search by	Constraint	Range
Comments	contains/does not contain	any text
Date created	is / is before / is after / is not	any date
Date modified	is / is before / is after / is not	any date
Label	is / is not	any label/ none
Lock	is	locked/unlocked
Name	contains/starts with/ends with/doesn't contain	any text
Size	is less than / is greater than	any # k
Version	is / is before / is after / is not	any number

Figure 3.20: The available search criteria and their respective constraints and ranges.

To specify your criteria, select an option from the first pop-up menu. Depending on the option you select, the second or third part of the Find specification will become either a pop-up menu, an option box or a date. Enter your search specification. (To change a date, click on the month, year or day and then use the Up and Down Arrows to reset that portion of the date.) Several sample criteria are shown in Figure 3.21.

Find and select items whose

| version ▼ | is before ▼ | 4.0 |

Find and select items whose

| date created ▼ | is before ▼ | 11/18/89 ⬍ |

Find and select items whose

| label ▼ | is ▼ | ■ Personal ▼ |

Figure 3.21: Several different search criteria as specified in the Find Item dialog box.

You can also specify the search range using the Search pop-up menu, shown in Figure 3.22.

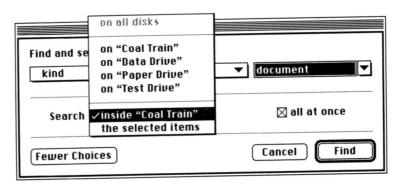

Figure 3.22: The Search pop-up menu.

The Search options are

- **On All Disks.** This will search all mounted volumes, including all folders and items appearing on the Finder desktop. With this option, the "All At Once" option isn't available.

- **On <any one currently mounted volume>.** Limits the search to one particular volume.

- **Inside <the current selection>/On The Desktop.** Limits the search to the currently selected volume or folder. If no volume or folder is selected, the option becomes "On The Desktop," which searches all mounted volumes.

- **The Selected Items.** Confines the search to those items currently selected. This is often used to further limit the results from a previous search resulting in a multiple-criteria search.

For example, suppose you need to free some space on your hard drive, so you search for all files larger than 250K, using the "All At Once" option, which will give you an open Finder window with all 250K or larger files selected. To locate only those larger than 250K that have not been changed in more than one month, choose the FIND command again and search the "Selected Items" for all files modified prior to 30 days ago. You can now back up and delete these files.

The "All At Once" option determines whether files matching your search criteria are presented individually or all together. A single window for the volume or window being searched is displayed, and all files matching the search criteria are selected. Files located in subfolders are displayed hierarchically. This option cannot be used when the "On All Disks" search-range option is selected.

If the "All At Once" option is not selected, clicking the FIND button locates the first file in the specified search range that matches the search criteria; the file window is opened and the file is selected. If the selected file is not the one you want, or if you want to find the next matching file after modifying the selected file, choose the FIND AGAIN command from the File Menu (Command-G) and the search will continue, using the same search criteria and range. Again, you can continue using the FIND AGAIN command as required.

After completing all the required options in the Find Item dialog box, click the FIND button to execute the search. If the search is going to be prolonged, a progress dialog box will appear indicating the percentage of range already searched.

When a matching file is located,

- The progress dialog box, if visible, disappears.

- A window opens for the folder or volume containing the matching file.

- If the "All At Once" option was selected, a window listing all files matching the specified criteria appears, as shown in Figure 3.23.

- If the "All At Once" option was not selected, the matching file's icon is selected, as shown in Figure 3.24.

Any time you're working in the Find Item dialog box, you can click the FEWER CHOICES button to return to the Find dialog box, described above.

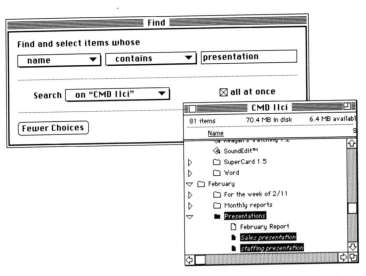

Figure 3.23: A group of files, located by the FIND command.

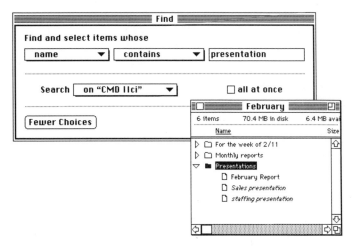

Figure 3.24: A single file, located by the FIND command.

Find Command Tips

- **Find does not look inside the System file.** Items such as fonts or sounds that have been placed inside the System file will not be located by the FIND command.

- **Find locates aliases as well.** Any alias that matches the specified search criteria can be found just like regular files.

- **The FIND AGAIN command (Command-g) can be used at any time.** The search parameters entered in the Find or Find Item dialog box remain until the Mac is restarted or the parameters are changed. You can always repeat the most recent search using the FIND AGAIN command.

- **Find also locates folders and volumes.** Any folder or volume matching the specified search criteria will be found, just like any other file.

- **Search By Kind to locate all data files created by one specific application.** To use the "By Kind" search criterion, specify the file kind (for example, all spreadsheet files) that the application assigns to its data files. (See the sample file kinds in Figure 3.25.)

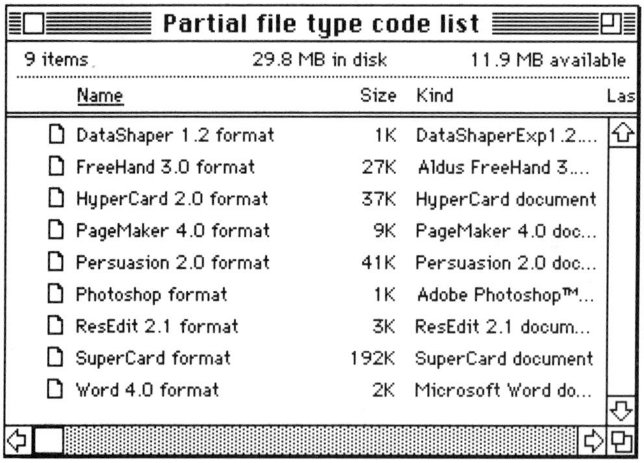

```
☰▢☰▬▬▬ Partial file type code list ▬▬▬☰⊞☰
 9 items         29.8 MB in disk        11.9 MB available
        Name                    Size   Kind              Las
   ▢ DataShaper 1.2 format        1K   DataShaperExp1.2....  ⇧
   ▢ FreeHand 3.0 format         27K   Aldus FreeHand 3....
   ▢ HyperCard 2.0 format        37K   HyperCard document
   ▢ PageMaker 4.0 format         9K   PageMaker 4.0 doc...
   ▢ Persuasion 2.0 format       41K   Persuasion 2.0 doc...
   ▢ Photoshop format             1K   Adobe Photoshop™...
   ▢ ResEdit 2.1 format           3K   ResEdit 2.1 docum...
   ▢ SuperCard format           192K   SuperCard document
   ▢ Word 4.0 format              2K   Microsoft Word do...  ⇩
 ⇦▢░░░░░░░░░░░░░░░░░░░░░░░░░░░░░░░░⇨⊟
```

Figure 3.25: The Kind column displays the name of the applications that create the file.

- **Use Find to do quick backups.** After you've used the Find command to locate all files on a volume modified after a certain date, you can drag those files to a removable volume for a "quick and dirty" backup. Of course, this procedure shouldn't replace a good backup utility—but you can never have too many backups.

- Use "The Selected Items" search range to perform multiple-criteria searches. For example, the FIND command will locate all file names beginning with S that are less than 32K in size and have the word "medicated" in their comments (or any other set of multiple criteria). The first criterion is searched for using the "On <any one volume>" range, then searching for each additional criterion using the "Selected Items" range.

Labels

The Label Menu is a great new System 7 tool that helps you categorize your files, identify certain types of files, locate these files and, in some cases, manipulate them as a group.

Configuring the Label Menu

The Label Menu is in the Finder menu bar; it's configured using the Labels control panel. Figure 3.26 displays the open Labels control panel. The text and color of your labels are configured in this control panel.

To set label text, click in each label text block, and enter the name of the label category you want to define. In label assignments, form must follow function; there's no advantage in having label assignments that don't help you use and manipulate your data more efficiently.

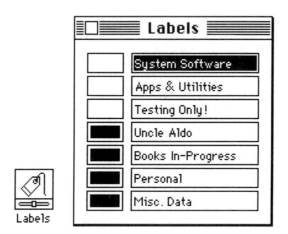

Figure 3.26: The Labels control panel.

There are several ways to use labels:

- **To categorize files.** Labels provide an additional level of categorization for files. Files are already categorized by type, creation and modification dates and related folders, but using aliases you can also classify them by topic importance and any other way you choose.

- **For visual distinction.** Color-coding icons helps you quickly distinguish one type of file from another on a color monitor. For example, all applications can be red, making them easier to spot in a folder full of dictionaries, Help instructions and other files. You can also use the Labels column in Finder windows, which lists label names next to file names.

- **To facilitate data backup.** You can find all files assigned to a specific label, then copy them to another disk or volume for backup purposes.

■ **To indicate security requirements**. Especially when using File Sharing, you can create labels that remind you of the security level of specific folders, files and volumes.

There are many ways to use the nine available label categories:

■ **Categories for logical subdivisions of data files**. If your work is project-based, you can specify large projects and use one Miscellaneous catch-all label for smaller projects. You could also have Long-Term Projects, Short-Term Projects and Permanent Projects.

■ **Categories for software applications**. You can differentiate launchable applications or label both applications and their ancillary files. You might want a separate label for utility programs, including third-party extensions, control panels, desk accessories and utilities that are launchable applications.

■ **Specify security levels**. If special security is required in your work environment, label one or two folders to identify them as secure. You can then use encryption utilities to safeguard these files, use them carefully with File Sharing or apply third-party security utilities to protect them.

Once labels are defined, you can alter label colors (available only on Color Macs). To do this, click on any color in the Labels control panel to make the Apple Color Wheel dialog box, shown in Figure 3.27, appear. Specify the color you want for the label. Because label colors are applied over existing icon colors, weaker colors with lower hue and saturation values (found toward the middle of the wheel) work best.

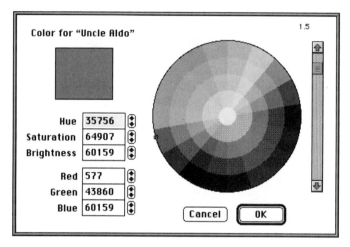

Figure 3.27: The Apple Color Wheel.

After you've modified the label names and colors, close the Labels control panel. The Label Menu and any files or folders affected are then updated. You can reopen the Labels control panel any time you need to reset the text or colors.

Comments

In the past, adding lengthy comments to Macintosh files has been unsatisfactory, to say the least. The main problem was that the comments were likely to disappear every time the invisible desktop file was replaced or rebuilt. Most people stopped using comments when they discovered that they could never be sure how long they'd last. In addition to that, they could only be seen by opening the Get Info dialog box, so they were inconvenient to use.

System 7 attempts to breath new life into file comments, correcting some of their their former shortcomings and adding some interesting possibilities that could make comments an important part of working with your Macintosh files.

In Finder 7, comments have been improved in two important ways:

- **Visibility.** You can now see comments in Finder windows. When the "Show Comments" option in the Views control panel is selected, as introduced earlier in this chapter, comments will display in all Finder windows. This makes them practical to use.

- **Searchability.** The new FIND command lets you search for text in file comments, making it possible to locate files by comment entries.

People will find other productive ways to use these new comment features. One idea is to use comments as cues: key words or phrases can provide information not already included in the file name, date, kind or other file information. Client names, project titles, related document names and obsolete by dates are a few examples. This additional information would be displayed in Finder windows via the FIND command.

Unfortunately, Finder comments are still lost when the desktop file is rebuilt. (The "desktop file" is actually a pair of invisible files that the Finder maintains on each disk or drive you use with your Mac.) The desktop file is sometimes automatically rebuilt by the System Software when minor disk problems are detected. Or, you can force the desktop to be rebuilt by holding down the Command and Option keys during startup.

Figure 3.28 shows some files with comments added. Complete comments make it easy to see at a glance what these files contain when browsing Finder windows; it also makes the files easy to retrieve with the FIND command.

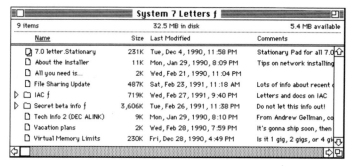

Figure 3.28: A Finder window as it appears when using the "Show Comments" option.

Moving On...

The power and importance of the capabilities introduced in this chapter cannot be overestimated. As you become more familiar with System 7, you'll use these features frequently:

- Aliases help you locate and launch files and access network data quickly and easily.

- The Find command will solve your "where is that file?" problem.

- Labels make it easier to keep important files organized.

- Comments remind you of details about particular file or folder content.

Next, in Chapter 4, we'll examine the most important folder on your hard drive, the System folder. In System 7 the System folder is still the home of your System Software, but it's organized a little differently. Innovations include automatic file placement, and a new way of working with fonts and other resources used by the System file.

Chapter 4: The System Folder

There's one folder on every Macintosh hard drive that's distinct from all others—the System folder, home of the Macintosh System Software and many other important files. The System folder is given special treatment by the System Software, by other software applications and by you as a Macintosh user.

While you can arrange files on your hard drive (and all other volumes) to suit your personal needs, you can only change the organization of the System folder in certain ways. That's because of the fundamental role software in the System folder plays in the operation of your Macintosh.

In this chapter, we'll take a brief look at the history of the System folder and examine the special role it plays. Then we'll focus on System 7's new System folder organization, and offer some suggestions to help you effectively manage this important resource.

System Folder Overload

System Software 1.0, released in January 1984 with the Macintosh 128K, included a System folder containing 22 items that consumed only 225K of disk space. In today's System Software that supports an array of applications and utilities, System folders often contain 100 or more files, and the size of these folders often soars above 1 megabyte.

These increases are partially due to the increasing complexity of the System Software itself, but also result from the growing number of non-System Software files that reside in the System folder. Beyond the obvious demands on disk space, these increases have resulted in chaotic System folder organization and some measure of system instability.

System 7 does little to reduce the pace of System folder growth, but it does provide new methods of maintaining System folder organization. It also introduces a few basic means of avoiding the instability caused by the old System folder organization.

System Software File Size

The growth of Apple's System Software, both in terms of the number of files it contains and the amount of disk space it consumes, has been steady but hardly unreasonable. In fact, considering the increased capabilities and additional hardware support that has been added, its relatively modest growth could even be applauded.

One System Software file, however, has been troublesome; the System file itself. The System file problem has not been due to its own growth, but rather because of its role as host to fonts, sounds and desk accessories. When stuffed with these items, a single System file could grow to 600K—and sometimes much larger. Often, the result of this overload was an unstable System file that would easily and frequently corrupt. It was both annoying and time-consuming to delete and rebuild the unstable file from scratch.

Fortunately, two utilities, Suitcase II and Adobe Type Manager (ATM), have come to the rescue. They have gained widespread popularity among Macintosh users and made large System files virtually obsolete. Suitcase II allows fonts and desk accessories to be used without being installed in the System file. ATM reduces the number of point sizes for fonts, thereby reducing the data needed to install a wide variety of type sizes.

But while these utilities relieve the pressure of large system files, they don't reduce the amount of disk space required—they simply shift resources (files) from inside the System file to another location. In other words, Suitcase II and ATM keep the System file small. But perhaps 50 screen font, printer font and desk accessory files must find space elsewhere—in the System folder or on the hard disk. Which brings us to the next problem—the cluttered System folder.

System Folder Files

In addition to the files Apple supplies with the System Software, two other types of files are generally placed in the System folder: system extensions, which add functions to the System Software, and miscellaneous files that enable other software applications to function properly.

System extensions modify the way the System Software works or extend the options provided by System Software features. They include inits, control panels and printer or network drivers. There are hundreds of examples of inits and drivers that modify your System Software. SuperClock, Pyro, Vaccine, AppleShare, DOS Mounter, NetModem, MailSaver, Autographix, PageSaver and SuperGlue are a few of the most popular. You've probably added files of this type to your System folder.

The miscellaneous files that applications store in the System folder don't interact directly with the System Software. They're placed in the System folder for other reasons:

- **Safety.** The System folder is the only "common ground" on a Mac hard drive that applications can rely on in every configuration.

- **Simplicity.** The Macintosh operating system can easily find the System folder, regardless of what it's called and where it's located. This allows applications quick access to files stored in the System folder.

- **Security.** The System folder is a safe place for applications to add files because most users are not likely to disturb files in their System folders.

Some of the many application-related files that use your System folder are Microsoft Word's Word Temp, Apple's CD-ROM Init, the PageMaker 4.0 Aldus Folder, and Stuffit Deluxe's Encryptors, Translators and Viewers.

Printer font files are also in this category. Printer fonts are placed in the System folder so they can be found by ATM, and so they are available when needed for automatic downloading to a PostScript printer. Usually, these are the most space-consuming files in the System folder—30K to 50K each. Even though utilities like Suitcase II and MasterJuggler make it possible to store printer and screen fonts in other locations, many people choose to keep them in the System folder anyway.

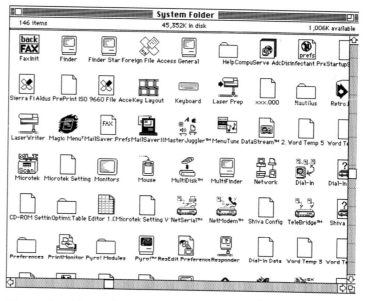

Figure 4.1: The author's large, messy System 6.0x System folder.

The main problem with "stuffing" the System folder is the resulting lack of organization, as shown in Figure 4.1. A crowded System folder is slow to open at the desktop, and finding what you want in the maze of files is a slow and tedious process.

System Folder in System 7

In System 7, Apple has completely redesigned the System Folder, providing a new organizational system that greatly reduces the potential for clutter. Predefined subfolders now exist, each containing a specific type of file. These folders are created by the System 7 Installer when System 7 is installed.

This organization of the System Folder uses folder designations and file arrangement based on the same logic you use in organizing your hard drive. Subfolders include the Apple Menu folder, Control Panels folder, Extensions folder, Preferences folder, Spool folder and Startup folder. A display of this new System folder organization is shown in Figure 4.2.

In some ways, the new System folder is more complex than the old. Fortunately, as we shall see, Apple has built in an "invisible hand" to help make sure that System folder files are always located correctly.

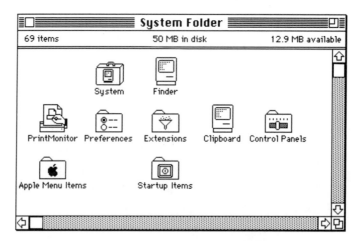

Figure 4.2: A standard System 7 System folder.

Because the new System folder and subfolders are so important to the operation of your Macintosh, it's important to understand what type of files should be placed in each folder. This section describes the folders and provides some basic tips for organizing and using them.

The Apple Menu Folder

One of the best things about desk accessories was their accessibility, via the Apple Menu, from inside any application. In System 7, the convenience of the Apple Menu has been extended beyond desk accessories to include applications, documents, folders and even volumes. And best of all, this powerful new Apple Menu is completely customizable.

When System 7 is installed, the Alarm Clock, Calculator, Chooser, Find File, Key Caps, Scrapbook desk accessories and a Control Panels folder alias appear in the Apple Menu. If you open the Apple Menu folder inside the System folder, these are exactly the files you find inside, as shown in Figure 4.3.

To modify the contents of the Apple Menu, add or remove files and aliases. The Apple Menu is updated immediately and displays the first 50 items (alphabetically) contained in the Apple Menu folder.

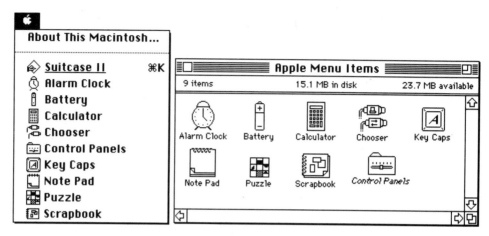

Figure 4.3: The System 7 Apple Menu and Apple Menu folder (as configured by Installer).

The four types of files you'll probably want to place in the Apple Menu folder are applications, documents, folders and volumes. Each is much easier to access in the Apple Menu than by using traditional desktop double-click methods. Choosing an item from the Apple Menu is equivalent to double-clicking on the item's icon: the selected DA or control panel is run, or the selected folder or volume is opened.

Most of the files added to the Apple Menu folder should be alias icons rather than original files, to avoid moving the file, folder or volume icon from its original location. In the Apple Menu folder, the file name remains displayed in italics but the file name appears in standard roman font in the Apple Menu—you can't tell by looking at the Apple Menu that the file in the Apple Menu folder is an alias.

(space bar)	. (.)	œ (Op-Q)	¶ (Op-7)	º (Op-9)
! (Sh-1)	/ (/)	w (W)	ß (Op-S)	ª (Op-0)
" (Op-[)	= (=)	z (Z)	® (Op-R)	Ω (Op-Z)
" (Op-])	? (Sh-/)	[(()	© (Op-C)	¿ (Sh-Op-/)
# (Sh-3)	@ (Sh-2)	] ())	™ (Op-2)	i (Op-1)
$ (Sh-4)	å (Op-A)	^ (Sh-6)	≠ (Op-=)	¬ (Op-L)
% (Sh-5)	A (Sh-A)	` (`)	∞ (Op-5)	√ (Op-V)
& (Sh-7)	œ (Op-')	{ (Sh-[)	≤ (Op-,)	ƒ (Op-F)
' (Op-])	B (Sh-B)	} (Sh-])	≥ (Op-x)	≈ (Op-X)
' (Sh-Op-])	c (c)	~ (Sh-`)	¥ (Op-Y)	Δ (Op-J)
((Sh-9)	ç (Op-c)	† (Op-T)	µ (Op-M)	... (Op-;)
) (Sh-0)	E (Sh-E)	¢ (Op-4)	∂ (Op-D)	- (O--)
* (Sh-8)	f (f)	£ (Op-3)	Σ (Op-W)	— (Sh-Op--)
+ (Sh-=)	G (SH-G)	§ (Op-6)	π (Op-P)	÷ (Op-/)
- (-)	ø (Op-o)	• (Op-8)	∫ (Op-B)	

Figure 4.4: The list above demonstrates, from top to bottom, left to right, the special characters that can be used to alphabetize files in the Apple Menu, and the keys you press to access them.

Because the Apple Menu displays files alphabetically, you can reorder the menu items by modifying their names with numerical or alphabetical prefixes. A list of the prefixes available appears in Figure 4.4. The results of using some of these is shown in the Apple Menu of Figure 4.5, in which applications, folders, desk accessories and control panels, documents and volumes are ordered separately.

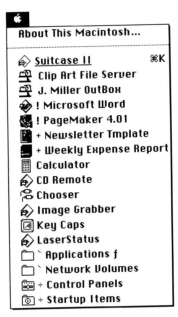

Figure 4.5: Files are arranged in this Apple Menu using file name prefixes.

The Control Panels Folder

Control panels are the evolution of control devices (cdevs) that used to appear in the System 6.0x Control Panel Desk Accessory. In System 7, a control panel is a small independent application launched by double-clicking on its icon. The only difference between a control panel and a regular application is that the control panel is implemented in a single window and provides no menus.

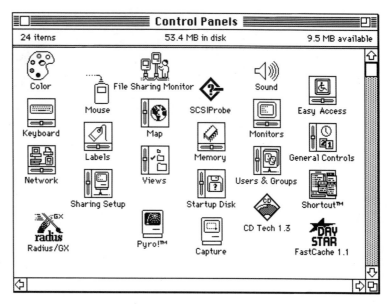

Figure 4.6: The Control Panels folder.

Control panels are stored in the Control Panels folder, which itself is stored inside the System folder—mainly because control panels often contain init resources that must be run during startup. If the init portion of the control panel isn't loaded at startup, the control panel won't function properly.

If you want to keep a copy of any control panel in another location, create an alias and move the alias to your preferred location. You could, for example, store aliases of frequently used control panels in the Apple Menu folder or in a folder containing other utility applications.

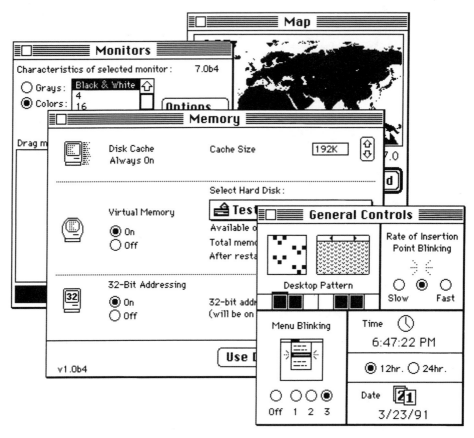

Figure 4.7: Control Panels appear in independent windows.

The Extensions Folder

As mentioned previously, inits, printer drivers and network drivers are major contributors to System folder overcrowding. In System 7, these files, which have invaded System folders in epidemic proportions since the introduction of System 6.0, now have a new home in the Extensions folder.

Most inits add features to the Mac's System Software, hence the name "Extensions." Drivers extend System Software capabilities in a less dramatic but important way.

During startup, the System Software looks in the Extension Folder and executes the code found there. These files can also be accessed during startup from the Control Panels folder, but separation of files between these two folders should be maintained. Inits and control panel files that aren't stored in the Extensions or Control Panels folder won't execute at startup and won't operate properly until they're correctly positioned and the Macintosh is restarted.

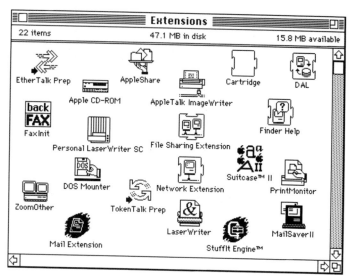

Figure 4.8: The Extensions folder holds inits, printer drivers and network drivers.

Because inits and control panels modify or enhance the System Software at startup, a new init or control panel may cause your Macintosh to crash if the init is incompatible with the System Software, some other init, another control panel or a certain combination of inits and control panels. If you have an incompatibility problem, hold down the shift key while restarting your Macintosh. This will disable all extensions and allow you to remove the incompatible file from the System folder.

When you restart, the words "Extensions Off" will appear under the "Welcome to Macintosh" message, as shown in Figure 4.9. As soon as these words appear, you can release the shift key, and the Macintosh will start up without executing any inits in the Extensions folder or the Control Panels folder.

Figure 4.9: The Welcome to Macintosh dialog box as it appears when the shift key is pressed at startup.

A final word about positioning inits: Although System 7 is designed to house inits in the Extension Folder or in the Control Panels folder, inits located directly in the System folder *will* execute during startup. This is necessary because some older inits and old cdevs don't operate properly when nested in System folder subfolders. New versions of these inits will undoubtedly be compatible with the new System folder structure; but until then, try placing inits directly in the System folder if they don't function properly in the Extensions folder.

The Preferences Folder

Preferences files created by application programs and utilities also became important contributors to System folder growth under System 6.0x. In System 7, these files are stored in the Preferences folder.

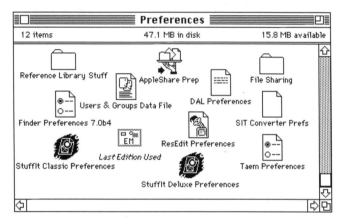

Figure 4.10: The Preferences folder.

As a user, you shouldn't have to do anything to the Preferences folder or its files. Your application programs should create and maintain these files automatically. However, you might want to check this folder occasionally and delete the preferences files of unwanted applications or utilities that you've deleted from your drives.

The Startup Folder

Applications, documents, folders and volumes in the Startup folder automatically run (or open) each time your Macintosh is restarted. This folder takes the place of the SET STARTUP command found in the

Special Menu of previous System Software versions. As with the Apple Menu folder, most of the icons in the Startup folder will probably be aliases.

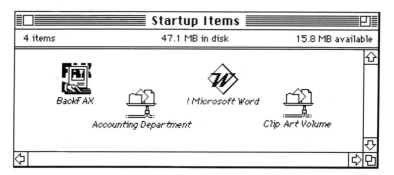

Figure 4.11: The Startup folder with alias icons that will be launched or mounted at startup.

While the Startup folder's main purpose is to open applications and documents, it's also a good place to put folder and volume icon aliases. These aliases will be opened, or mounted, at startup—a simple but useful function. (Of course, before mounting any networked volumes, any required passwords will be requested.)

The System File

The System file remains the centerpiece of Macintosh System Software, overseeing all basic Macintosh activities and assisting every application and utility run on the Macintosh. As a user, you can remain blissfully ignorant of most of the work performed by the System file, but there are some aspects of this file that you should understand in order to use it productively.

Among other things, the System file holds fonts, sounds and keyboard files. In previous System versions, fonts and desk accessories were moved in and out of the System file via the Font/DA Mover utility. Thankfully, this is no longer necessary in System 7; fonts and other resources can be moved in and out of the System file by dragging file icons. (Desk accessories are no longer stored in the System file; see *Chapter 5, System 7 and Your Software.*)

To check fonts, sounds and keyboard configurations in the System file, open the System file by double-clicking on it as if it was a folder. A window opens, as if it were a folder, displaying icons for all fonts, sounds and keyboard configurations it currently contains.

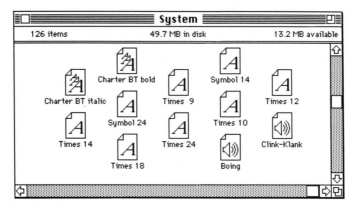

Figure 4.12: An open System file window.

While the System file is open, you'll see that font, sound and keyboard files have unique icons. Double-clicking on any of these icons will open the resource file, displaying a font sample or playing the sound, respectively.

System 7 supports both older style bit-mapped or PostScript screen fonts and the new TrueType fonts. You can tell whether it's a standard

screen font or a TrueType font by the font file icon and the accompanying display. A traditional screen-font icon displays a single letter "A"
and only one type-size sample is shown. A TrueType font icon shows
three "A"s and displays three sample type sizes when opened. (See
Figure 4.13. For more information about fonts, see *Chapter 8, Fonts
in System 7.*)

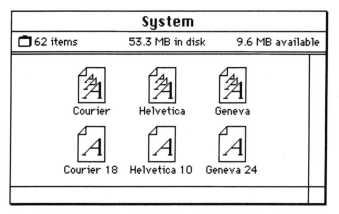

*Figure 4.13: Both bit-mapped and TrueType fonts can be
installed in the System file.*

Adding and Removing Fonts and Sounds

To add fonts or sounds to the System file, drag their icons into the
open System file window or onto the System file icon. (All other applications must be closed before adding to the System file.) To remove
fonts or sounds, drag their icons out of the open System folder window
and into another folder or volume, or directly into the Trash Can.

Modifying the System Folder

Although the System folder and its subfolders are initially defined and configured by the Installer, the System folder is changed as you add new computer software, add or remove fonts and sounds, customize your Apple Menu, change startup files and use other features.

Adding Files to the System Folder

There are several ways to add files to the System folder after its initial creation:

- **By the Apple Installer.** To add additional printer drivers, network drivers or keyboards, you can rerun the Apple Installer application at any time. The Installer adds the selected files to your System folder, placing them into the proper subfolders.

  You don't have to use the Installer to add drivers or files from the System Software disks; also, you can drag copy files directly from these disks into your System folder.

- **By application software installers.** Many software applications use installation programs that copy the software and its associated files to your hard drive. Installers that have been specifically written or updated for compatibility with System 7 can place files correctly into the System 7 Folder or subfolders.

  Older installer applications often place all files directly in the System folder, ignoring the subfolder structure. In these cases, the application may require that the files remain as positioned by the installer. However, most inits should be moved to the Extensions folder, and control panels should be moved to the Control Panels folder, regardless of how they were originally positioned. (Although all inits should be placed in the Extensions folder or Control Panels folder, inits located directly in the System folder will be executed at startup.)

- **By software applications**. Historically, many software applications read and write temporary and preferences files to the System folder. Others use the System folder for dictionaries and other ancillary files. Applications updated for System 7 should properly read and write files in the System folder and System folder subfiles.

  Older applications not rewritten for System 7 may not use the subfolders, but files placed directly in the System folder will be accessed properly and won't cause any problems for your System Software or other programs. New program releases will address subfolder location, in the interest of further System folder simplification.

- **By the Macintosh user**. Since some programs and utilities don't use installer applications, many files must be placed into the System folder manually. These files can be dragged onto the System folder icon or dragged into an open System folder window.

  When files are dragged onto the System folder icon, the Macintosh automatically positions them in the correct System folder or subfolder. This Helping Hand helps you manually

add files to the System folder correctly, even if you know
nothing about the System folder structure.

Before positioning files, the Helping Hand informs you it's at
work and tells you how it's positioning your files, as shown in
Figure 4.14. The Helping Hand works only when files are
dragged onto the System folder icon.

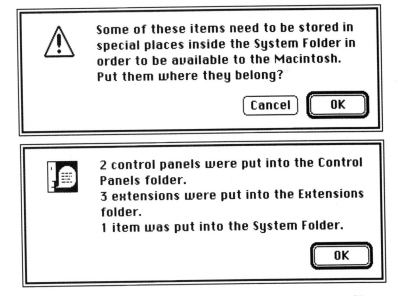

*Figure 4.14: The System folder's Helping Hand makes sure files
are positioned properly.*

Of course, once files are in the System folder, you can reposition them freely. The Helping Hand will not affect the movement of files within the System folder.

You can also avoid the action of the Helping Hand by dragging files directly into an open System folder window. When you drag files this way, you can place files into any System folder subfolder, or into the System folder itself, without interference.

Deleting Files From the System Folder

Files in the System folder for the most part can be deleted just like any other file, by dragging them into the Trash Can. However, some files cannot be deleted because they're "in use." "In use" files include the System file; the Finder; any extensions or control panels with init coding that ran at startup; open control panels and any temporary or preferences files used by open applications.

To delete the System file or Finder, you must restart the Macintosh using another boot disk. To delete an "in use" extension or control panel, move the file out of the Extension or Control Panels folder, restart the Mac, then delete the file. To delete open control panels or temporary or preferences files from open applications, simply close the control panel or open application and drag the file to the trash.

Moving On...

Working in the System folder used to be like playing with a house of cards, but as we've seen, System 7 brings new order and stability to this important part of your hard drive. The new subfolders are especially useful:

- The Apple Menu folder lets you customize your Apple Menu.

- The Extensions folder contains all the inits and drivers that add features to your Mac and the System Software.

- The Control Panels folder holds special "mini-applications" that set preferences for System Software features, utilities and even hardware peripherals.

- The Startup folder lets you determine which files and applications are opened each time your Mac is turned on.

In the next chapter, we turn our attention to the effects this new System Software has on Software applications used on the Mac—from new ways of accessing your software to a new document type that makes it easier for you to create frequently used files. We'll also look at the enhanced dialog boxes you will encounter whenever you open or save files with System 7.

Chapter 5: System 7 and Your Software

Thus far, the System 7 features we have discussed are those that change the way you organize and manipulate data files on your Macintosh. But as important as file management is, it's not the reason you use a Macintosh. You use the Mac because its software applications—word processors, spreadsheets, databases, graphics programs and the rest—help you accomplish your work productively.

In this chapter, we'll look at some of the ways System 7 affects software applications, beginning with the important issue of compatibility. Then we'll see the expanded launching methods, new Stationery Pads and desktop-level enhancements System 7 provides. Other major enhancements that affect software applications, including data sharing, program-to-program communication and support for TrueType fonts, are discussed in *Chapter 7, The Edition Manager and IAC,* and in *Chapter 8, Fonts in System 7.*

System 7 Compatibility

It's always exciting to get a new software upgrade—it means more features, better performance and an easier-to-use interface. But as seasoned computer users know, along with improvements and solutions, software upgrades often introduce bugs and incompatibilities.

System Software is particularly susceptible to upgrade compatibility problems because every Macintosh application is so heavily dependent on the System Software. Each application must be fine-tuned and coordinated to work together smoothly with the system. The relationship between System Software and an application is like that of two juggling partners, each throwing balls into the air that the other is expected to catch. Upgrading System Software replaces a familiar partner with a new one, without changing the routine or allowing time to practice, while still expecting each toss and catch to occur precisely.

Apple's goal has been to ensure that System 7 is compatible with as many existing applications as possible. In fact, it claims that any application running under System 6.0.x can operate under System 7 without alteration, as long as it was programmed according to its widely published programming rules. For the most part, this appears to be true.

Generally speaking, to be considered System 7-compatible, an application must run under System 7 and provide the same features, with the same degree of reliability, that it did under System 6.0x. But System 7 compatibility is not black and white—it will exist in varying degrees in different applications. Most will successfully launch and provide basic operations under System 7, and many will operate correctly in

System 7's multitasking environment; but problems with 32-bit memory and File Sharing will probably become more common.

Applications that are not System 7-compatible will have to be upgraded by their developers in order to be System 7-compatible. If you find that one of your applications doesn't operate properly in System 7, contact the software developer to obtain a System 7-compatible upgrade.

Let's Be Friendly

If a System 7-compatible application is (more or less) no better under System 7 than it was under System 6.0x, compatibility is obviously not the ultimate accomplishment. The ultimate goal is to take full advantage of all new System 7 features, a status which Apple calls "System 7-Friendly," or "System 7-Savvy." To be System 7-Friendly an application must be specifically written, or updated, for technical compatibility with System 7 and support for its new features.

To put it another way, applications that are System 7-compatible will survive, but applications that are System 7-Friendly will thrive. To be considered System 7-Friendly, applications must

- **Support multitasking.** System 7 lets multiple applications be open and processing data simultaneously. Applications should be able to operate in both the foreground and the background, and should support background processing to the greatest degree possible. (More information on multitasking and background processing later in this chapter.)

- **Be 32-bit clean.** When the "32-Bit Addressing" option is turned on in the Memory control panel, certain Macintosh models can utilize large amounts of memory (discussed in *Chapter 11, Memory Management*). Applications should operate correctly when this option is used.

- **Support the Edition Manager's Publish and Subscribe features.** The Edition Manager, described in *Chapter 7, The Edition Manager and IAC*, allows data to be transferred from one application to another while maintaining a link to the original file. Applications must include the basic Publish and Subscribe commands.

- **Support AppleEvents and Core events.** System 7's Inter-Application Communication (IAC), also described in *Chapter 7, The Edition Manager and IAC*, defines a basic set of Apple Events that allow one application to communicate with another.

- **Impose no limit on font sizes.** Applications should support all font sizes, from 1 to 32,000 in single-point increments. (See *Chapter 8, Fonts in System 7.*)

- **Provide Help Balloons.** As described in *Chapter 2, Finder 7*, Help Balloons offer quick pop-up summaries of an application's menu commands, dialog box options and graphic elements.

- **Be AppleShare-compliant.** System 7 allows any user to access files shared on AppleShare servers or files from other System 7 Macintoshes using File Sharing. Applications should operate correctly when launched over an AppleTalk network, or when reading or writing data stored on File Sharing or AppleShare volumes (see *Chapter 9, Introduction to File Sharing*).

- **Support Stationery Pads**. Applications should be able to take full advantage of Stationery Pads, a new type of document template featured in System 7. (See the Stationery Pads discussion later in this chapter.)

Most major software developers should be offering System 7-Friendly upgrades within three to six months after System 7's release. Of course, all future software will be written with System 7 in mind, and eventually all Macintosh applications will be System 7-Friendly.

Launching

Double-click, Double-click, Double-click. That's how most Macintosh users launch their software applications. Two clicks to open the drive or volume, two to open the application folder, and a double-click on the application icon to launch the software.

This method can quickly grow wearisome when it means clicking through many volumes and folder layers to reach an icon. As alternatives, a wide range of application launching utilities, including On-Cue, PowerStation, DiskTop and MasterJuggler, have appeared in recent years. With these utilities, you can launch by selecting application names from a list instead of searching through folders for icons.

Applications can still be launched in System 7 by double-clicking on icons, but more icons are available, including aliases and stationery documents. It's now also possible to launch applications or documents from the Apple Menu or by dragging a document onto an application icon.

In fact, you can now launch applications in all of the following ways:

- **Double-click on an application icon.** You can double-click on an application icon, or the alias of an application icon, to launch that application.

- **Double-click on a document icon or its alias.** If the application that created a document is unavailable, the Application Not Found dialog box, shown in Figure 5.1, will appear. To open a document that presents this dialog box, you must either locate the original application or use another application that's capable of opening that type of document.

  For example, suppose a MacWrite II file displays the Application Not Found dialog box when double-clicked. You could open Microsoft Word, then access the file with the OPEN command. Similarly, SuperPaint can open MacPaint files and many applications can open TIFF or EPS files. In fact, most applications can open documents of several different file types.

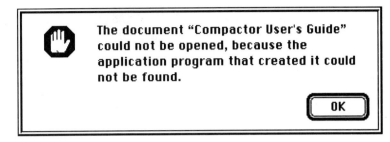

Figure 5.1: The Application Not Found dialog box.

- **Double-click on a Stationery Pad document or its alias.**
  Stationery Pad documents are template documents that create
  untitled new documents automatically when opened. (More
  on Stationery Pads later in this chapter.)

- **Drag a document icon onto an application icon.** This
  method of launching will work only when the document is
  dragged onto the icon of the application that created it.

  If an application *will* launch, the application icon highlights
  when the document icon is above it. Application icons will
  highlight only when appropriate documents are positioned
  above them, as shown in Figure 5.2.

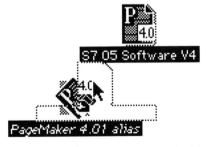

*Figure 5.2: Application icons highlight when documents they can
launch are dragged onto them.*

■ **Add applications or documents to the Startup folder inside the System folder.** To launch an application or open a document and its application, add the application or document icon or an alias of one of these icons, to the Startup folder inside the System folder. This will cause the application or document to be launched automatically at startup. (See *Chapter 4, The System Folder* for more information on using the Startup folder.)

■ **Choose an application or document name from the Apple Menu folder inside the System folder.** The application or document name will then appear in the Apple Menu and can be launched by choosing the application or document name. (Information on configuring the Apple Menu is found in *Chapter 4, The System Folder.*)

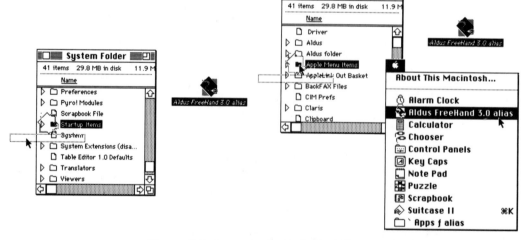

Figure 5.3: Items are launched at startup when added to the Startup folder (left), or when selected from the Apple Menu.

Launching Methods

There's no one best way to launch applications. You'll probably find
that a combination of methods is the most efficient. Keep the following
launching tips in mind:

- **The Apple Menu**. Add the applications and documents you
  use most frequently to the Apple Menu. (See *Chapter 4, The
  System Folder* for more on the Apple Menu.)

- **Alias folders**. Assemble groups of application aliases into folders
  according to application type; add aliases of frequently used folders
  to the Apple Menu.

  You can select the folder name from the Apple Menu to open
  the folder and double-click on the application you want to
  launch. Hold down the option key while you double-click on
  the application icon to close the open folder window automatically during the launch.

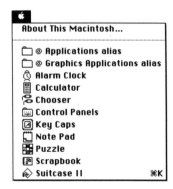

*Figure 5.4: Adding folders full of application icons
to the Apple Menu makes them easy to access.*

Figure 5.4 shows an Apple Menu configured using this method. An @ character has been added before the name of each folder alias, which forces these folders to group near the top of the Apple Menu.

- **Double-click on icons.** When browsing in Finder windows to locate specific files, use the tried-and-true double-click method to launch applications, aliases, documents or stationery icons.

- **Drag icons onto applications**. If you store documents and applications or their aliases in the same folder, or if you place application icons or aliases on the desktop, dragging icons onto applications may prove useful, although in most cases double-clicking on the document would be easier.

Stationery Pads

Another innovation in System 7 is Stationery Pads, which is a fancy name for quickly making an existing document into a template. Templates, as you may know, give you a head start in creating new documents.

For example, the documents in your word processor probably fall into a handful of specific formats—letters, reports, memos, chapters, etc. Rather than starting each document with a new, unformatted file, the stationery document for a letter, for example, would provide date, salutation, body copy, closing character and paragraph formatting, correct margins and other basic formatting.

Template support has been available in several Macintosh applications for some time, but by adding the Stationery Pad feature to System 7, Apple makes templates available in every software package you use to create documents.

7/15/91

Dear Mr. Cimmoh,

This is your lucky day! I am pleased to inform you that your name has been selected in our weekly grand-prize drawing, and you have won a new car and dream vacation valued at $20,000.
In order to claim your prize, please stop by our store, and complete a Prize Winner Registration form, available from our Store Manager, Ms. Juni Enrich. You will then be allowed to select your automobile and vacation from the prize-winner catalog.
Once you receive your prizes, our contest photographer will contact you to arrange to have promotional pictures taken of you and your prizes. (You agreed to such photo's in your signed entry form.)

Sincerely,

Robert Scrunge
Store Manager

Figure 5.5: A letter that will become a Stationery Pad.

Creating a Stationery Pad

A Stationery Pad (a document that is going to be stationery) is usually created in three steps:

- First, you find an existing typical example of a document you commonly create.

- Then you modify the typical document to make it a good generic representation and save it to disk.

- Finally, select the "Stationery pad" option in the file's Get Info dialog box.

As an example, to create a memo Stationery Pad, open an existing representative memo, like the one shown in Figure 5.6 Although this memo is typical, it does have one unusual element, the embedded graphic. So we remove that element, since most of the memos we create do not call for such graphic elements. The remaining memo elements are left to serve as placeholders.

Before saving the memo Stationery Pad, it's a good idea to edit the text in all placeholders, so that they're appropriate to use in final documents. Replace placeholder text with nonsensical data ("greeking"), which helps ensure that no placeholder elements are accidentally used in finished documents. For the memo date, for example, use 0/0/00, and the memo address can read To: Recipient.

A date such as 7/15/91 might be overlooked and not replaced with the current date each time the Stationery Pad is used. The 0/0/00 date, on the other hand, is almost certain to be noticed when the document is proofread. Figure 5.6 shows our sample memo with generic placeholders inserted.

Figure 5.6: After being edited, the document contains placeholders.

After editing the memo, the S͟A͟V͟E͟ A͟S͟ command saves the template document to disk. Use names that are easily identified in Finder windows and dialog box listings: for example, add the letters "STNY" to the end of each document name. You're not required to use naming conventions; you'll be able to distinguish Stationery Pads by their icons alone, but using distinct file names gives you an extra advantage.

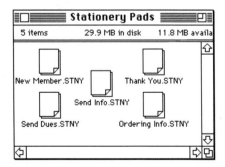

Figure 5.7: A folder full of Stationery Pads.

There's one final but critical step in creating a stationery document. In the Finder, after the edited and saved Stationery Pad document is selected and the GET INFO command is chosen, the Stationery Pad option in the lower right corner of the Get Info dialog box is then selected, so its check box is filled. Notice that the icon inside the Get Info dialog box changes to show that the document is now a Stationery Pad. When the Get Info dialog box is closed, the conversion is complete.

The stationery document's icon at the Finder will also be updated to reflect its new status, but the icon that appears depends on the application used to create the document. These icons are discussed more completely later in this section.

Using Stationery

After you've created Stationery Pad documents, you can either launch them by double-clicking on their icons from the desktop, or you can open them with the OPEN command in an application's file menu.

When a Stationery Pad is launched from the desktop, the dialog box shown in Figure 5.8 appears, prompting you to name and save the new document being created. After entering a new name, you can click the OK button, to create a copy of the Stationery Pad, save it in the same location as the Stationery Pad and open this new document; or you can use the SAVE IN button to save the file in a new location before it's opened.

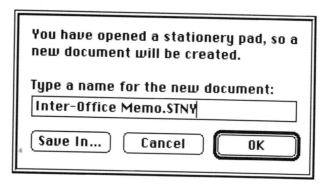

Figure 5.8: The Open Stationery Pad dialog box.

Since the Stationery Pad file is duplicated and renamed before it's opened, if you later decide you don't need this new document, you'll have to manually delete it from your disk.

Stationery Pad works differently when opened from within an application. In this case, a copy of the Stationery Pad is not created; instead, the original Stationery Pad file is opened. In Open dialog boxes, you can tell Stationery Pad documents by their icons, as shown in Figure 5.9. Since opening a Stationery Pad from the Open command modifies the original file, you can't use Stationery Pads as templates for new documents when opening them in this way. A warning dialog box appears when Stationery Pads are opened from the Open command, to remind you that you'll be modifying the Stationery Pad itself.

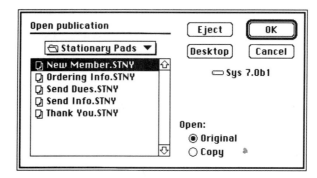

Figure 5.9: An Open dialog box with Stationery Pads visible.

Figure 5.10: This dialog appears when a Stationery Pad is opened from inside an application.

If you want to use a Stationery Pad as a template, you must open it from the Finder. Of course, even when your application is already running, you can return to the Finder from the Applications Menu, and launch your Stationery Pad without quitting the application.

Once you've opened a copy of a Stationery Pad document, you can customize it as required. Be sure to edit all placeholders that you set when creating the Stationery Pad document. You can delete unnecessary elements, add new ones, and edit the document in any other way you choose.

Stationery Pad Tips

- **Stationery Pad aliases.** Whether they were created before or after the "Stationery Pad" option was set, aliases of Stationery Pad documents access the Stationery Pad normally. The alias icon does not display the Stationery Pad icon.

- **Stationery comments.** Comments are transferred to any new document created with the Stationery Pad. To take advantage of this, you can write the name of each Stationery Pad document in the Stationery Pad's comment field. Later you can determine which Stationery Pad was used to create a document by simply checking the document's GET INFO comment.

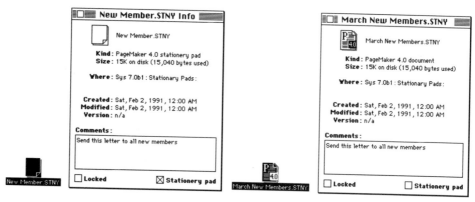

Figure 5.11: Comments are carried over to Stationery Pads.

- **Stationery Pad Folder.** Create a Stationery or Templates Folder and keep aliases of all your Stationery Pad documents in this folder. Keep the original documents organized as they were originally. This makes it easy to access Stationery Pads when you need them. If you use them frequently, you can also put an alias of this folder in your Apple Menu folder.

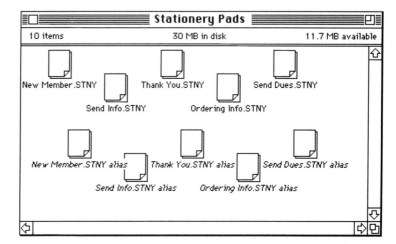

Figure 5.12: A folder containing Stationery Pads and Stationery Pad aliases.

- **Application support for multiple documents**. If an application does not support more than one open document at a time, opening a Stationery Pad from the Finder when the application and a document are already open may not work. In this case, close the current open document, then reopen the Stationery Pad using the OPEN command.

- **Opening Stationery from the OPEN command**. Opening a Stationery Pad document from inside an application that isn't Stationery Pad Aware may cause problems. An application may open the Stationery Pad itself rather than creating a new Untitled copy. When you open Stationery Pads using the OPEN command, be sure to use a new file name and the SAVE AS command, so you don't accidentally overwrite your Stationery Pad document.

■ **Editing Stationery Pads**. Deselecting the "Stationery Pad" option in the Get Info dialog box will turn any Stationery Pad document back into a "normal" document—it will lose its Stationery Pad properties. You can then edit the Stationery Pad document, making changes to your Master. After editing and saving this document, reselect the "Stationery pad" option in the Get Info dialog box to turn the file back into a Stationery Pad.

The Desktop Level

It is impossible to work on the Macintosh and not hear, and use, the word "desktop." In Macintosh terminology, the word "desktop" usually refers to the Finder desktop, which is the on-screen area where volume icons, windows and the Trash Can appear. Also, files and folders can be dragged from any mounted volume or folder and placed directly on the desktop.

In previous System Software versions, the Finder desktop was ignored by the Open and Save dialog boxes. In these dialog boxes, each mounted volume was discrete, and all files were on disks or in folders.

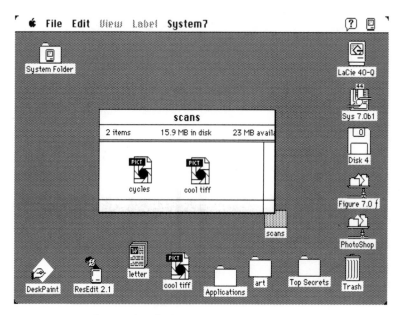

Figure 5.13: The Finder desktop.

In System 7, dialog boxes provide access to the Finder desktop and all
volumes, files and folders that reside there. In fact, the DRIVE button has
been replaced with a DESKTOP button that causes a new desktop view
to appear in the scrolling file listing. This desktop view displays
the name and icon of each volume, file and folder that exist on the
Finder desktop.

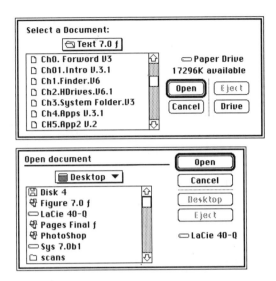

Figure 5.14: A sample dialog box from System 6.0x (top) and one from System 7 (bottom).

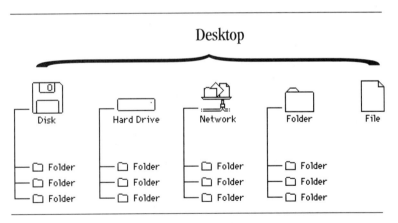

Figure 5.15: The Desktop level offers a birds-eye view of the available volumes, files and folders.

From the desktop view in these new dialog boxes, you can move into any volume, folder or file on the desktop by double-clicking a name in the scrolling list, or save files directly onto the desktop. Once any volume or folder is open, the list of files and folders at that location is displayed, and the dialog box operates normally. Saving a file onto the desktop causes its icon to appear on your Finder desktop, and leaves you free to later drag it onto any volume or folder.

Dialog Box Keyboard Equivalents

In addition to the new DESKTOP button, all Open and Save dialog boxes now support a number of keyboard equivalents that make it faster and easier to find and create files:

- **Desktop express.** Command-D is the equivalent of clicking the DESKTOP button.

- **Next or previous volume or drive.** To cycle through available volumes (formerly done by the DRIVE button), press Command-Forward Arrow. You can now also cycle backward by pressing Command-Back Arrow.

- **File listing / File name options.** In Save As dialog boxes, pressing the tab key toggles back and forth between the scrolling file listing and the file name option. You can tell which is activated by the presence of an extra black border and control the active window from the keyboard. (In earlier versions of the System Software, pressing the tab key was the equivalent of pressing the DRIVE button.)

When the file name option is active, you can control the cursor position with the arrow keys, and of course enter any valid file name. When the scrolling file listing is active, use the keyboard equivalents listed below to locate, select and manipulate files and folders.

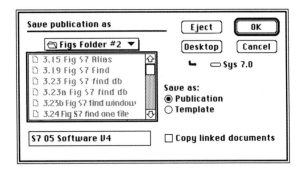

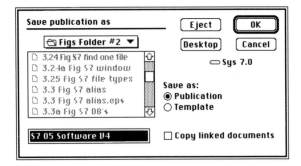

Figure 5.16: A dialog box with the scrolling list active (top) and with the Name option box active (bottom).

The following keyboard equivalents are available in the scrolling file listing of either Open or Save As dialog boxes:

- **Jump alphabetically.** Typing any single letter causes the first file name starting with that letter, or the letter closest to it, to be selected.

- **Jump alphabetically, then some.** If you type more than one letter, the Mac will continue to narrow down the available file names accordingly. In other words, typing only the letter F will jump you to the first file name that starts with an F; typing FUL will pass by the file "Finder 7 Facts" and select the file "Fulfillment Info." When typing multiple characters to find files, you must not pause between characters, or the Mac will think you're starting a new search—instead of interpreting your second character as the second letter of a file name, it will treat it as the first letter of a new search.

- **Open folder.** While a folder is selected, press Command-Down Arrow to open that folder and view its contents.

- **Close folder.** While a folder is selected, press Command-Up Arrow to close that folder and view the contents of its enclosing folder or volume.

Desk Accessories

Desk accessories have always had a fond place in the hearts of Macintosh users. As they were originally designed, DA's came to symbolize the unique nature of the Mac—its customizability and much of its fun.

The main benefit of using desk accessories was being able to run an additional application (even if it was a small one) without quitting the main application—you could open a calculator, or delete files from your disk, without leaving your word processor, for example. With System Software 5.0, MultiFinder became an inherent feature of the System Software, giving users the ability to run large and small multiple applications.

The introduction of MultiFinder meant that desk accessories' days were numbered. System 7 pounds the last nail into the coffin, but not before assuring them an afterlife. The cause of death is System 7's inability to launch or install desk accessory files from the DA Suitcase format. The resurrection is provided by System 7's ability to easily turn these old desk accessories into new double-clickable applications.

Existing desk accessories appear at the Finder with their familiar Suitcase icons, as shown in Figure 5.17. In previous System Software versions, these suitcases were opened and installed into the System file using the Font/DA Mover, or attached to the System file via utilities like Suitcase II and MasterJuggler. In System 7, however, these DA suitcases are relics whose only purpose is to store desk accessories until they're converted for use in System 7.

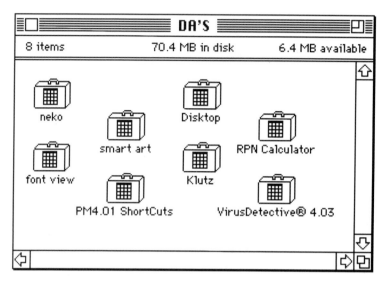

Figure 5.17: DA icons.

To convert desk accessories into System 7-compatible applications, double-click on the Suitcase icon, and a window will open, as shown in Figure 5.18. This window displays each desk accessory in the Suitcase, with its own Application icon. At this point, you may run the DA by simply double-clicking on it, or you can permanently convert the DA into an application by dragging it out of the Suitcase and into any other folder or volume. As you copy the DA into a new folder or volume, it's transformed into a stand-alone application. From this point forward, it functions as an application, although it's still listed by the Finder's Kind item as a desk accessory.

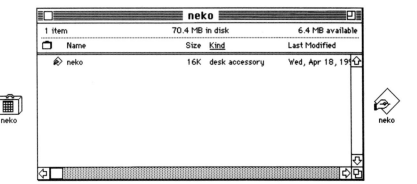

Figure 5.18: A DA icon, open DA window and DA application.

This process (removing DA's from their Suitcases) is the only way to use DA's in System 7. Once "converted" into System 7-compatible applications, you can't use them as applications in System 6.0x or earlier. If you try to launch a converted desk accessory into earlier System Software, the Name dialog box will appear. For this reason, you should keep copies of all your desk accessories, in their original desk accessory format, on disk in case you ever need to use them with an older version of the System Software.

Once a DA has been converted into an application, it can be used just like any application. You can store it in any folder, and you'll usually launch it by double-clicking on its icon. Of course, you can launch the converted DA with any of the launching methods described earlier in this chapter. You'll also want to install the DA, or an alias of it, in the Apple Menu folder so you can launch it from the Apple Menu.

After opening a converted DA, you can either close it when you're finished, hide it with the Applications Menu's HIDE command, or bring another application to the foreground and leave the DA open in the background. Most converted DA's are closed by clicking the close box in their window title bar, but you can also use the File Menu's QUIT command.

Moving On...

Even the oldest Macintosh programs are improved by System 7, as we've seen throughout this chapter. Some improvements are dramatic and substantial, while others are more subtle or incidental:

- There are now even more ways than ever to launch your applications and their document files.

- A new document type, the Stationery Pad, is provided by the System Software to every application.

- The Desktop level is given official presence in all Open and Save dialog boxes.

- Desk accessories leave the shelter of the Apple Menu and can now be used like normal applications.

Another important aspect of System 7 is the ability to open and use several applications simultaneously. Chapter 6 focuses on multitasking, describing the commands and features it supports, and looking at the ways it can be used to work more productively.

Chapter 6: Working With Multiple Applications

One "exciting new feature" of System 7 is actually an exciting old feature that some Macintosh users have been taking advantage of for more than two years. Known as MultiFinder in previous System Software versions, this feature lets you

- Run multiple applications at once.

- Switch between open applications as necessary.

- Leave one program working while you switch to another.

MultiFinder was a separate utility file, kept in the System folder of previous System Software versions. Because MultiFinder's features have been incorporated into System 7, the MultiFinder utility is no longer used. As you'll see, System 7 provides all the features of MultiFinder, plus some new ones.

Since the MultiFinder utility file is no longer used, the name "MultiFinder" is no longer appropriate. In this book, the set of features that allows you to open multiple applications simultaneously will be referred to as the *multitasking features of System 7*. Other people and publications will continue to refer to these as MultiFinder features, or you may also hear them described as the "Process Manager." Some may avoid using any specific name, simply referring to them as part of the System Software or the Finder.

Technically speaking, it should be pointed out, there are two kinds of multitasking: *cooperative* and *preemptive*. System 7 provides cooperative multitasking, which means that all open applications have equal access to the Macintosh's computing power. Some purists consider preemptive multitasking, which ascribes priority to specific applications or tasks, to be the only "real" multitasking. The distinctions between these two are unimportant, and probably uninteresting, to most Macintosh users. For convenience, we'll use the term multitasking to describe the Mac's ability to open and operate multiple applications simultaneously.

What Is Multitasking?

Multitasking allows several application programs to be opened and used simultaneously. You can have your word processor, page layout software and graphics package all running at the same time, and you can switch between them freely. It's even possible for an application to continue processing information while another application is being used. Figure 6.1 shows Adobe Illustrator, Microsoft Word and Aldus PageMaker all open simultaneously on the Macintosh.

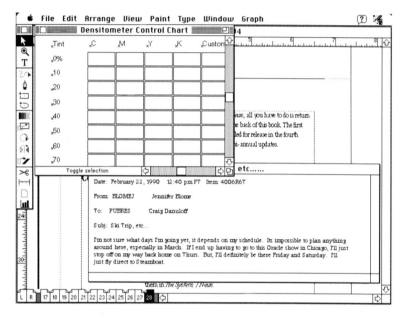

Figure 6.1: A Mac as it appears with several open applications.

Multitasking is a fantastic productivity booster, allowing you to use time and resources with maximum efficiency. For example, you're working in your word processor when you receive a telephone call from your mother. She wants to know whether she'd be better off investing the $10,000 she just won playing bingo in a 7-year CD paying 8.25 percent, or if she should sink it into T-bills paying 6.15 percent tax-free. To help dear old Mom out of her dilemma, you need access to a spreadsheet. So you quit your word processor, launch your spreadsheet, perform the necessary calculations, offer your advice, quit the spreadsheet, launch the word processor, reload your file and say goodbye to your mother.

All of this is fine—of course you want to help your mother—but all the time it took to quit your word processor, launch the spreadsheet, quit the spreadsheet, relaunch the word processor and reload your file could have been avoided. Multitasking would have allowed you to run your spreadsheet without quitting your word processor.

This example points to one of the most obvious benefits of multitasking—the ability to handle interruptions with minimum loss of productivity. For most people, interruptions are an unavoidable part of working, and whether they're in the form of a ringing telephone, a knock on the door, an urgent Email message or your own memory lapses (you forgot to print that report and drop it in the mail), the least disruption possible is the key to productivity.

The second major benefit of multitasking is its ability to use two or more applications together to complete a single project. To prepare a mail merge, for example, you can export data from your database manager, prepare the merge lists, then execute the merge. In most cases, the raw data exported from your database will require some cleaning up before it's ready to be merged; and often you'll encounter a minor data formatting problem that requires you to repeat the whole export and data cleanup process. But by using multitasking, you avoid the unnecessary delay and frustration of quitting the word processor to return to the database, then quitting the database to return to the word processor.

As other examples, you may need to read reports and view database or spreadsheet data while preparing presentation graphics; update graphic illustrations in a drawing package before importing them into a page layout; or use an optical character recognition package to read in articles for storage in a database. In these and many other cases, quickly switching from one application to another and using the Mac's CUT, COPY and PASTE commands to transfer data between these open applications often allow transfer of information between applications that cannot otherwise share data.

The third benefit of multitasking is the most exciting—and certainly the one yielding the largest productivity gains: multitasking supports *background processing*. This means that an open application can continue to process data even when you switch away from that application to work in another. Any task that ties up your computer, forcing you to wait for it to finish, can probably benefit from background processing. Common examples are printing, transferring files to or from bulletin boards, large spreadsheet calculations and database report generation. Examples of background processing and ways you can take advantage of this tremendous capability are discussed later in this chapter.

MultiFinder in System 6.0x

If you're familiar with MultiFinder from earlier versions of the System Software, you'll find only a few differences between MultiFinder and the multitasking features of System 7. The most notable difference is that multitasking is always available and, unlike MultiFinder, cannot be turned off.

If you didn't use MultiFinder in previous versions of the System Software, it was probably for one of the following reasons:

- **Insufficient memory.** MultiFinder required two megabytes of RAM and four or more megabytes of RAM to be useful. The same is true of the multitasking capabilities in System 7, although the recent dramatic lowering of RAM prices and the addition of virtual memory capabilities in System 7 make this less of an issue than it was in the past. (System 7 memory requirements are discussed later in this chapter, and in *Chapter 11, Memory Management.*)

- **Reputation.** MultiFinder had a reputation for instability. Many people believed that using MultiFinder made the Macintosh prone to frequent crashes. As often happens with software and hardware, this reputation was undeserved—the rumors of crashes were not based on the real facts.

When MultiFinder was first released, many applications were crashing when they were launched under MultiFinder. This was not the fault of MultiFinder; it was usually because the application had not been written according to Apple's programming rules. Once these incompatible applications were made MultiFinder-compatible, almost all problems vanished.

Another problem—again not MultiFinder's fault—was the increasing use of init programs, which caused a memory conflict in the System Heap (an area of RAM used by the operating system), often resulting in crashes when using MultiFinder. This problem was easily cured with utilities such as HeapFix or HeapTool, which are freely available from user groups and bulletin boards. In any case, this type of problem is not apparent in System 7.

■ **Complexity.** MultiFinder was considered too complex by many
novice Macintosh users. This perception was understand-
able—after all, MultiFinder was offered as a virtually un-
documented utility program. A Macintosh user had to be
somewhat daring and adventurous just to turn it on and learn
how to use it. For the majority of users who don't spend their
free time attending user groups, browsing on CompuServe or
reading about Macintosh, MultiFinder seemed intimidating
and too risky.

In System 7, multitasking is seamlessly integrated into the System
Software, making the simultaneous use of multiple applications a
fundamental part of the working routine. Everyone who uses the
Macintosh should take the time to learn, understand and benefit from
this powerful tool.

Working With Multiple Applications

System 7 allows you to open multiple applications automatically,
without any special configuration or initiation. In fact, when you
launch your first application from the Finder, you'll immediately
notice the effect: the Finder desktop (the volume icons, Trash Can,
etc.) does not disappear as the new application is launched, as was the
case in previous versions of the System Software. The Finder remains
visible in System 7 because both your new application and the Finder
are now running simultaneously.

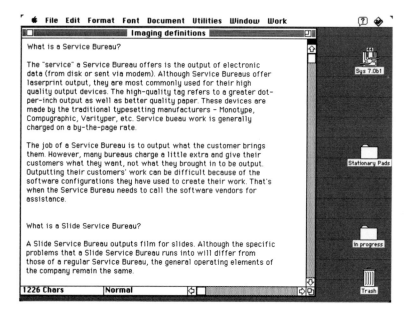

Figure 6.2: MS Word running with Finder elements visible.

Launching additional applications continues to demonstrate the abilities of multitasking. As each additional program opens, its menu bar and windows are displayed, and other open applications are unaffected.

When you first start using multiple applications simultaneously, the sight of several windows on-screen at the same time may be a little disconcerting. As you learn to arrange and manipulate these windows and enjoy the benefits of multiple open applications, you'll soon find yourself wondering how you ever got along using just one program at a time.

The number of applications you can launch simultaneously is limited only by the amount of memory you have available. If your launch will exceed available memory, a dialog box will alert you to the problem

and the additional application will not be launched. (More on memory
and running multiple applications later in this chapter.)

Foreground and Background Applications

Although more than one program can be open at once, only one
program can be active at any one time. The active program is the
foreground application, and other open but inactive applications are
background applications, even if you can see portions of their windows or if they're simultaneously processing tasks.

You can tell which program is currently active in several ways:

- The menu bar displays the menu commands of the active
  program only.

- The active program's icon appears at the top of the Applications Menu.

- The active program name is checked in the Applications
  Menu.

- The Apple Menu ABOUT THIS MACINTOSH command lists the
  active program name.

- Active program windows overlap other visible windows or
  elements.

- Active program windows display a highlighted title bar, which
  includes horizontal lines, the Close box and the Zoom box.

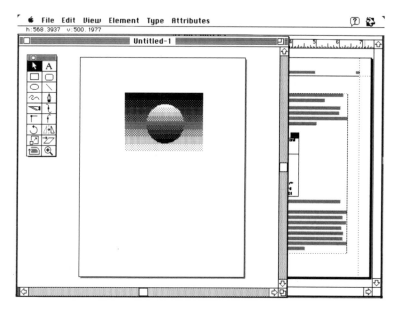

Figure 6.3: Aldus FreeHand is the active program in this window; PageMaker is in the background.

In contrast, a background application's menu bar does not appear, its icon is not checked in the Applications Menu, none of its windows are highlighted, and some or all of its windows may be hidden or obscured.

Since only one program can be in the foreground, it's important to be able to quickly and easily switch from one foreground program to another. Switching between applications is commonly referred to as "sending to the back" and "bringing to the front."

There are two ways to switch between open applications:

- Use the **Applications Menu**. Located in the upper right corner of the menu bar, the Applications Menu lists the names of all applications currently running. Choose the name of the application you want to switch to, and that application will bring its menu bar and windows to the front.

For example, to switch from an application to the Finder, choose the word Finder from the Applications Menu: the Finder's menu bar will appear, and any icons and windows on the Finder desktop will become visible.

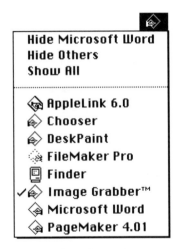

Figure 6.4: The Applications Menu as it appears with numerous open applications.

- **Click the mouse on any visible window.** Clicking the mouse on any visible element on the screen brings the application owning that element to the front. For example, while working in your word processor, if you can still see the icons on the Finder desktop, clicking on one of these icons will bring the Finder to the front, making it the current application. After working in the Finder, return to the word processor by clicking on the word processor window.

Background Processing

You can bring any application to the foreground, sending any other to the background, at any time except when dialog boxes are open. You can even send most applications to the background while they're calculating or otherwise processing data—they'll continue to calculate or process in the background. Background processing adds an entirely new dimension to simultaneously using open multiple applications.

If multiple open applications could be used only sequentially, one after the other, productivity increases would be limited to the time saved by avoiding repeated opening and quitting of applications. Background processing, however, lets you print a newsletter, calculate a spreadsheet and communicate a telecommunications package with a remote bulletin board at the same time. This is the ultimate in computer productivity.

Background processing is easy. Start by doing a lengthy process, like a spreadsheet calculation or a telecommunication session, then bring another open application to the foreground. The background task continues processing while the computer is used for another task in another application. Because foreground and background applications are sharing the hardware resources (there's only one central processing unit in the Macintosh), you may notice a slowdown or jerky motion in the foreground application. The severity of this effect will depend on your Macintosh's power and the number and requirements of the background tasks being performed; but there should be no detrimental effect on your foreground application.

You may need to periodically attend to a task left running in the background, or you may be given notice when it completes its task. If so, an Alert dialog box will be displayed, or a diamond will appear before the application's name in the Applications Menu.

Using the Print Monitor for Background Printing

The first background processing most people use is printing. Background printing is not quite the same as using two applications at once, but it's similar.

Without multitasking, you have to wait for the entire file to be printed—because of the time it takes for the printer to mechanically do the job. In background printing, files are printed to disk as fast as the application and printer driver can handle them, then a utility called a *print spooler* sends the print file from the disk to the printer. The advantage is that the print spooler takes over the task of feeding the pages to the printer and waits as the printer performs its slow mechanical tasks, while you continue working in your main application or even use another software application.

Background PostScript printing support is built into System 7 and controlled via the Chooser control panel's "Background Printing" option. By default, Background Printing is turned on, but you can turn it off at any time by clicking the Off radio button, as shown in Figure 6.5.

With Background Printing turned on, files printed using the LaserWriter driver are spooled to your hard drive. At the same time, the Print Monitor utility, automatically running in the background, begins printing the spooled file to the selected PostScript printer. While Print Monitor is printing, you can bring it to the foreground by selecting its name from the Applications Menu. (See Figure 6.6.)

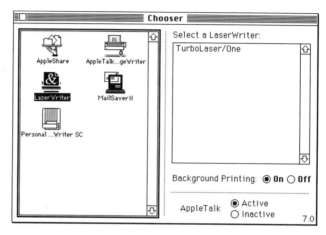

Figure 6.5: Chooser and "Background Printing" Option.

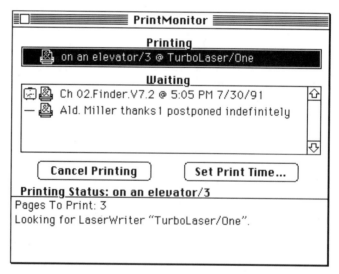

Figure 6.6: The Print Monitor dialog box.

Print Monitor provides several options: you can delay the printing of any spooled file for a specific or indefinite period of time; you can rearrange the printing order if several files have been spooled; and you can cancel the printing of a spooled file. Print Monitor can also be used to simply monitor the status of background printing as it occurs.

To delay or postpone the printing of any spooled file, click its file name and then click the SET PRINT TIME button. (See Figure 6.7.) When the Set Print Time dialog box appears, select the portion of the time or date you want to change, then click the Up or Down Arrow next to that time or date to reset it. Click the POSTPONE INDEFINITELY radio button if you're not sure when you want to print the file but wish to save it so it can be printed later. After completing these settings, click the OK button to return to the PrintMonitor dialog box.

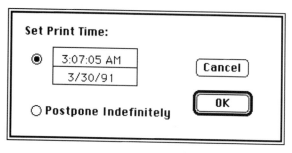

Figure 6.7: The Set Print Time dialog box.

To cancel after printing has begun, click the CANCEL PRINTING button. It will take a few seconds for printing to stop, at which time the file name will be removed from the Printing message area at the top of the PrintMonitor dialog box. To cancel printing a file waiting in the print queue, select the file name from the Waiting area, then click the REMOVE FROM LIST button.

Normally, Print Monitor completes its job invisibly in the background. If your Macintosh happens to crash, or be shut off, while Print Monitor is handling a print job, Print Monitor will run automatically when your Macintosh is restarted and advise you (by flashing its icon at the top of the Applications Menu) that an error has occurred. Bring the Print Monitor to the foreground, and it will tell you which file it was unable to finish printing, and ask if you want to re-attempt printing that file.

Copying Files in the Background

Copying files from one location to another is a basic tool the Finder has always provided, but through the successive Finder versions, the activity has continued to evolve.

Early versions of the Finder provided only a simple dialog box during file copying. Later, a counter of files being copied was added. Then names of copied files were added, and finally the progress bar became a part of this dialog box. Despite these improvements, which seemed to make time pass more quickly, you were still forced to wait while files were copied.

In System 7, the process of copying files takes a huge step forward: the wait has been eliminated altogether. You can now work in any open application while the Finder copies a file in the background. To use this feature,

- Open the application you want to use while the Finder is copying.

- Switch to the Finder using the Applications Menu or by clicking on the Finder desktop.

- Start the copy process in the normal way by dragging the desired files from their source location to the icon of the destination folder or volume. The copying process will begin and the Copying dialog box will appear.

- Then select the Applications Menu with the Stop Watch cursor and the name of the open application you want to use while the file copy is in progress. This application will come to the foreground and is ready for you to use, while the Finder continues its copy operation in the background.

- Switch back to the Finder any time you like, using the Applications Menu or clicking on the Finder desktop.

Hiding Applications

Running several applications concurrently can result in an on-screen clutter of windows displayed by open applications. To alleviate this problem, System 7 lets you "hide" open application windows, thus removing them from the screen without changing their status or the background work they're doing. You can hide an application at the time you leave it to switch to another application, or while it's running in the background.

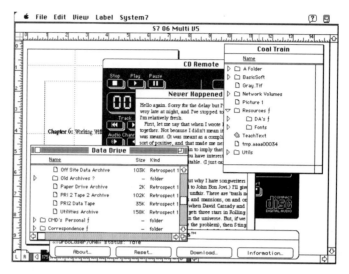

Figure 6.8: Without hiding, running multiple applications can result in a crowded display.

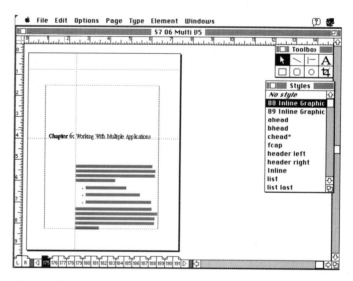

Figure 6.9: Using hiding, the same open applications result in a clear display.

The Applications Menu provides three Hide commands, HIDE CURRENT APPLICATION (Current Application being the name of the current foreground application), HIDE OTHERS and SHOW ALL.

- **HIDE CURRENT APPLICATION.** Removes all windows of the current application from the screen, and brings another window of an open application to the foreground. Usually, the Finder is brought to the foreground; but if the Finder itself has been hidden, the next application in the Applications Menu is brought forward instead.

  A hidden application's icon is dimmed in the Applications Menu to signify that it's hidden. To unhide the application, either select its name from the Applications Menu, which will bring it to the foreground, or choose the SHOW ALL command.

- **HIDE OTHERS.** Removes all windows from the screen except those of the current application. This is useful when on-screen clutter is bothersome, or if you're accidentally clicking on windows of background applications and bringing them forward. After the HIDE OTHERS command has been used, all open applications icons, except those of the foreground application, are dimmed in the Applications Menu, as a visual reminder that these applications are hidden.

- **SHOW ALL.** Using this command makes all current applications visible (not hidden). (You can tell which are currently hidden by their dimmed icons in the Applications Menu.) When the SHOW ALL command is chosen, the current foreground application remains in the foreground and the windows of hidden background applications become visible but the applications remain in the background.

While an application is hidden, it continues to operate exactly the same as it would if it were running as a background application and not hidden. If an application can normally perform tasks in the background, it will still perform these tasks in the background while it's hidden. In fact, because of the effort saved by not having to upgrade the screen display, some tasks operate faster in the background when their application is hidden.

You can also hide the current foreground application when you send it to the background, by holding down the option key while bringing another application forward (either by choosing its name from the Applications Menu or by clicking the mouse on its window). Applications hidden in this manner can be retrieved with the SHOW ALL command or by selecting their dimmed icons from the Applications Menu.

Multitasking Tips

Once you start using the Hide commands to reduce on-screen clutter, you should be very comfortable working with multiple open applications. The following tips can help:

- **Save before switching**. Before bringing another application to the foreground, save your work in the application you're leaving, so that if your Mac crashes or is turned off accidentally, you won't lose your work.

- **Resuming after crashing**. If an application crashes in System 7, you can usually force the Mac to close that application and regain access to your other applications without losing your work by pressing command-option-escape.

Note that after resuming from this kind of a crash, your system may be unstable and prone to additional crashes. You should save any unsaved work in other open applications, and you may want to restart your Macintosh, just to be safe.

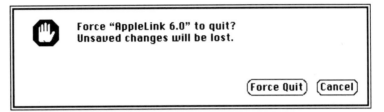

Force "AppleLink 6.0" to quit?
Unsaved changes will be lost.

[Force Quit]   [Cancel]

Figure 6.10: The Force Quit dialog box.

- **Shutting down or restarting**. Selecting the Shut down or Restart commands from the Finder's Special Menu while multiple applications are open will cause all open applications to be quit. If any open documents contain changes that haven't been saved, the application containing the document will be brought to the foreground, and you'll be asked if you want to save those changes. Click OK to save, No to discard the changes, or Cancel to abort the Shut down or Restart operation.

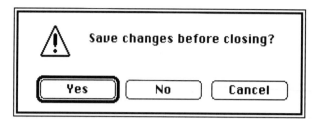

Figure 6.11: Save Changes dialog box.

- **Efficiency for background applications**. Applications in the background often run more efficiently if hidden with one of the Hide commands from the Applications Menu. This is true because often the on-screen display can't keep up with the application's processing rate; as a result, the application has to wait for the screen to be drawn. The extent of this delay depends on your computer system and video display. Using the Hide command eliminates all video-related delay.

- **Switch and hide**. To hide an application while switching to another open application, hold down the option key while clicking on the open application's window, or while selecting the name of another open application from the Applications Menu.

The Memory Implications of Multitasking

Everything has its price. Macintosh users know this well (especially experienced Macintosh users). Multitasking is no exception—its price is *memory*.

Put simply, you can run only as many applications at once as your available Macintosh memory can handle. This is because a predefined amount of memory must be dedicated to the application while it's open. Running multiple applications simultaneously requires enough memory to satisfy the cumulative amounts of those applications. Your total amount of System 7 available memory includes what's supplied by the RAM chips installed on your computer's logic board or on Nubus cards, plus any virtual memory created with the Memory control panel. (*See Chapter 11, Memory Management* for more information about virtual memory.)

When Macintosh System 7 is first turned on, some of your memory is taken up immediately by the System Software and the Finder. This amount varies depending on how many fonts and sounds you've installed, your RAM Cache setting, the extensions you're using and whether you're using File Sharing. As many as three or four megabytes of memory can be consumed by the System Software itself in some circumstances. Your Macintosh's memory usage is documented in the About This Macintosh dialog box, shown in Figure 6.12. If you would like to reduce the amount of memory your System Software consumes, remove unused fonts or sounds, reduce the size of your RAM Cache, and turn off File Sharing.

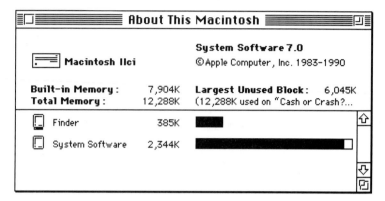

Figure 6.12: The About This Macintosh dialog box.

Each time you launch an application, the application requests the amount of memory that it needs in order to run. If enough memory is available, the application is launched. If enough memory is not available, one of two dialog boxes will appear. The first, shown in Figure 6.13, informs you there's not enough memory available to launch the selected application. The second, shown in Figure 6.14, tells you the same thing but it also gives you the option of launching the application in the amount of RAM that is available. Normally, launching the application under these circumstances will allow you to use the application without incident.

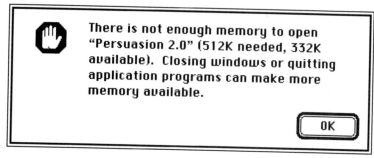

Figure 6.13: This dialog appears when launching an application with limited memory available.

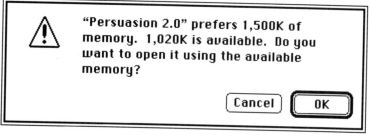

Figure 6.14: This dialog box appears when launching an application with almost enough memory available.

If available memory is insufficient to launch an application, quit one or more applications currently open to free up additional memory. Then try again to launch the application you want. If this isn't enough, quit additional open applications and retry the launch until you're successful.

(For more information on your Macintosh's memory, including ways you can expand available memory, tips on reducing the amount of memory each application consumes and more about using the About This Macintosh dialog box, see *Chapter 11, Memory Management*.)

Moving On...

Working with several applications at once takes some getting used to, but ultimately it's the best way to make the most of your time and computing resources. As we've seen in this chapter, System 7's multitasking support is impressive:

- You can launch as many different applications as your available memory permits.

- Many applications can continue to process data while they're running in the background.

- "Hiding" open applications reduces on-screen clutter without affecting the operation of the applications themselves.

Like many other System 7 features, multitasking is available to every System 7-compatible program. Next, Chapter 7 introduces two advanced features available only System 7-Friendly applications, the Edition Manager and Inter-Application Communication.

Chapter 7: The Edition Manager and IAC

Launching several applications simultaneously can dramatically improve your productivity on the Macintosh, as you saw in Chapter 6. But System 7 makes it possible to integrate your applications even more closely: text and graphic elements can be shared between documents; messages and commands can be passed from one application to another. These exciting capabilities are made possible by the Edition Manager and Inter-Application Communication (IAC), respectively.

Although the power of the Edition Manager and IAC are provided by System 7, neither feature is automatically available to System 7-compatible applications. Edition Manager and IAC are like toolkits of new capabilities that developers can add to their applications—but only after updating such applications to make them System 7-Friendly. As a result, the number of available applications supporting these features will start small but will grow steadily over the coming months and years. IAC will lag behind Edition Manager for reasons explained later in this chapter.

The Edition Manager

Creating text and graphic elements within one application and using them in other applications has always been a hallmark of the Macintosh. Its legendary CUT and COPY commands are even being offered by other me-too graphical operating systems. But while others are matching the 1984 Macintosh's capabilities, System 7 raises the ante considerably for this type of feature with the introduction of the Edition Manager's PUBLISH and SUBSCRIBE commands.

By using PUBLISH and SUBSCRIBE in your System 7-Friendly applications, elements can be moved between applications, then manually or automatically updated as they're modified. In other words, when text or graphic elements are moved from one document to another, original and duplicate elements remain linked. When the originals are changed, so are the duplicates.

The benefits are obvious:

- Charts created in spreadsheets or database programs and used in word processors or page layout applications can be automatically updated any time the data changes.

- Legal disclaimers and other boilerplate text commonly used in documents can be automatically updated if the language changes (dates on a copyright notice, for example).

■ Illustrated publications can be created using preliminary versions of graphic images that are automatically updated as these graphics are completed.

And PUBLISH and SUBSCRIBE commands can be used for more than simple "live copy and paste" between two applications on your own Macintosh. They support Macintosh networks (using System 7's File Sharing feature or other networking systems), so your documents can include components created, manipulated and stored by many people on many network file servers.

(Note: While the term Edition Manager is the technical programming term for this set of capabilities, we'll use the term "Publish/Subscribe" for the remainder of this chapter to refer to the entire set of Edition Manager capabilities.)

How Publish/Subscribe Works

While Publish/Subscribe is a powerful feature, its basic premise is simple: any elements—text, graphics or combinations of text and graphics—can be transferred from one document to another using Publish/Subscribe. The transfer begins when elements to be shared are selected then published to a new edition file. (See Figure 7.1.) This process is similar to the CUT or COPY process, except that instead of being transferred into memory, the selected elements are saved to the edition file on disk. At the time you publish these elements, you name the edition file and specify where on your hard drive it will be stored.

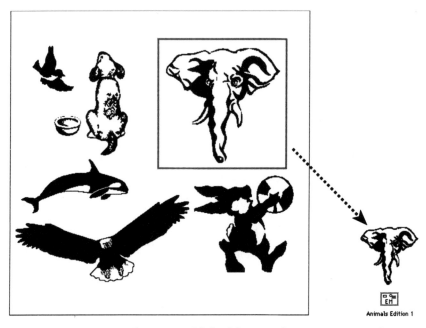

Animals Edition 1

Figure 7.1: An element published from a document is stored in an edition file.

The section of your document used to create an edition is referred to as the Publisher. A link is automatically maintained between an edition file and the document that created it. When changes are made in the Publisher, the edition file is updated to reflect these changes. (See Figure 7.2.) Updates can be made any time the original document is changed, or at any other time you initiate them.

Animals Edition 1

Figure 7.2: The edition file is automatically updated when the document changes.

To complete the transfer of elements between documents, the receiving document subscribes to the edition file by importing the edition file elements and establishing a link between the edition and the subscribing document. The document section imported from an edition becomes a Subscriber (to the edition). Figure 7.3 illustrates this process.

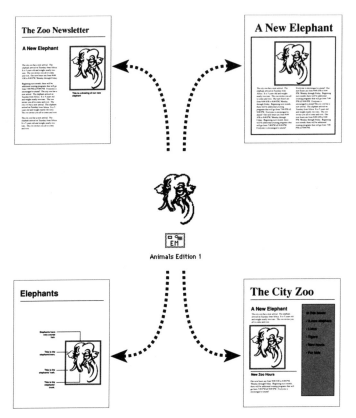

Figure 7.3: Edition files can be subscribed to by any number of other documents.

At this point, the edition file is an independent disk file, linked to the document that published it and any documents subscribing to it. (Any number of documents can subscribe to a single edition.) As elements in the publisher document change, the edition file is updated according to options set in that original document. As the edition file is updated, the edition data used by subscribers is also updated according to options set in the subscribing document. This entire process is shown in Figure 7.4.

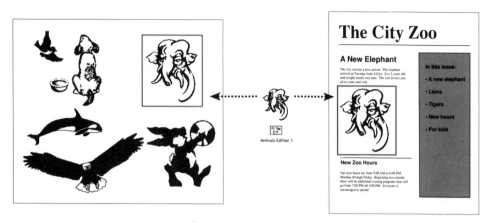

Figure 7.4: Both the publishing document and the subscribing document are linked to the edition file.

Publish / Subscribe Commands

In applications that support Publish/Subscribe, four new commands usually appear in the Edit Menu: CREATE PUBLISHER, SUBSCRIBE TO, PUBLISHER OPTIONS/SUBSCRIBER OPTIONS and SHOW BORDERS. Some applications use other command names for these functions, but they should work essentially the same as that described below.

The Create Publisher Command

CREATE PUBLISHER creates a new edition file, which you name and store in any desired location on any available volume. The edition file contains the text and graphic elements selected when the command is chosen. To publish any elements, select the areas of the current document that you wish to share, and choose the CREATE PUBLISHER command. The Create Publisher dialog box, shown in Figure 7.5, then appears.

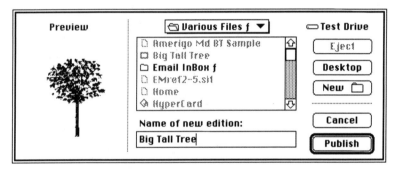

Figure 7.5: The Create Publisher dialog box.

The left side of this dialog box previews the elements that will be included in the edition. The edition contents depend not only on which elements were selected with the CREATE PUBLISHER command, but also on the "Select How Publisher Decides What To Publish" option setting. This option is described below along with the Publisher Options dialog box.

To complete the creation of the edition, enter a name in the "Name of New Edition" option box, and select a destination to which the file will be saved. Then click the PUBLISH button, which saves your new edition to disk.

There's now a new file on disk, separate from the document you're currently working in that contains a copy of the elements you selected to publish. It's this file—this edition—that will be placed into other documents and applications using the SUBSCRIBE To command. The edition will be updated to include any changes made to the elements it contains, according to the options set in the Publisher Options dialog box.

The Subscribe To Command

The SUBSCRIBE To command, the Publish/Subscribe equivalent of the PASTE command, imports a copy of an edition file into the current document. When this command is chosen, the Subscribe To dialog box appears, as shown in Figure 7.6. The names of edition files appear in the scrolling list, and a preview of any edition appears when you select the file name. Select the edition you want, click the SUBSCRIBE button, and the chosen edition appears in your document.

Figure 7.6: The Subscribe To dialog box.

When working in text-based applications, the edition appears at the place where the cursor was positioned when the SUBSCRIBE To command was chosen. In graphics applications, the edition file usually appears in the current screen display area. Details on how to use and manipulate these included editions follows.

The Publisher Options Command

The third Edition Manager command is either PUBLISHER OPTIONS or SUBSCRIBER OPTIONS, depending on the current selection. The PUBLISHER OPTIONS command, available only when the rectangle surrounding published elements is selected, presents the dialog shown in Figure 7.7.

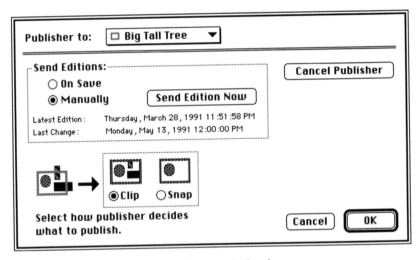

Figure 7.7: The Publisher Options dialog box.

The Publisher Options dialog box can also be accessed by double-clicking on the border of any published elements.

This dialog box presents five important options:

- **Publisher To**. This is not really an option, since it offers no alternatives; it simply shows you where the edition is stored and the path to that location. To see the storage location, click on the Publisher To pop-up menu.

- **Send Editions**. This lets you choose when the file associated with the selected edition will be updated. If you choose "On Save," the edition file is updated each time the current document is saved; if you choose "Manually," the Send Editions Now button must be clicked to update the edition file.

  This option also displays the date and time the edition file was last updated. If "On Save" is selected, this is probably the date and time the creating file was last saved. If "Manually" is selected, the time the elements included in the edition were last changed is also listed, letting you know how up-to-date the edition is in relation to the file's current status.

- **Send Editions Now**. Clicking this button updates the edition file to reflect the current status of the published elements. This button is normally used only when "Send Editions Manually" is selected.

- **Select how publisher decides what to publish**. As mentioned earlier, the light rectangle that appears after a publisher has been created defines the portions of the current document to be included in the edition. With this option you decide whether the edition will include only objects that are completely inside the box, or all elements (those partially enclosed as well as those fully enclosed).

Select "Clip" if you want the edition to include all elements.
Select "Snap" to include only fully enclosed elements.

Figure 7.8: Using the "Snap" option would exclude the whale from the edition created by the top example, and the eagle from the edition file created by the bottom example. The "Clip" option would include both animals in both examples.

Because the content of an edition is defined by a rectangle, you may notice some elements in the preview that were not selected when the CREATE PUBLISHER command was selected. There's no way to exclude these elements, other than by altering the "Select How Publisher Decides" option.

■ **Cancel Publisher.** The Cancel Publisher button removes the link between the published elements in the current application and the edition file. Cancelling the publisher does not delete the edition file, so it has no direct effect on any documents that subscribe to that edition.

You can't re-establish the link to an edition once it's been cancelled (although you can use the Create Publisher command to create a new edition with the same name, saved in the same location), so the Cancel Publisher button should be used only in certain circumstances. It would be better to use the "Send Editions Manually" option, to temporarily prevent editions from being updated.

If you accidentally use the Cancel Publisher button, you may be able to undo it by exiting your document with the Close command, clicking the Don't Save button to avoid saving your changes, then re-opening the document with the Open command. (Of course, doing this means you lose any changes you've made.) The Revert command offered by some applications may also return your document to the state it was in before you cancelled the publisher.

The Subscriber Options Command

The Subscriber Options command can be selected only when a subscribed edition is selected, as evidenced by the dark rectangle surrounding the edition. When selected, the Subscriber Options dialog box, shown in Figure 7.9, appears.

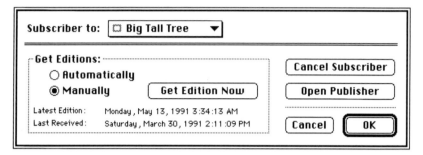

Figure 7.9: The Subscriber Options dialog box.

The Subscriber Options dialog box can also be accessed by double-clicking on the subscribed elements.

This dialog box presents five options:

- **Subscriber To**. This offers no alternatives; it simply lets you see where the edition is stored and the path to that location. To see the storage location, click on the Subscriber To pop-up menu.

- **Get Editions**. This lets you choose when the edition elements will be updated to reflect any changes made to the edition file. The "Automatically" option causes any changes to the edition file to be imported each time the document is opened or whenever the edition file changes; the "Manually" option requires the GET EDITIONS Now button to be clicked in order for changes to the edition to be reflected in your document.

  If you choose "Automatically," your document will always have the latest version of the text or graphic elements contained in the edition file. If you choose "Manual" your document may not always reflect updates to the edition file, but you can choose when those updates are made.

The date and time the current edition was last changed by the application that created it are displayed below the "Get Editions" option. If "Manually" was selected, the date and time the edition was imported into the current document are also listed. If these dates and times are not the same, the edition data contained in the current document is not up-to-date with the current edition file.

If the dates and times are dimmed, the edition file can't be located: it's either been deleted or moved to another volume. This means that the link between the current document and the edition file has been broken. More information on re-establishing this link is provided later in this chapter.

- **Get Edition Now.** Clicking this button imports the current edition file contents into your document. It's normally used only when the "Manually" option is selected

- **Cancel Subscriber.** The Cancel Subscriber button removes the link between the imported elements and the edition file. The imported elements remain in the current application, but future changes to the edition will not be reflected in the current publication.

You cannot re-establish the link to an edition once it's been cancelled (although you can use the Subscribe To command to create a new link to that same edition), so using the Cancel Subscriber button should be limited to particular circumstances. A better strategy would be to use the "Get Editions Manually" option to temporarily prevent editions from being updated in the subscribing document.

If you accidentally use the Cancel Subscriber button, you may be able to undo it by exiting your document with the Close command, clicking the Don't Save button to avoid saving your changes, then re-opening the document with the Open command. (Of course, following these steps means you lose any changes you've made.) The Revert command offered by some applications may also return your document to the state it was in before you cancelled the subscriber.

■ **Open Publisher.** The Open Publisher button performs an impressive task indeed, launching the application that created the selected edition and opening the document from which the edition was published. This allows you to edit the contents of the edition using all the tools and abilities of the application that originally created it.

There is no difference between using the Open Publisher button to launch an application and open the document that created an edition, and performing these same tasks using the Finder. But the Open Publisher button makes the process more convenient. Any changes you make to the open document will be reflected in the disk file and any related edition files, depending on the settings you use in the Publisher Options dialog box and whether you use the Save command.

It's possible to modify the edition file without changing the original document, using the following steps after launching the application with the Open Publisher button: 1) Set the Publisher Options for the edition to "Send Editions Manually"; 2) Make the necessary changes to the text or graphic elements; 3) Click the Send Editions Now button in the Publisher Options dialog box; 4) Close the document or quit the application without saving your changes. The edition file will now be updated, but the original document and any other editions will remain unchanged.

The Show Borders Command

Rectangular borders distinguish elements in your document that have been published in an edition file from elements that are part of another edition file that's been subscribed to. The border around published elements is light (about a 50 percent screen); the border around subscribed elements is dark (about a 75 percent screen), as shown in Figure 7.10.

Figure 7.10: Borders surround published elements (left) and subscribed elements (right).

The SHOW BORDERS command toggles the display of these borders, allowing you to hide or display them as necessary. Regardless of the SHOW BORDERS command setting, borders always appear when a publisher or subscriber is selected. Borders never appear on printed versions of your documents—they're for on-screen use only.

Editing Subscribers

Because the contents of a subscriber are provided by an edition file, and are usually updated periodically (according to the setting in the Subscriber Options dialog box), there are limits to manipulating a subscriber within any document. In general, you can't make any changes that would be lost when a new version of the edition becomes available.

These are some of the limitations in editing subscribers:

- **Text subscribers.** With subscribers that include only text, you can't edit the text when subscribing to the edition. The only exception is that you can set the font, type size or type style of the text, as long as the change applies to the entire subscriber text. You can't make one word in the edition bold or set one sentence in a different font.

- **Graphic subscribers.** When using subscribers that include graphics, you can reposition the editions you've subscribed to, but in most cases you can't resize them. (If you *are* permitted to resize the subscriber, graphic handles appear on the corners of the subscriber border.)

- **Text in graphic subscribers.** The text in a graphic subscriber cannot be modified in any way. In the subscriber, the text is considered a part of the graphic element.

The correct way to edit a subscriber is to reopen the document that published the edition, make changes in that document, then save those changes or use the SEND EDITION Now button to update the edition. You can quickly access the original document for any edition by clicking the OPEN PUBLISHER button found in the Subscriber Options dialog box.

Edition Files at the Finder

The edition files created with the Create Publisher command look just like any other files on your disks. They use a small shaded rectangle icon similar to the one that surrounds editions in publishing or subscribing applications; you can add comments to them using the GET INFO command.

Double-clicking on an edition file in the Finder opens a small window (shown in Figure 7.11) that contains the edition contents, the edition type (PICT, Text, etc.) and the OPEN PUBLISHER button. The OPEN PUBLISHER button launches the application that created the document the edition file was created from, and opens that document.

You work only on the document that created the edition, not on the edition file. Any changes made to the edition elements are then updated to the edition file (based on the options in the Publisher Options dialog box). This means that deleting a file that has published editions makes it impossible to ever modify or update those editions again— the data in the editions cannot be accessed from either the edition file or the subscriber document.

 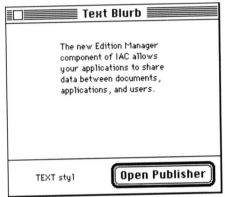

Figure 7.11: These windows are opened by clicking on edition files.

Edition File Links

The link between edition files and their publishers and subscribers is automatically maintained, even if these documents are (renamed) or moved to new locations on the current volume. If an edition file, publishing document or subscribing document is moved to a new volume and the copy on the original volume is deleted, the links to and from the file will be broken.

When links to or from an edition file are broken, it's impossible to automatically or manually update the edition file or the version of that edition file used in any subscribing documents. You can tell that a link is broken by the grayed-out appearance of certain type elements in the Publish To or Subscribe To dialog boxes, as shown in Figure 7.12.

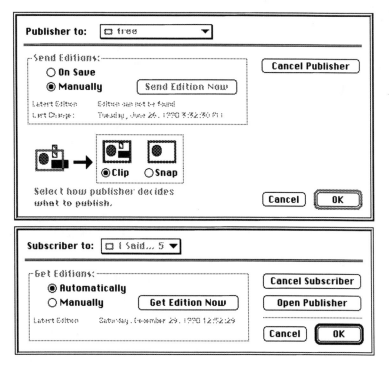

Figure 7.12: The Latest Edition and Last Change lines are dimmed when the edition has been deleted or moved to another volume.

Although there's no direct way to "reconnect" a broken Publisher or Subscriber link, you can re-create a link between an application and an edition published from it:

- Open the application and select the border surrounding the previously created edition. Even though the link has been broken, the border will still be visible.

- Select the CREATE PUBLISHER command, and save the edition with the same name as the previous edition, to the same location as the previous edition, overwriting the unlinked copy that remains there.

- Any Subscribers using this edition will now update, according to their option settings, using the information in this new version of the edition.

To recreate a link between an edition and a subscribing application:

- Open the subscribing application and select the element that was imported as a subscribed edition.

- Select the Subscribe To command, locate the edition file you want to recreate a link to. Click the Subscribe button.

- The data from the edition file as it now exists will appear in your document, replacing the older version that was selected. This edition is now linked to the edition file on disk, and will update according to the settings of the Publisher and Subscriber options.

Unavailable Edition Files

When a document containing subscribers is opened, the Macintosh attempts to locate edition files linked to each subscriber. If any of these edition files reside on unmounted floppy disks or removable volumes, you'll be prompted to insert the disks or volumes. Then the document will open normally and the links between the subscribers and their edition files will be maintained.

If you don't wish to insert the requested disks or volumes, click the Cancel button in the Please Insert the Disk... dialog box. The subscriber elements will still appear in the document, but the Subscriber Options dialog boxes will display an Edition Cannot Be Found dialog box. To establish a link to the edition, insert the correct disk, then click the Get Edition Now button.

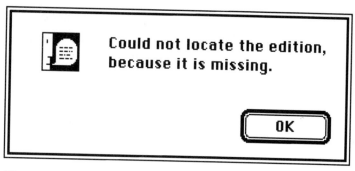

Figure 7.13: The Edition is Missing dialog box.

Edition Files and Your Network

Edition files can be published to or subscribed from any available network or File Share volume. There's no real difference in the way they operate on network/File Share volumes, except that documents containing publishers and subscribers must access the editions over the network in order to keep all files updated properly.

To expedite sharing editions via a network, you can create aliases of editions stored on network volumes that you access frequently. You can then browse these aliases on your local hard drive (from the Subscribe To dialog box) and when the editions are used, the aliases will automatically connect to the appropriate network volumes and access the actual edition files.

To subscribe directly to editions on network volumes, these will also mount automatically when documents subscribing to the editions are opened.

Figure 7.14 shows one sample network: in this case, edition files could be stored on the AppleShare file server, or on either File Sharing Mac, and be used either directly or through aliases, by any network user.

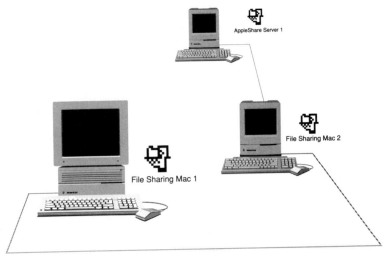

Figure 7.14: A sample network with an AppleShare server and File Sharing Macs.

Edition Manager Tips

- **Republishing an edition.** If you overwrite an existing edition (by creating a new edition with the same name in the same location as an existing edition), the new edition will be linked to all documents that subscribed to the old edition.

For example, if you wanted to replace an existing edition file named "Corporate Logo" with a new graphic, you could create a new edition named "Corporate Logo," using the CREATE PUBLISHER command, and save it in the same volume and folder as the old "Corporate Logo" edition. (When you're asked to confirm that you want to overwrite the old file, click the YES button.) At this point, all documents that subscribed to the old "Corporate Logo" edition file will begin using the new "Corporate Logo" edition file the next time they're updated.

■ **Nested editions**. You can create editions that contain text or graphics subscribed to from other editions. After appropriate updating options are set in all associated Publish To and Subscribe To dialog boxes, changes made to elements in original documents will be correctly updated everywhere they occur.

For example, if your page layout program subscribed to your "Corporate Logo" for the purpose of using it, along with some text and ornamental graphics, to create a corporate insignia, you could use the Create Publisher to save an edition file named "Corporate Insignia." This edition could then be subscribed to for use on the first page of all corporate reports created in your word processing programs. If the "Corporate Logo" edition was updated, this update would appear in the page layout file (where the insignia was created), and extended to the "Corporate Insignia" edition when the page layout document was opened (assuming the Publisher Options and Subscriber Options are set correctly). The updated Corporate Insignia edition would then be updated in all documents it was used in (if the appropriate Subscriber Option was set).

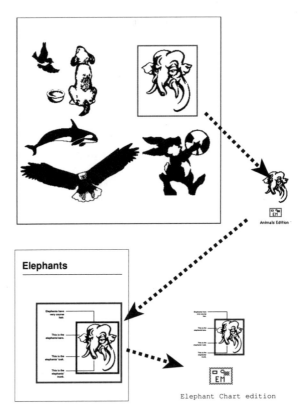

Figure 7.15: Edition files can contain other editions.

- **Double-click on edition borders to open option dialogs.**
  Double-clicking on a subscriber in a document will open the
  Subscriber To dialog box. Double-clicking on the border
  around any publisher will open the Publisher To dialog box.

- **Saving Publisher documents.** When an edition is created,
  the edition file appears on disk and can be subscribed to
  immediately. If the document that published the edition is
  closed without being saved, however, the edition file will be
  deleted, and all subscriber links will be broken.

An example: You open a drawing application and quickly create an illustration of a cow jumping over the moon. Using the CREATE PUBLISHER command, you create an edition named "Cow Over Moon," then switch to your word processor where you subscribe to the Cow Over Moon edition and continue to work on your text document. Later, when you're ready to quit for the day, you choose the SHUT DOWN command from the Finder, and your drawing application asks if you want to save the Untitled file you used to create Cow Over Moon. At this point, if you don't name and save this file, the Cow Over Moon edition will be deleted from your disk. The image will remain in the word processing document that subscribed to it, but the link between the word processing document and the deleted edition file will be broken. It will be impossible to edit the graphic in the future without recreating it.

If you try to close a document with published editions without saving, the dialog box shown in Figure 7.16 will appear.

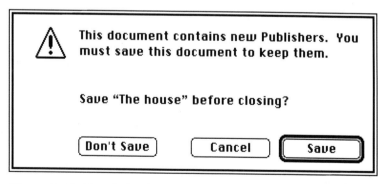

Figure 7.16: This dialog box appears to warn you that quitting the unsaved document will result in the loss of edition files.

■ **Edition aliases**. Edition file aliases can be subscribed to just like standard edition files. As always, the alias file will maintain a link to the original file, even if the alias or the original is moved or renamed. If the alias's original document is on a network file server or File Sharing volume, the volume will be mounted automatically.

Inter-Application Communication

Publish/Subscribe, like the Cut, Copy and Paste commands, are examples of how the Macintosh System Software lets applications share data and communicate indirectly with each other. System 7 also provides even broader application-to-application communication, known as Inter-Application Communication (IAC).

IAC provides a structural framework within which software applications can send messages and data to other software applications. These capabilities make the Macintosh more powerful in many ways. They reduce the pressure on any one application to "do it all," allowing each application to specialize in what it does best and let other applications do other tasks.

Spell-checking is a good example. Almost every Macintosh application allows text to be created, and over the last few years many have added built-in spelling checkers, each with its own version and its own dictionary files. You have to learn and remember how each one works and make room for each data file on your hard drive. And the developers of each program have to spend time and money developing and testing utilities.

Suppose, instead, that one independent spelling checker was the best of them all, offering the biggest dictionaries, the most features and the best user interface. Using IAC, all your software applications could access this one spelling checker, saving you the hassle of learning multiple commands, customizing multiple dictionaries and wasting hard-drive space on duplicate files. And your software developers could spend their time and money on other things, such as improving their applications features.

Understanding Apple Events

The mechanics of IAC are quite technical, but fortunately you don't need to know anything about them unless you intend to write your own Macintosh programs. You'll be aware of IAC in the future when your updated software versions take advantage of its features; but even then, the entire IAC operation will be translated into friendly Macintosh commands and dialog boxes you're already familiar with. (So you can skip the rest of this section, if you'd like.)

Just in case you're interested, however, lets take a brief look at the way System 7 provides IAC capabilities to software applications.

IAC is a protocol that defines a new type of communication between applications, and provides a mechanism for the delivery and implementation of that communication. You can think of IAC as a set of grammatical rules that comprise an acceptable format for messages sent between applications. A message in this format is an Apple Event.

In addition to the Apple Events format, IAC provides a messenger service, to transmit the properly formatted message from one application to another.

While IAC defines the communication format, it doesn't specify the message content. The "language" of Apple Events is being defined by Apple and by the Macintosh software developer community, in cooperation with Apple. This is very important; a computer language designed to communicate between a variety of software applications developed by different companies must be carefully constructed in order to accomplish its goal of facilitating precise communication.

In order for an application to send an Apple Event, or to understand an Apple Event it receives, the program must be specifically programmed to handle that Apple Event properly. This is why it's impossible for non-System 7-Friendly applications to use IAC, and why even System 7-Friendly programs will provide only limited IAC support for some time to come. Only when the Apple Events language is clearly defined can software developers update their programs to properly engage in an Apple Events dialog.

To help software developers implement program support, Apple has classified Apple Events into four categories:

- **Required Apple Events**. Open Application, Open Document, Print Document and Quit Application are the four basic Apple Events and the only ones required for System 7-Friendly applications. (Think of them as the *Hello*, *Please*, *Thank You* and *Goodbye* of Apple Events.)

- **Core Apple Events**. These are not as universal or fundamental as the Required Apple Events, but they're general enough so that almost every Macintosh application should support them. The list of Core Apple Events, quite large already, is growing as Apple and its software developers work to make sure every type of communication that may be needed is provided for.

- **Functional-area Apple Events**. Specifically addressed to a class of similar applications (like word processors or graphics programs), this type of Apple Event supports functions that are common within that class but not universal. Apple Events for word processing might include pagination, footnotes and hyphenation, for example, while Apple Events for graphics programs could support lines and curves, masking and custom fill patterns.

- **Custom Apple Events**. A Macintosh software developer might have a need for Apple Events designed for proprietary or cooperative use by their own applications. If a developer's word processor included a unique feature not controllable with any existing Core or Functional-area Apple Events, the company could define its own Custom Apple Event. This Apple Event could be kept secret and used only by the software developer's applications, or it could be shared with other software developers.

The entire current list of Apple Events, along with detailed descriptions of each, is regularly sent to all Macintosh software developers so they can incorporate these events into their software updates. Only time will tell whether defined Apple Events gain universal support.

Apple Events and Program Linking

When an application sends an Apple Event to another program, the receiving program is usually launched, then asked to perform a task. Of course, this assumes that the receiving program is available. In addition to programs that exist on the same hard drive, Apple Share events, through IAC, can communicate with programs that reside on other parts of the network as well.

Chapter 9, Introduction to File Sharing, introduces the System 7 capability that lets any user on the network share data with any other user on the network.

In *Chapter 10, Working on a Network*, you'll learn about the Program Linking option, which allows you to access software from other Macintoshes on the network via IAC commands. Using this option, applications on one Macintosh can use Apple Events to communicate with applications on other Macs across the network. As with other aspects of IAC, it remains to be seen how this capability will be translated into new Macintosh software features.

Moving On...

Some people are predicting that over time the lines between individual applications will blur as the powers of the Edition Manager and IAC are fully utilized. As we've seen, the Edition Manager allows you to transfer text and graphics between applications, while maintaining a "live link" to the original data, using just a few simple commands:

- **Publish to**. This command saves the selected data to a new edition file on disk.

- **Subscribe to**. This command imports an edition file from disk into the current document.

- **Publisher/Subscriber options**. These commands control the way changes to original documents are updated to the edition file and documents subscribing to the edition file.

From the sophistication of Publish/Subscribe and IAC, we now return to an old familiar Macintosh topic—fonts. Chapter 8 looks at using fonts in System 7, including existing bit-mapped and PostScript fonts, and the new font technology, TrueType.

Chapter 8: Fonts in System 7

Fonts are the blessing and curse of the Macintosh. No other computer offers such a variety of fonts or typographic capabilities; but because of technical problems and corporate politics, no other aspect of the Mac has caused so many headaches for so many people.

System 7 expands both the benefits and drawbacks of Macintosh font technology, introducing a new font standard called TrueType. In this chapter, we'll look at all of the existing Macintosh font standards— bit-mapped fonts, PostScript fonts and the new TrueType fonts. Finally, we'll focus on the practical implications of font life in System 7.

Bit-Mapped Fonts

The original Macintosh introduced many exciting innovations to the world of computing. One of the most important was the enhanced appearance of type. Documents created on the Macintosh could use a variety of typefaces, or fonts, as tools of communication. Earlier personal computers reduced all communications to the drab, mechanical and impersonal look of pica-12 (the original dot-matrix font). But the Macintosh made it possible to produce text in a wide range of typefaces—on printed pages and on-screen.

It wasn't long before the original Macintosh fonts (New York, Monaco, Geneva and Chicago) were joined by many other bit-mapped fonts that could be used in any Macintosh software and printed on the Apple ImageWriter. There were, unfortunately, limitations to working with Macintosh fonts even at this early stage:

- **Dot-matrix bit-mapped quality was unacceptable for most business uses.** While typeface variety was certainly a welcome improvement, most people still considered ImageWriter output quality unacceptable for business use regardless of the fonts. And the only acceptable business alternative available, letter-quality printers, were nearly impossible to connect to early Macintosh systems.

- **Font variety was limited.** Although bit-mapped fonts proliferated, almost all were "novelty" faces with little value beyond advertisements, invitations and entertainment. The lack of interesting "body copy" faces probably resulted from the difficulties in showing subtle type designs on-screen and printing them on the ImageWriter.

- **400K system disks could hold only a limited selection of fonts.** Since hard drives were not generally available at that time, it was necessary to boot the Macintosh from a 400K floppy disk. After squeezing the System folder plus an application or two onto a floppy, only a small amount of room was left for font styles and sizes. To get around this, most people created several startup disks, each containing a System file customized with different fonts. They would then selectively reboot, changing System disks as necessary.

- **Macintosh applications could support only a limited number of fonts at one time.** When too many fonts were installed in the System file, applications acted strangely, often providing only a random subset of the installed fonts. This problem was ultimately cured by System Software and application upgrades.

At the time, these typographic "challenges" were taken in stride; most people were thankful to have any typographic variety at all. The limitation posed by the fact that the Apple ImageWriter was the only available printer was also important, because it meant that even with font variety, Mac documents couldn't shake the "dot-matrix look." Fortunately, this limitation didn't last long.

PostScript Fonts

The introduction of the Apple LaserWriter printer brought a new type of font to the Macintosh; the PostScript font. These fonts were required in documents created for output to the LaserWriter (and all later PostScript printers) in order for type to be printed at high resolution.

Eventually, PostScript fonts came to be known by a variety of names, including laser fonts, outline fonts and type 1 fonts.

Each PostScript font consists of two files: a screen font file and a printer font file.

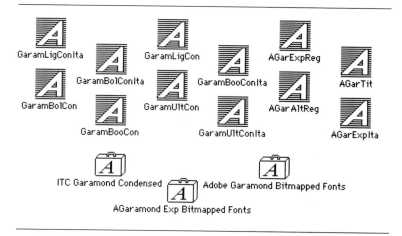

Figure 8.1: Icons for some of the screen font files (below) and printer font files (above) used in this book.

PostScript screen fonts are handled the same as non-PostScript screen fonts:

- They appear with the Font/DA Mover Suitcase icon.

- They're provided in different styles and sizes.

- They're installed with the Font/DA Mover (or Suitcase II or MasterJuggler).

- They appear in the Font Menu or dialog box in all applications.

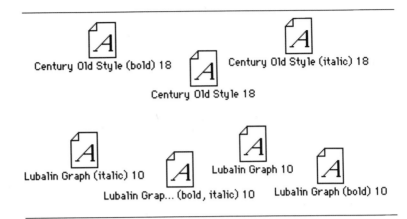

Figure 8.2: Each PostScript screen font represents a single font, size and style.

PostScript printer fonts have no non-PostScript equivalents. Here's how these printer fonts work:

- As described below, printer fonts provide the PostScript printer with mathematical descriptions of each character in a font, as well as any other information it needs to create and produce high-resolution characters.

- They're separate files that generally exist in one-to-one correspondence with screen fonts (there's a unique printer font file for each unique screen font name). In some cases, however, printer fonts outnumber screen fonts, and vice versa.

  Regardless of whether all screen fonts and printer fonts are matched, it's usually not necessary to use all available screen fonts, but it is necessary to use all available printer fonts. (Without using the Helvetica Bold screen font, you can still create Helvetica Bold; but without using the Helvetica Bold printer font, it's impossible to print Helvetica Bold.)

- They display an icon that looks like the LaserWriter in most cases, but not always. The icon depends on the way the printer font was created.

- They're usually about 50K in size, but can range from a minimum of 10K to a maximum of 75K.

- Printer font files can be built into the printer's ROM chips, stored on printer hard disks or kept on the Macintosh hard disk and downloaded manually or automatically to the printer as they're needed. They must be available to the PostScript printer at print time.

PostScript Font Challenges

For a variety of reasons, using PostScript fonts in the real-world Macintosh environment has never been easy. The main problem is that the software and hardware environment in which PostScript fonts are used and the PostScript fonts themselves have been in a constant state of evolution. Most of these problems have been overcome through System Software upgrades, new font-management utilities or "work-around" methods that have become well known and commonly accepted as necessary for font survival.

The list below describes many of the challenges PostScript font users have faced, along with their resolutions:

- **PostScript fonts vs. non-PostScript fonts.** A PostScript screen font is not noticeably different from a non-PostScript screen font, which makes it very difficult for inexperienced users to distinguish between them in documents that will be output on high-resolution PostScript printers.

For the most part, PostScript's dominance in the Macintosh world has alleviated this problem; most Macintosh users now have access to PostScript printers. And PostScript fonts are now the rule rather than the exception.

It would be helpful if Apple and Adobe had designed PostScript screen fonts to indicate their PostScript status— perhaps a symbol character displayed before or after their font names. This would simplify the difficult task of determining which fonts can be used to prepare documents to be output on PostScript printers.

- **Screen font availability.** Once a document is created, there's usually no easy way to determine which fonts it contains, in order to be sure all necessary screen and printer fonts are available at print time—especially if the person printing the file is not the one who created it.

Over time, individual software vendors have developed schemes to help identify screen fonts used in a document. PageMaker displays the dimmed names of used but not-currently-available fonts in its font menu, and Xpress produces a list of fonts used, for example. Only Adobe has addressed the problem of screen font availability, allowing Illustrator to correctly print files even if the screen fonts used to create the file aren't available at the time the file is printed. Unfortunately this solution has never caught on with other vendors. (It's possible that Adobe's proprietary font knowledge allows them this advantage.)

■ **Printer font availability.** The most fundamental requirement of PostScript fonts is that for each screen font used in a document, a corresponding printer font must be available at print time. This requirement has caused tremendous difficulty for Mac users, because there's no automated way to track the screen font/printer font correspondence.

The advent of large font-storage printer hard drives, the Suitcase II and MasterJuggler font management utilities, PageMaker's Download Screen Fonts option and the NFNT font resource have made the "Font Not Found: Substituting Courier" messages less common. But unfortunately, the only real solution to this problem lies with users and service bureau operators.

■ **Too many font names in the font menus.** For non-PostScript screen fonts, a single font is provided in several different sizes, but bold and italic versions must be created using the STYLE command. PostScript fonts, on the other hand, provide a separate screen font for each size and style. This means that font menus are very long. For example, Helvetica includes four entries (B Helvetica Bold, I Helvetica Italic, Helvetica, etc.), Times has four as well, and so on.

Utilities like Suitcase's Font Harmony and Adobe's Type Re-union combine these font styles into a single font menu entry, reducing the four different Helvetica entries to one, and reinstating the STYLE command for additional font styles. But sometimes, during the process, the FONT/NFNT ID numbers are altered, resulting in fonts being "lost" when you move documents from one Mac to another.

```
┌─────────────────────────────┐      ┌──────────────────┐
│ Font                        │      │ Font             │
├─────────────────────────────┤      ├──────────────────┤
│  B Helvetica Bold           │      │  Chicago         │
│  BI Helvetica Bold Italic   │      │  Courier         │
│  B Times Bold               │      │  Geneva          │
│ ✓ BI Times Bold Italic      │      │ ✓ Helvetica      │
│  Chicago                    │      │  Monaco          │
│  Courier                    │      │  New York        │
│  Helvetica                  │      │  Times           │
│  I Helvetica Italic         │      └──────────────────┘
│  I Times Italic             │
│  Monaco                     │
│  New York                   │
│  Times                      │
└─────────────────────────────┘
```

Figure 8.3: Each style of a font is listed separately (left) when fonts are not harmonized, but not when they are harmonized (right).

- **Font ID Conflicts.** The original Macintosh system was designed to handle only a small number of fonts. With the font explosion that followed PostScript's introduction, there were soon more fonts than available Font ID numbers.

  Fortunately, the Apple Font/DA Mover resolved Font-ID conflicts as new fonts were added to the System File. But unfortunately, the Font/DA Mover did this by randomly renumbering the fonts. This caused problems because some applications tracked fonts by Font ID number, and as a result, the same font would have different ID numbers on different Macintoshes. Because many applications used the Font-ID numbers to keep track of font assignments within documents, Font-ID instability caused documents to "forget" which fonts were used to create them when they were transferred from one

Macintosh to another. Working with a wide range of fonts on the Macintosh bore a striking resemblance to a low-stakes game of Russian roulette.

This problem was partially solved with the release of System Software 6.0, which added more complete support for a Macintosh resource called NFNT (pronounced N-Font). NFNT offered a font-numbering scheme capable of handling over 32,000 different fonts. Of course, implementing the new system meant that millions of non-NFNT fonts already in use had to be replaced with new NFNT versions, and that a master set of new NFNT fonts had to be distributed for use in this replacement.

To make matters worse, Apple and Adobe used the same uneven, unplanned and unprofessional distribution methods for the new font ID system that they used for Apple System Software and shareware updates—user groups, bulletin boards and friendly file-sharing. Therefore, the problem was only partially solved.

To further complicate the introduction of NFNT fonts, Apple and Adobe chose not to "harmonize" the NFNT fonts by allowing only a single Font Menu entry to appear for each font (as discussed previously). So it was left to users to perform this harmonization with their own utilities, which as mentioned above results in a non-universal set of fonts.

- **Different fonts with the same names.** As more vendors produced more PostScript fonts, another problem appeared: different versions of the same fonts released by different vendors.

This not only caused Macintoshes to become "confused" about which screen fonts and printer fonts were used in documents; it also made it hard for service bureaus to know if the Garamond specified in a document was the Adobe, Bitstream or other font vendor version of the typeface. This point was crucial because font substitutions wouldn't work. And, even if they did, character width differences would play havoc with the output.

■ **The Type 1 font secret.** Since Adobe Systems had developed PostScript, they kept the specifics of the optimized format known as "Type 1" for themselves. The Type 1 font format provided fonts with "hints" embedded in the font outline that made them look better when output in small type sizes on 300 dpi laser printers.

The Type 1 format was also the only format compatible with Adobe's TypeAlign and Adobe Type Manager (ATM) utilities. This excluded all other vendors' PostScript fonts from using these utilities, since all non-Adobe PostScript fonts were in the "Type 3" format.

After the political turmoil surrounding the announcement of TrueType, Adobe released the specification for the Type 1 font format, and most other font vendors have begun upgrading their fonts to the Type 1 format.

Fonts on Screen

The success of PostScript fonts was due in large part to their ability to print type at any output device's ultimate resolution. But when viewed on-screen, PostScript fonts looked no better than non-PostScript fonts—which is to say, they were legible only in screen-font sizes and were jagged, more or less, at all other sizes.

Soon after the acceptance of PostScript as a font standard, Adobe offered a solution to the problem of poor on-screen font display—a solution it called Display PostScript. Display PostScript was an entirely new display technology that Adobe hoped to sell to Apple for use in the Macintosh, and to other hardware vendors as well. Apple, not wanting to become even more dependent on Adobe, said "no thanks." After all, if two companies have a phenomenally successful first joint venture, the last thing they should do is try a follow-up, right?

Following Apple's rejection of Display PostScript, Adobe set to work on another method of improving PostScript fonts' on-screen display. The result was the Adobe Type Manager, which is a Macintosh init document that allows PostScript screen and printer font data to be viewed on-screen. When ATM is installed, PostScript fonts display at the best possible resolution on-screen at any point size, as long as both the screen and printer fonts are installed.

ATM also improves the output quality of PostScript fonts on non-PostScript printers. With ATM, almost any PostScript font can be printed successfully at any size on any dot matrix, ink jet or QuickDraw laser printer.

The primary drawback of ATM is that a printer font corresponding to each installed screen font must be kept on your hard drive. This requires more space and increases the cost. Screen fonts can be obtained without charge from service bureaus or on-line sources, but printer fonts must be purchased at costs of up to several hundred dollars per type family.

PostScript Printing

When a document containing PostScript fonts is printed to a PostScript printer, the LaserWriter or Aldus Prep print driver queries the PostScript printer to determine if the required PostScript fonts are resident in the Printer. These fonts may be built into a printer's ROM chips, or they may have been previously downloaded into the printer's RAM or onto the printer's hard disk. If the fonts are resident, the document is sent to the printer for output. If the fonts are not resident, the print driver checks to see if the printer font files are available on the Macintosh hard disk. If they are, they're downloaded into the printer's RAM temporarily. If they aren't, an error message in the Print Status dialog box alerts you that specific fonts are unavailable.

When the document is printed, the PostScript printer uses the printer font information to create each character. The information from the PostScript screen font is translated into new printer-font characters. The screen fonts serve only as placeholders on-screen. The process of creating the printed characters is called *rasterization*—the most complex part of the PostScript printing process. During rasterization, PostScript uses the PostScript printer font file's mathematical character descriptions to select the output device pixels necessary to produce the requested character at the highest possible resolution.

When a document containing PostScript fonts is printed to a non-PostScript printer, such as a QuickDraw or dot-matrix printer, screen font information is transferred directly to the printer and is the only source used to produce the printed characters. None of the advantages of PostScript are utilized. There is no difference between the use of a PostScript font and a non-PostScript font (except when ATM is being used, in which case PostScript fonts are superior).

PostScript Fonts in System 7

PostScript fonts and the Adobe Type Manager are fully supported in System 7. There's no need to change your reliance on PostScript type or PostScript output devices.

It is important, however, that fonts and their support files be stored in the proper locations:

- **Screen fonts**. As described in *Chapter 4, The System Folder*, PostScript screen fonts are now installed directly in the System file, and the Font/DA Mover is no longer used. You can still attach PostScript screen fonts with utilities like Suitcase II, if you wish.

- **Printer fonts**. Printer font files must be kept in the System folder in order to be downloaded automatically or used by ATM. When printer font files are dragged onto the System Folder icon, they're installed in the Extensions folder, but (at least at the time of this writing) they don't work properly if left there; they must be moved out of the Extensions folder and back into the System folder itself.

■ **ATM**. The ATM control panel should reside in the Control Panels folder, and the ATM 68000/68020 file should reside in the System folder itself.

TrueType

TrueType is the new font format Apple introduces in System 7. It's designed to bring to the Macintosh all the best aspects of PostScript, as well as the benefits of operating system-level outline font support.

TrueType offers several benefits:

■ High-resolution text display on any device, including Macin-tosh displays and various output devices.

■ Support for outline fonts in all applications.

■ An open type format whose font specifications have been published for use by all type vendors.

■ Full freedom for type designers, because of its quadratic curve basis and support provided by System 7.

■ Compatibility with existing font standards, primarily by operating in a mixed-font environment without altering existing documents.

■ Type industry support (AGFA Compugraphic, Bitstream, Inc., International Typeface Corp., Monotype Corp. and others).

■ Microsoft support in future versions of Windows and OS/2, providing cross-platform compatibility.

TrueType fonts don't use separate screen and printer fonts, and don't require separate screen fonts for different sizes. A single TrueType font file allows a font to be displayed on-screen clearly and without jagged edges at any size, and printed at full resolution to any dot matrix, QuickDraw or PostScript printer. TrueType fonts will likely be compatible with film recorders, full motion video and other output sources in the not-too-distant future.

TrueType and PostScript

TrueType is an alternative to PostScript, not a replacement for it. PostScript is fully supported in System 7, as described above. Neither is necessarily better than the other; let's just say they're different. Later in this chapter we'll examine the realities of working in a world of mixed PostScript and TrueType fonts, and offer some suggestions on the best ways to organize and utilize these font technologies on your system.

Although TrueType is a competitor for PostScript fonts, it's not a competitor for the complete PostScript language. TrueType printers use TrueType for fonts but QuickDraw descriptions for all other page elements. QuickDraw has proven itself on the Macintosh screen, but its use as a high-resolution printing model is new. It's unlikely that the PostScript standard will be replaced in the near future; it has firm support from developers of high-end software, hardware developers, service bureaus and end users. The PostScript language will likely continue to dominate personal computer printing.

TrueType Technology

TrueType fonts, like PostScript printer fonts, are outline fonts, which means that each character is described mathematically, as opposed to the bit-by-bit description used by existing screen fonts. TrueType mathematical descriptions are based on quadratic bezier curve equations rather than PostScript's standard bezier curve equations. The difference between these equations is in the number of points used to determine the position of the lines and curves that make up each character. Apple claims TrueType's method creates better-looking characters at a wider range of output and display resolutions.

Because TrueType uses mathematical descriptions for on-screen and printer font versions, a single file can serve both the display and any output devices. As mentioned above, PostScript requires two files, a screen font file and a printer font file, in order to print or display at full resolution. Although it is true that it's easier to manage one font file than two, Adobe claims that putting its screen fonts and printer fonts in separate files is an asset, since either can be updated or enhanced independently at any time without affecting existing documents or printer configurations.

When a document containing TrueType fonts is printed, the sequence of events depends on the type of printer used:

- **Dot matrix printers.** When a document containing TrueType fonts is printed to a dot matrix printer, the characters are reproduced in their natural contours, just as they appear on-screen. The output images are the results of the on-screen rasterization process, not the TrueType outlines. Therefore, dot matrix output can only provide a more exact representation of the Mac's on-screen display.

- **QuickDraw printers.** When a document containing TrueType fonts is printed to a QuickDraw printer such as the LaserWriter II SC, the same process as described above for Dot matrix printers occurs — information from the on-screen rasterization process is sent to the printer.

- **68000-based PostScript printers with 2 megabytes of RAM.** When a document containing TrueType fonts is sent to a PostScript printer or output device using a Motorola 68000 CPU and at least 2 megabytes of RAM (such as the LaserWriter IINT, and most of today's imagesetters), the print driver queries the device to see if the TrueType font scaler is available. The TrueType font scaler may be built into the printer's ROM (in pre-System 7 PostScript printers) or it may have been previously downloaded onto the printer's hard disk or into printer RAM (using the LaserWriter Font Utility). If the TrueType font scaler is not available, it is automatically downloaded into the printer's RAM, where it will reside until the printer is reset. This font scaler will consume approximately 80K of printer memory.

  With the font scaler in place, the page is sent normally. Mathematical descriptions of any included TrueType fonts are sent to the printer and processed by the TrueType font scaler. The page is then output at full resolution, using any TrueType fonts rasterized by the font scaler software.

- **68000-based PostScript printers with less than 2 megabytes of RAM, or RISC-based Adobe PostScript printers.** When a document containing TrueType fonts is printed to a PostScript printer or output device using a Motorola 68000 CPU and less than 2 megabytes of RAM (such as the

LaserWriter Plus), or to a RISC-based Adobe PostScript printer, TrueType fonts are encoded into PostScript Type 1 font format and sent to the printer where they're processed just like all other PostScript fonts. The encoded Type 1 fonts do not contain PostScript "hints."

- **Printers with built-in TrueType scaling**. When a document containing TrueType fonts is sent to a printer containing a built-in TrueType font scaler, such as the LaserMaster 400XL, or MicroTek TrueLaser, the TrueType outline information is sent directly to the printer where the font is rasterized and imaged.

TrueImage

TrueImage is a PostScript-clone interpreter, developed by Microsoft. It allows printers to output documents described in PostScript or QuickDraw, using either PostScript or TrueType fonts. Like other PostScript-clone interpreters, TrueImage was developed to allow printer manufacturers a way to support PostScript without paying royalties to Adobe Systems. Becoming involved with this development allowed Apple to find an alternative source for the PostScript controllers it was licensing from Adobe and ensure that support for TrueType fonts would be included in the TrueImage controllers.

Currently only a few TrueImage printers are available. But over the coming years, numerous TrueImage printers will likely be sold into both the Macintosh and PC markets.

Biffo

ABCDEFGHIJKLMNOPQRSTIVWXYZ
abcdefghijklmnopqurstuvwxyz123456789

Braggadocio

ABCDEFGHIJKLMNOPQRSTIVWXYZ
abcdefghijklmnopqurstuvwxyz123456789

Gil Sans Ultra

ABCDEFGHIJKLMNOPQRSTIVWXYZ
abcdefghijklmnopqurstuvwxyz123456789

Old Style

ABCDEFGHIJKLMNOPQRSTIVWXYZ
abcdefghijklmnopqurstuvwxyz123456789

Geneva • New York • Chicago • Monaco

*Figure 8.4: Sample TrueType fonts from Monotype (above), Bitstream (right page)
and Apple's TrueType versions of the standard Mac fonts (above).*

Amerigo

ABCDEFGHIJKLMNOPQRSTIVWXYZ
abcdefghijklmnopqurstuvwxyz123456789

Bernhard Modern Italic

ABCDEFGHIJKLMNOPQRSTIVWXYZ
abcdefghijklmnopqurstuvwxyz123456789

STENCIL

ABCDEFGHIJKLMNOPQRSTIVWXYZ
ABCDEFGHIJKLMNOPQRSTUVWXYZ123456789

American Text

ABCDEFGHIJKLMNOPQRSTIVWXYZ
abcdefghijklmnopqurstuvwxyz123456789

Futura Black

ABCDEFGHIJKLMNOPQRSTIVWXYZ
abcdefghijklmnopqurstuvwxyz123456789

Embassy

ABCDEFGHIJKLMNOPQRSTIVWXYZ
abcdefghijklmnopqurstuvwxyz123456789

A Mixed World

In a laboratory environment, where some Macintoshes used only PostScript fonts and some used only TrueType fonts, where all documents using PostScript fonts were created only on the PostScript machines and those using TrueType fonts were created only on the TrueType machines, the daily use of these systems from a font-technology perspective would be very straightforward.

Unfortunately, none of us live or work in such a laboratory. Most Macintosh computers are more likely to be configured with PostScript fonts, TrueType fonts and non-PostScript non-TrueType bit-mapped fonts. And most people will have some documents created with only PostScript fonts, some with only bit-mapped fonts, some with only TrueType fonts and many documents with mixes of TrueType, PostScript and bit-mapped fonts. So how is all of this going to work in the real world?

It depends — on the way you install fonts in your System file, the printer(s) you use and how software developers implement fonts in their updated System 7-compatible applications.

Configuring Your System

Fonts (TrueType fonts, bit-mapped fonts and PostScript screen fonts) are installed in System 7 by simply dragging them into the System file. They can be dragged onto the System folder icon, the System file icon or directly into an open System file window. Fonts cannot be installed while any application other than the Finder is open. If you try to drag fonts into the System file or the System folder while applications are open, the Alert dialog box shown in Figure 8.5 will appear.

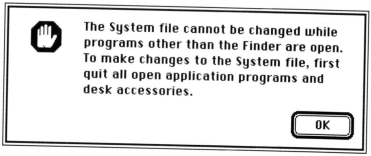

The System file cannot be changed while programs other than the Finder are open. To make changes to the System file, first quit all open application programs and desk accessories.

OK

Figure 8.5: The System file Cannot Be Changed dialog box.

Because bit-mapped fonts and the screen fonts provided for PostScript fonts include font size numbers at the ends of their file names, TrueType files will not usually conflict with existing screen fonts, and vice versa. It is normal and even preferable to install and keep both the TrueType version and the PostScript screen font version of a font in your System file. In other words, don't delete the existing screen fonts from your System file just because you're installing the TrueType version of the same font. If you do, the text in your documents may shift when you reopen them because the character widths of the TrueType font and the old PostScript screen fonts are different. (The way applications select fonts is discussed later in this section.)

You can distinguish TrueType fonts from PostScript screen fonts or bit-mapped fonts by the icon they display. TrueType fonts use an icon with three A's, and PostScript screen fonts or bit-mapped fonts use an icon with a single A, as shown in Figure 8.6.

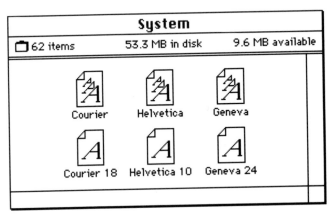

Figure 8.6: Font icons for TrueType and PostScript.

When you double-click on a font icon in System 7, a display of the font appears. For TrueType fonts, this sample shows the font at 9-, 12- and 18-point sizes. Non-TrueType fonts display only a single sample.

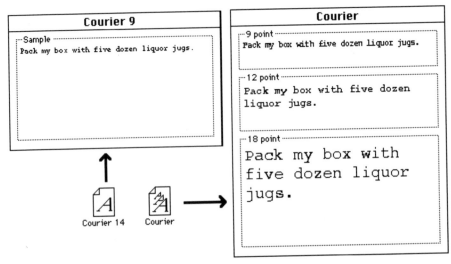

Figure 8.7: A TrueType sample window and non-TrueType sample window.

Fonts are removed by dragging them out of the System file window: double-click on the System file to open the System file window and drag the icons of any fonts you want to remove to another location or into the Trash Can. You cannot remove fonts while applications other than the Finder are open.

Fonts in Your Applications

Once you've installed your TrueType fonts, their names will appear in the Font Menus or dialog boxes of all applications just like other available screen fonts. There's no way to recognize a TrueType font just by looking at its name in a Font Menu. If you have PostScript screen fonts and the TrueType font in a single font listing in your System folder, the font name will appear only once. The Macintosh will decide whether to use the PostScript screen font or a scaled TrueType font for each occurrence, depending on the point size at which the font is used.

Assume, for example, that you have the PostScript screen fonts for Helvetica, Helvetica Bold, Helvetica Italic and Helvetica Bold Italic installed in your System file, each in 10-, 12- and 14-point sizes. Assume that the TrueType Helvetica, Helvetica Bold, Helvetica Italic and Helvetica Bold Italic files are also installed. In this case, most applications would use the PostScript versions of Helvetica for any instances of 10-, 12- or 14-point type, and the TrueType version of Helvetica in all other cases. In other words, PostScript screen fonts are used when they're available at the size specified, and TrueType fonts are used for all other sizes.

Of course, when no TrueType font has been installed, PostScript versions are used at all sizes, just as they were before the introduction of TrueType. If ATM is installed, ATM will scale the on-screen font display to provide smooth character representations. PostScript outlines will be used at print time to produce smooth type at the resolution of the output device (assuming the output device is equipped with a PostScript interpreter).

This process of alternating PostScript screen fonts and TrueType fonts is controlled by each application. Some software developers choose to use TrueType fonts even when PostScript screen fonts of the exact size requested are available. There's no way to tell whether TrueType or PostScript fonts are being used until the document is printed, so consult your application manuals for more information. It's doubtful that many developers will choose to use TrueType fonts when PostScript fonts are available.

The importance of this somewhat confusing system is that documents created on your Macintosh before the installation of TrueType will still use the same PostScript screen fonts they used before, with only minimal repositioning of text required when the old documents are opened in System 7. If, on the other hand, you remove all your PostScript screen fonts when you install TrueType versions of those fonts, old documents will be forced to use TrueType fonts, and more extensive text repositioning may occur as a result. The same thing will happen if you're using an application that ignores PostScript screen fonts and uses the TrueType fonts in all situations.

Text repositioning occurs because character widths for TrueType fonts will not always exactly match PostScript font character widths, even in the same font and family. The width of a 14-point Helvetica Bold "H" may be slightly different in TrueType than it was in PostScript. The cumulative result of the character width accommodations in your document will be text repositioning.

Moving On...

Fonts continue to be an exciting part of the Macintosh, and as shown in this chapter, font technology remains a source of innovation and controversy. System 7 supports three different font formats:

- **Bit-mapped fonts**. The end may be near for these fonts, which lack any type of outline and therefore have limited ability to produce smooth characters either on-screen or in print.

- **PostScript fonts**. This current standard is fully supported in System 7, but facing pressure from the abilities, or at least the publicity, of TrueType.

- **TrueType fonts**. The new font format developed by Apple, TrueType remains a promising rookie at the time of this writing. It has already contributed by forcing innovations in PostScript, and will likely develop into an import font technology in its own right.

Another aspect of the Macintosh that has been in constant evolution is support for work on networks. In Chapter 9, you'll learn how to share the data on your Macintosh with others on the network.

Chapter 9: Introduction to File Sharing

Fonts were not the only area where the Macintosh was ahead of its time in 1984. The first Macintosh had a built-in AppleTalk port, allowing any number of Macintosh computers to be strung together with inexpensive twisted-pair cable to form a network. Back then, there was no compelling reason to create a Macintosh network.

Today, an AppleTalk port remains standard equipment on every Macintosh, and there are many good reasons for putting a Mac on a network. But AppleTalk is no longer the only network available for the Mac; Ethernet and Token Ring networks are available as well.

The three main reasons why you might want to put your Macintosh on a network:

- **Computer-to-computer communications.** Networked Macintoshes can utilize electronic mail, messaging systems and transfer files directly from one computer to another.

- **Shared peripherals.** Laser printers, color printers, slide recorders, high-speed modems, fax/modems and scanners are all expensive peripheral devices that can be shared among networked Macintoshes.

- **Centralized or distributed file servers.** Storing large amounts of data on file servers provides an easy way to share information, allows a number of people to participate in work-group projects and reduces the data storage requirements of individual users. Apple's AppleShare is the dominant file-serving software, but other servers compliant with the AppleShare Filing Protocol (AFP) can also be used.

It's in this last category that System 7 provides greatly expanded abilities. In System 7, Macintosh users can share files from their hard drives with other computers on the network, and access files being shared by these other computers. This new feature is called File Sharing. In this chapter, you'll learn the basics of File Sharing, and how to use it to allow others to access your files. *Chapter 10, Working on a Network*, discusses additional File Sharing features, including accessing the data shared by other Macs and ways you can connect to your own Macintosh from another computer on your network.

What Is File Sharing?

File Sharing is a System 7 feature that lets you designate up to 10 folders and volumes on your computer to be shared with other computers on your network. For each shared folder or volume, you can assign access privileges, which can limit the use of your shared data to only the network computers you specify.

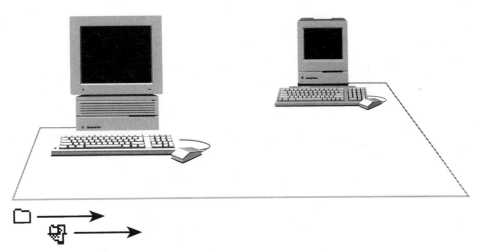

Figure 9.1: File Sharing lets you share your data with others.

File Sharing also lets you access folders and volumes other Macintoshes are sharing, provided you've been granted access privileges. Once accessed, folders and volumes from other Macs appear on your desktop and can be used as if they were your own.

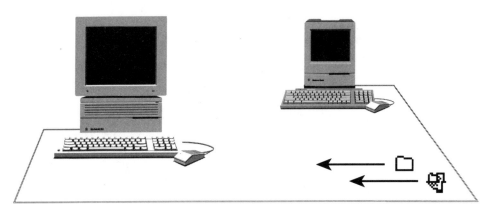

Figure 9.2: File Sharing lets you access data from other computers.

In networking parlance, when your computer is sharing files, it's
acting as a server; when it's accessing files from another computer, it's
acting as a client. File Sharing allows every user on a Macintosh
network to become a server, a client or both server and client.

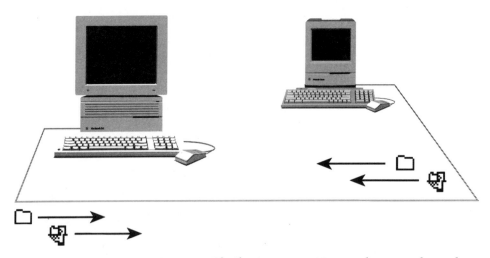

*Figure 9.3: Using File Sharing, every Mac on the network can be
both server and client.*

Sharing data from your Macintosh, and accessing data shared by others on your network, can increase your capabilities and productivity in many ways. Here are some examples of resources that can be shared.

- **Central libraries**. Reference files such as clip art, templates (or Stationery Pads) and historical records can be kept in one location and shared with the entire network.

- **Drop-box folders that send and receive files**. Each network user can define an electronic "In box" and "Out box." By assigning access privileges, the In-box lets everyone add files, but not look at the folder content, while the Out-box does not allow files to be added, but does allow designated users to "pick-up" the files they need.

- **Shared edition files that create living "work-group" documents**. The Edition Manager features (described in Chapter 7) together with File Sharing give network users access to edition files created by many users and stored on several hard drives.

The Limits of File Sharing

Although the capabilities of File Sharing are impressive, it's important to understand that File Sharing is only a "personal" version of AppleShare, Apple's dedicated file-server software. While small networks can usually satisfy their file-serving needs with File Sharing's feature, larger or heavily used networks should use a combination of AppleShare and File Sharing. In these situations, File Sharing will supplement AppleShare, not replace it.

There are several reasons why File Sharing in some cases should be limited in this way:

- **Administration requirements**. As you'll see later, the administrative requirements of sharing files are not incidental. When many users need frequent access to numerous files and folders, centralized file-sharing administration, provided by central file servers such as AppleShare, is usually more efficient than distributed administration.

- **Security risks**. To avoid the burden of administrative requirements, users often neglect security issues, leaving confidential or sensitive data unprotected and available to anyone on the network. This is less likely to occur on centralized professionally managed file servers.

- **Performance degradation**. Even with a very fast Macintosh and a very fast hard drive, File Sharing takes a noticeable toll on computer performance. Macintoshes or peripherals that aren't particularly speedy to begin with make the problem even worse. The benefits outweigh the inconveniences for the casual or infrequent user; but continually having to deal with long delays can be annoying and counterproductive. A centralized server with resources dedicated to the burdens of serving network users is the practical alternative in these circumstances.

- **Access limitations**. File Sharing can serve only 10 folders or volumes from one Macintosh at a time, and support only 50 users at one time (and that would be pushing it). These constraints are too restrictive in many cases. Also, the sharing

Macintoshes must be left on all the time to ensure files are always available on the network (files on a shut-down Mac are not accessible for file sharing).

A File Sharing Quick Tour

File Sharing's capabilities are powerful, and therefore require more preparation and attention than most other System 7 features. Here are the steps necessary to use File Sharing:

- **Prepare your Macintosh.** This includes physically connecting to a network, installing the File Sharing files and activating AppleTalk.

- **Start File Sharing.** The Sharing Setup control panel provides basic configuration information and the master switch.

- **Configure Users & Groups.** Users must be defined, and user preferences and access privileges set in the Users & Groups control panel. In most situations, user groups will also need definition. You must also specify access privileges your Macintosh will enforce when network "guests" log on.

- **Specify folders/volumes to share.** To share any folder or volume, the SHARING command must be applied, and sharing options set.

- **Connect with others using File Sharing.** In order to access folders and volumes being shared by others, the Chooser is used to complete a log-on process.

- Use the File Sharing Monitor to track access to your
  shared data. A new control panel, called the File Sharing
  Monitor, constantly gives you updates on who's accessing what
  on your computer.

The remainder of this chapter looks in detail at the first four of these
steps. The last two are covered in *Chapter 10, Working on a Network*.

Preparing for File Sharing

File Sharing success depends on correctly connecting your Macintosh
computers and installing network drivers. The simplest and most
common Macintosh networking scheme uses LocalTalk or PhoneNet
connectors and cabling that plug directly into the AppleTalk port on
the back of the Macintosh.

More sophisticated networks require Ethernet or Token Ring adaptors
via NuBus or PDS slots (available in most Macintoshes). After adaptors
and appropriate extensions into the System folder are installed, network availability and the presence of network software drivers must be
verified by opening the Network control panel, which displays the
available network drivers (shown in Figure 9.4).

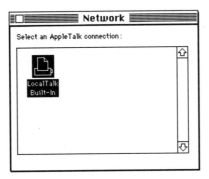

Figure 9.4: The Network control panel displays the icons for available networking systems.

After verifying installation, open the Chooser and call AppleTalk by clicking the "Active" radio button. If your network is divided into zones, the Chooser also displays a list of available AppleTalk zones, as shown in Figure 9.5.

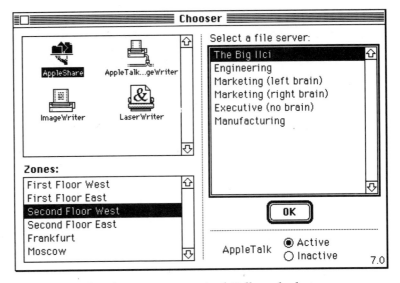

Figure 9.5: The Chooser turns on AppleTalk and selects network zones.

File Sharing also requires, not surprisingly, that the File Sharing be installed by the Installer application. You can tell that File Sharing software has been installed when the SHARING command appears in the File Menu. If it's not there, run the Installer again and choose the "File Sharing" option. (See Appendix A for more information on using the Installer to add File Sharing.)

Starting File Sharing

With your network physically ready and File Sharing installed, you can configure and turn on File Sharing with the Sharing Setup control panel located in your control panels folder. The Sharing Setup control panel (shown in Figure 9.6) lets you define your "network identity," turn File Sharing on and off, and start and stop Program Linking, using the Network Setup dialog box.

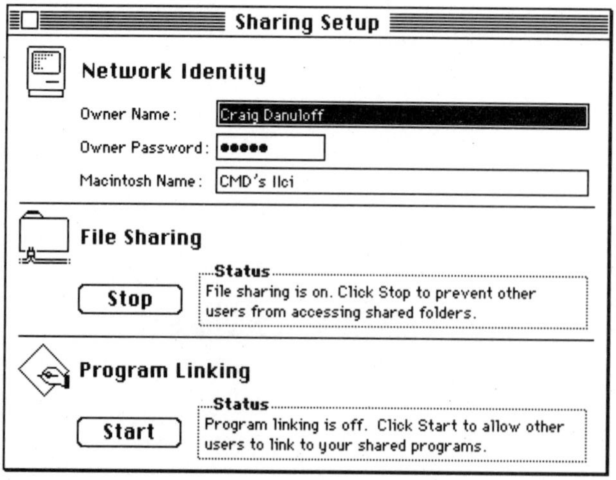

Figure 9.6: The Sharing Setup dialog box.

The options in this dialog box are

- **Owner Name**. The name your Macintosh displays to others when you seek access to their computers via File Sharing. It's also the name you use to access your computer from any other on the network. Any name of up to 32 characters is acceptable, and you can change the Owner Name at any time.

- **Owner Password**. A security gate, allowing you as owner to access this Macintosh's entire hard drive from anywhere on the network when File Sharing is turned on. It also allows you as an assigned owner to access any shared folders or volumes. (By default, you're assigned ownership of all folders and volumes shared by your Macintosh. You can then assign this ownership to others, if you wish, as described later in this chapter.)

  Note that this password can be changed at any time, and it's not necessary to know the old password to define a new one. This means you don't have to worry about forgetting your password—which may seem like a breach of security, and it is. But File Sharing controls only remote-user access to your Macintosh. It doesn't apply to you or anyone else who sits down at your Mac's keyboard. Thus, the ability to change the password at any time is consistent with the Mac's total lack of local security.

- **The Macintosh Name**. The name other network users see when looking at your Macintosh from the network. It appears in the Chooser when they click on the AppleShare icon, and when they print to network printers. This "Macintosh Name" is the equivalent of the Chooser name used in earlier System Software versions.

- **File Sharing (Start/Stop)**. The master control switch. When the Sᴛᴀʀᴛ button is clicked, File Sharing is turned on and the folders and volumes on your Macintosh become available to the network, based on the access privileges assigned to them. As File Sharing starts, the message in the Status area documents the startup process.

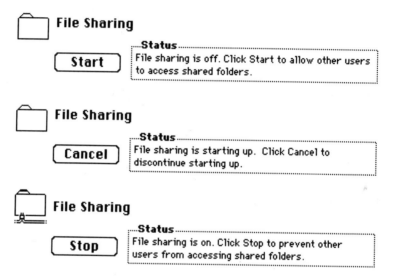

File Sharing

┌─ Status ──────────────────────────┐
│ File sharing is off. Click Start to allow other users │
│ to access shared folders. │
└──────────────────────────────────┘

[Start]

File Sharing

┌─ Status ──────────────────────────┐
│ File sharing is starting up. Click Cancel to │
│ discontinue starting up. │
└──────────────────────────────────┘

[Cancel]

File Sharing

┌─ Status ──────────────────────────┐
│ File sharing is on. Click Stop to prevent other │
│ users from accessing shared folders. │
└──────────────────────────────────┘

[Stop]

Figure 9.7: After the Start button is pressed, the Status message documents the progress of File Sharing.

Once File Sharing is running, the Sᴛᴀʀᴛ button becomes the Sᴛᴏᴘ button. When the Sᴛᴏᴘ button is clicked, you're asked how many minutes until shutdown. Enter a number between 0 (for immediate shutdown) and 999 (for delayed action).

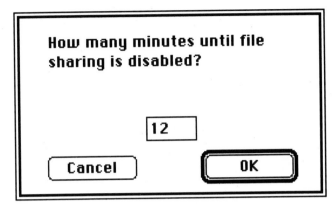

Figure 9.8: The Shut down dialog box.

After you click OK in this dialog, the Status message tells you how many minutes remain before File Sharing is turned off. As turn-off time approaches, other users accessing your Macintosh files are warned of impending shutdown, so they can save their work and release any volumes or folders they're using. It's not necessary for users to release your files before the shutdown; contact with your Macintosh is terminated immediately in any case. However, the Mac simply extends the courtesy of warning other users, so they won't lose work or be abruptly interrupted. If you choose the 0 minutes option, cutoff will occur without warning. (To check the number of users currently connected to your Mac, use the File Sharing Monitor control panel, as described later in this chapter.)

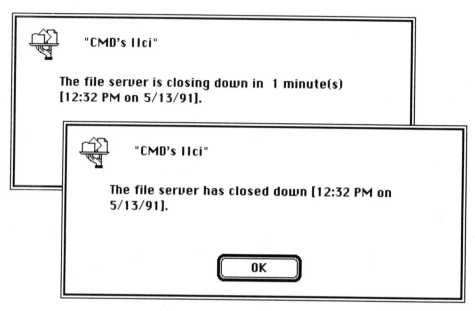

Figure 9.9: Clients are warned before a File Sharing server closes, and after it has closed down.

When File Sharing is on and users are connected to your Macintosh, the Shut Down or Restart command brings up the Alert dialog box shown in Figure 9.10. Again, be sure to give your network users enough time to save their work before shutting down. If possible, cancel the Shut Down or Restart and leave your Macintosh running so network use can continue.

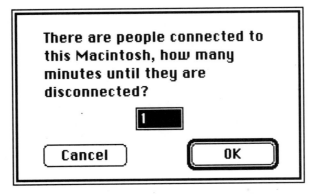

Figure 9.10: The alert that appears at Restart or Shut Down.

- **Program Linking** (Start/Stop), discussed in depth in *Chapter 10, Working on a Network*, allows inter-application communication (IAC) commands of remote users to control programs residing on your Macintosh.

Registering Users & Groups

If you plan to use File Sharing to make your Macintosh folders and/or volumes available to other network users, you must decide who may and may not share your files. You may want to share your files with every user on your network, but it is more likely that you will want to restrict access to some or all of your shared files.

To designate access, you open the Users & Groups control panel (shown in Figure 9.11), which displays a window containing one icon for each user and one icon for each group registered to access your Macintosh, in addition to a Guest icon and an icon for you, the Macintosh Owner.

Of course, when you open the Users & Groups control panel for the first time, no users or groups are yet defined, so only the Guest and Macintosh Owner icons will appear.

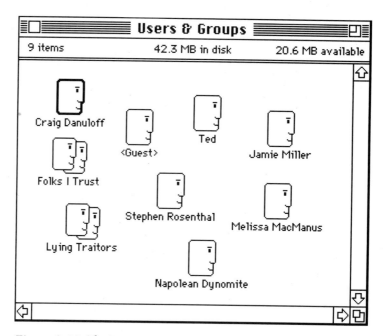

Figure 9.11: The Users & Groups control panel.

Although this control panel looks like a normal Finder window, it's not. You cannot drag-copy user icons or group icons out onto the desktop or to another folder or volume. Nor can you copy other files into this window. If you try to do so, an Alert dialog box will remind you that you can't.

Via the Users & Groups control panel, you can grant access to four user categories:

- **Registered Users.** These are specific people you want to have access to your shared folders or volumes. Registered Users are given access to your data as individuals or as members of a defined Group.

- **Groups.** A Group is a collection of defined Registered Users. Individual Registered Users can be included in any number of groups.

- **Guests.** Any user on your network who has not been defined as a Registered User can attempt to log onto your shared folders or volumes as a Guest. You define whether you want these non-Registered Users to have access to your data.

- **Macintosh Owner.** As the owner, you can give yourself special remote abilities and access privileges to your computer.

In addition to the definitions and privileges mentioned so far, the Sharing dialog box provides additional security safeguards. This dialog box specifies Registered Users and Groups who have access privileges to particular folders and volumes. (More on the Sharing dialog box later in this chapter.)

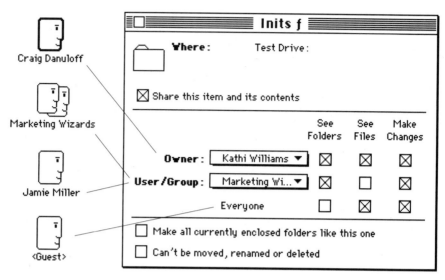

Figure 9.12: The defined users and groups are assigned access privileges via the Sharing dialog box.

Creating New Users

To create a new user, open the Users & Groups control panel, and choose the NEW USER command from the File Menu. This creates a new "untitled" Registered User icon in the Users & Groups window. Enter the name of the user you want this icon to represent.

It's best to enter the person's actual name, rather than a code name. A code name is more likely to be misspelled when the Registered User logs on.

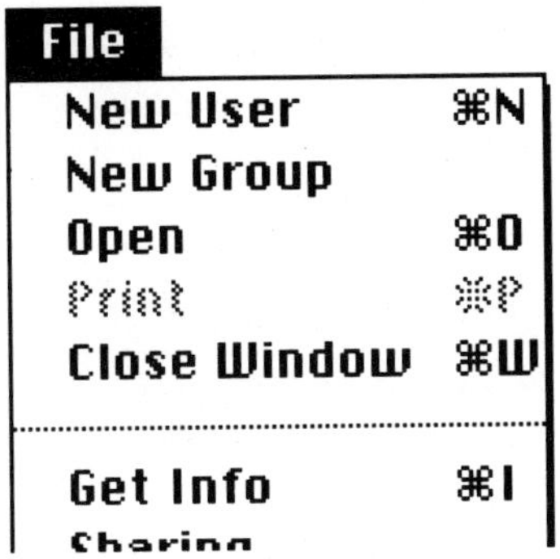

```
┌─────────────────────────────┐
│ █File█                      │
│  New User           ⌘N     │
│  New Group                  │
│  Open               ⌘O     │
│  Print              ⌘P     │
│  Close Window       ⌘W     │
│ ·························   │
│  Get Info           ⌘I     │
│  Sharing                    │
└─────────────────────────────┘
```

Figure 9.13: The File Menu provides the NEW USER and NEW GROUP commands.

Up to 100 Registered Users can be defined, but Apple recommends staying near 50. If more than 50 people need regular access to certain shared folders or volumes, consider moving that data to a dedicated AppleShare server, or allowing all Guests access to that data. (There is no limit to the number of Guests who can access your Macintosh, only to the number of Registered Users.)

You don't need to register users individually unless you want to limit access privileges. If you're going to allow everyone on the network to see and change your data, they can all log on as Guests. If not, you should define Users and Groups.

Configuring User Preferences

After registering a new user, or to alter a user's password or preferences, double-click on the user icon to open the File Sharing options window, as shown in Figure 9.14. This dialog box sets the user's password and allows or disallows the user to connect via File Sharing or Program

Linking. This dialog box also displays a list of all groups the user is included in (you can't change or modify group memberships in this dialog box).

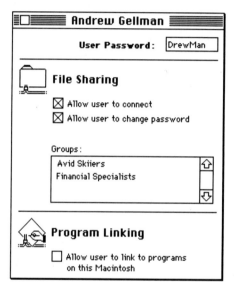

Figure 9.14: The User Preferences dialog box.

Lets look at the options in this dialog box:

- **User Password.** In order to access your data from another Macintosh on the network, user name and, in most cases, a password must be entered. By default, the user has no password, and logs on by simply entering the user name and leaving the password option blank. (More information on the log-in process later.) This obviously doesn't provide much security assurance that the user logging on is supposed to have network access.

To add a password, type one into the User Password option box. For security, eight bullets will appear, instead of the password itself.

When you add or change a user password, you must notify the user, for obvious reasons. Another approach is to leave the user without a password, letting them define their own passwords the first time they log on. They can then change their password periodically after that. This is done with the "Allow User To Change Password" option, described below. A variation would be to start with an obvious password like the user's first name, then encourage the user to change it at the first opportunity.

You can change any user password at any time. For example, if a user forgets his or her password, there's no way for you to find it; you must "change" it to resolve this problem. Changing a password also lets you bar a particular user's access until you provide a new password.

Avoid using obvious passwords like names, zodiac signs and birthstones, and change passwords regularly.

- **Allow User to Connect.** This check box is the "personal" master switch for File Sharing that makes it possible or impossible for a user to connect as a Registered User (they still may be able to connect as a Guest). This option is on by default, but occasionally you may want to turn in off. Using this option to revoke access privileges is less drastic than deleting the user, which makes later reinstatement more difficult.

■ **Allow User to Change Password.** This option allows Registered Users to change their passwords using the CHANGE PASS-
WORD button that appears in the Chooser as they log onto your
Macintosh. In most cases, this option should be selected,
because changing user passwords frequently increases the
security of your data. Of course, since you as the Owner can
always change passwords directly in this dialog box, you lose
no privileges by allowing users this option.

■ **Program Linking.** Users can take advantage of this option if
the feature is turned on in the Sharing Setup control panel.

Creating and Working With Groups

Since a network comprises many individual users, assigning access
privileges to each individual for each item would be a very tedious job.
To avoid this, File Sharing lets you define Groups, add Registered Users
to these groups, then assign access privileges that apply to all Group
members.

New Groups are created by selecting the File Menu's NEW GROUP command while the Users & Groups control panel is open, which places a
new "untitled" Group icon in the Users & Groups window. Enter the
name of the group you want this icon to represent (descriptive names
are best). Registered Users never see the group names you assign, nor
do they need to know which groups they're assigned to.

Groups cannot be combined and you can't make a Guest icon a member of any group; but you can add yourself as the Macintosh Owner to
any group. This isn't as useless as it may seem: if you assign ownership

of folders or volumes to another user or group, you won't have access to that folder (over the network) if you're not a member of a group that has access privileges (unless you add yourself to that group) or use the "Allow User To See Entire Volume" option in your Owner Preferences (described later).

To add Registered Users to the group, drag their icons onto the Group icon and release them. Or you can double-click on the Group icon to open the group's window and then drag user icons directly into this window. Adding a user to a group does not remove the user icon from the main Users & Groups window. You can drag a single user icon into any number of groups. To check which groups a user is part of, double-click the Registered User's icon and see the list in the User Preferences dialog box.

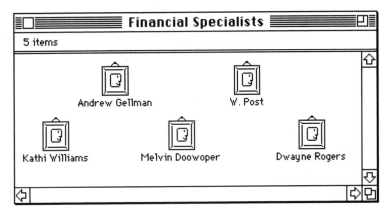

Figure 9.15: A defined Group containing five Registered Users.

To remove a user from a group, open the group window and drag the user's icon to the Trash Can. This deletes the user from the group; it does not remove the user entirely, and it doesn't remove the user from any other groups he or she belongs to. Similarly, you can delete an entire group by dragging the group icon to the trash, which removes the group but doesn't affect any group member individually.

Configuring Guest Preferences

You may occasionally want to share files with someone on your network who isn't a Registered User. This is made possible by File Sharing's support of Guests. A single Guest icon is automatically included in the Users & Groups control panel, and this icon is used to control access to your shared data for all non-Registered Users. The Guest icon cannot be deleted. Double-clicking on the Guest icon brings up the Guest Preferences dialog box, as shown in Figure 9.16.

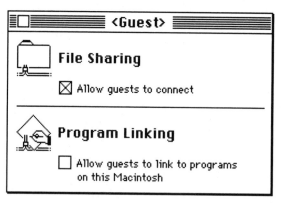

Figure 9.16: Guest Preferences.

There are only two options in this window:

- **Allow Guests to Connect.** This option (the default) is the master switch that lets guests log onto your Macintosh. When this option is deselected, network users can't log onto your Macintosh as guests.

Allowing guests to log on does not automatically give them access to data. Guests can access folders and volumes based only on the "Everyone" access privileges in the Sharing dialog box, as described later in this chapter. If no folders or volumes are available to Everyone, guests who attempt to log on will find no data available.

■ **Allow guests to link to your programs**. Program Linking, as described in Chapter 10, is used by System 7's IAC feature. If you select this option, guests can link to your programs; if you deselect it, they can't.

Configuring Owner Preferences

The preferences you set for yourself, the Macintosh Owner, affect the way you can access your Macintosh from elsewhere on the network. They have no affect on what you can do directly from your keyboard (and mouse). The Macintosh Owner icon is created automatically, and named with the Macintosh Owner Name, as set in the Sharing Setup control panel. The owner icon appears with a bold border in the Users & Groups window. Double-clicking on this icon opens the Macintosh Owner Preferences dialog, shown in Figure 9.17.

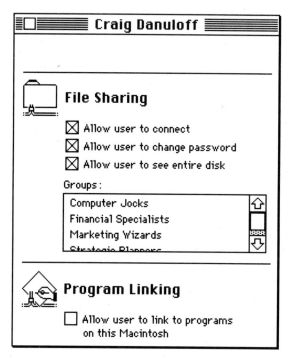

Figure 9.17: The Macintosh Owner Preferences dialog box.

The options in this dialog are the same as those described previously for any Registered User, with the exception of the "Allow User To See Entire Volume" option. This option lets you access entire volumes on your Macintosh from anywhere on the network at any time—even when the volumes have not been specifically shared with the SHARING command. When accessing volumes in this way, you have full access privileges to all files, folders and applications.

This feature is very powerful—and potentially dangerous. It allows you to work on your Macintosh, or access any data stored on your Macintosh, from any Mac on the network just as if you were at your own keyboard. The danger is that anyone else who knows your Owner Name and password could gain the same access.

If you don't need this feature, leave it deselected. If you do use this option, be very discreet with your password, and change it frequently. If you won't need to use this feature over an extended period of time, temporarily deselect it. Of course, there's always the possibility that someone might sit down at your Macintosh keyboard and access your data or change your password, then remotely access your Mac. File Sharing should not lull you into a false sense of security. If you have good reason to believe this could happen, other security measures should be taken.

Sharing Folders or Volumes

For any folder or volume to be shared with others on your network, the Sharing command must initiate sharing and specify access privileges. Any mounted volume, including hard disks, hard disk partitions, removable cartridges, CD-ROMs and any folder on any mounted volume can be shared. Floppy disks and folders on floppy disks cannot.

To initiate sharing, select the folder or volume and choose the Sharing command from the File Menu, which brings up the Sharing dialog box (shown in Figure 9.18). This dialog box is used to turn on Sharing and assign access privileges to this item. Access privileges, as you learned earlier, determine who can see the folders and volumes, who can see the files inside those folders and volumes, and who can make changes to existing files or store new files. (More on access privileges later in this chapter.)

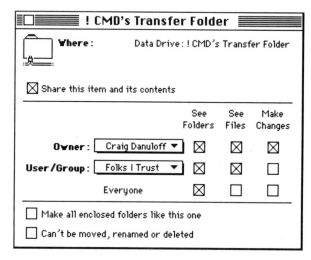

Figure 9.18: A Sharing dialog box.

The Sharing dialog box presents a number of important options:

- **Share this folder and its contents**. This check box is the master switch that turns sharing on or off for the selected folder or volume and the contents of that folder or volume. Until this option is selected, all other options in this dialog box are dimmed.

- **Owner**. This option specifies the owner of the selected folder or volume and the owner's access privileges. In most cases, you (as the Macintosh Owner) will remain the owner of shared folders and volumes.

  However, using the pop-up menu, you can designate any other Registered User as the owner of the selected folder or volume. The assignee can then reset access privileges for the item. Your access to the folder or volume from another Macintosh on the network is then dependent on your inclusion in the "User/Group" option (discussed in the following subsection). Of course, your access to the folder or volume from your own Macintosh will not be affected; these options affect only network access.

Once an owner has been specified, use the check boxes to assign access privileges. (More on available access privileges and their use in the next section of this chapter.)

- **User/Group.** This option grants one user or one group access to the selected folder or volume (via the pop-up menu), and defines the access privileges available to this user or group. In many ways, this is the most important Sharing option, because it usually designates the person or group of users that will most frequently access the shared data. (See "Access Privileges" in the next section of this chapter for the many powerful ways this feature can be used, including bulletin boards, drop boxes, read-only filing systems and true workgroup file sharing and storage systems.)

- **Everyone.** This option specifies access privileges granted to Guest users on your Macintosh. As mentioned before, anyone on your network can log onto your Mac as a Guest, providing you've specified that Guest log-ins are permitted. In that case, the "Everyone" option determines which volumes and folders they can access.

- **Make all enclosed folders like this one.** When you share a folder or volume, all enclosed folders are also automatically accessible to users with access privileges. You cannot "unshare" a folder enclosed in a shared folder or on a shared volume, but you can change the access privileges of an enclosed folder so that they don't match those of the enclosing folder. This option also can reset the access privileges of the enclosed folders so they match those of the currently selected folder or volume.

For example, a folder called Out-box is shared, with full access privileges, by everyone on the network. Inside this folder is a folder called Project A. We want to limit access to Project A so that only members of the Project A group can share it. To do this, after using the SHARING command for the Out-box folder, you'd select the Project A folder and choose the SHARING command again. Now, access privileges are reset, limiting access to group members only. Figure 9.19 displays the Sharing dialog box for the "CMD's Outbox" Out-box and "Project A" folders.

Notice that the "Share This Folder And Its Contents" option has been replaced in the "Project A" folder dialog box with a "Same As Enclosing Folder" option. This occurs because the "Project A" folder is inside a folder that's already shared. By default, this new option is selected, and the access privileges match those specified for the enclosing "CMD's Outbox" folder. Deselecting this option makes it possible to change the access privileges.

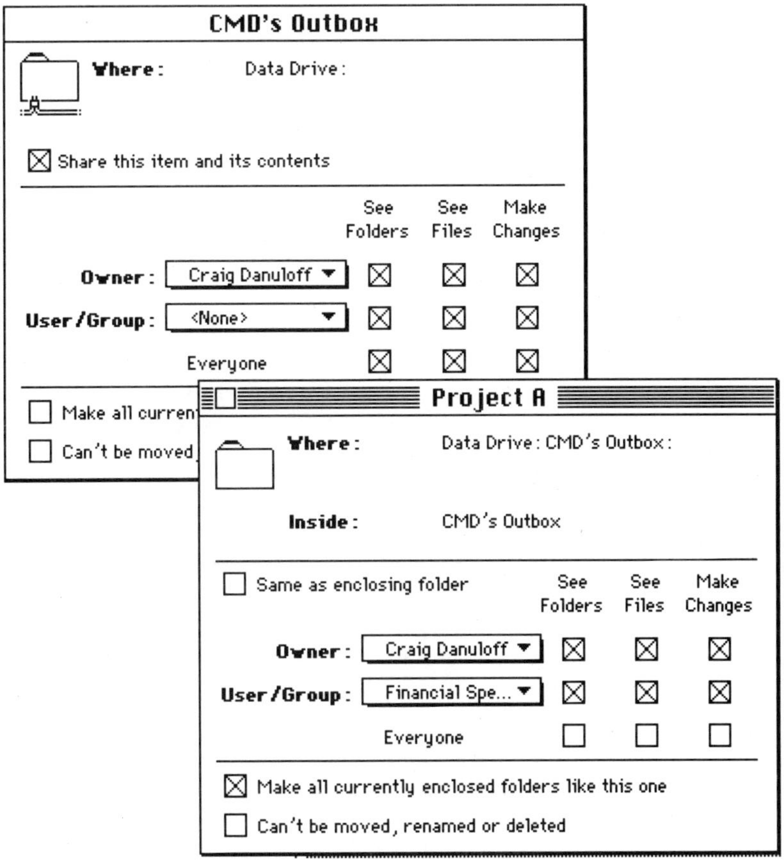

Figure 9.19: The Sharing dialog box for a parent and child folder.

- **Can't be moved, renamed or deleted.** This option gives you a safety net to ensure that the folder or volume you share is not moved, renamed or deleted by any network user— including the owner. It's a good idea to select this option in all cases, unless you know that repositioning, renaming or deleting the item will be necessary. This will prevent accidental changes with unpleasant results.

After completing these options, click the close box in the title bar to close the dialog box, and apply these options to the selected item. If you've made changes to the ownership or access privileges of the item, dialog boxes appear asking you to confirm or cancel the changes requested. A dialog box will also appear if you chose the "Make All Enclosed Folders Like This One" option. Figure 9.20 displays these warning dialogs.

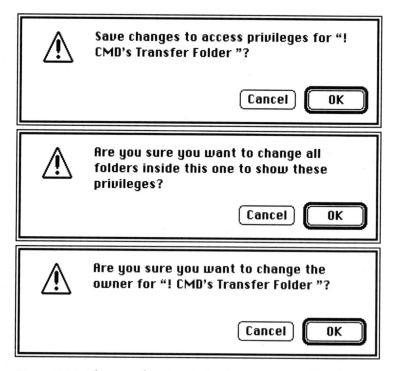

Figure 9.20: Three confirming dialog boxes appear after changing Sharing options.

Icons of Shared Items

After you have specified and implemented sharing options, icons of the shared folders will modify, confirming their shared status. Figure 9.21 shows a folder icon and its changes.

Figure 9.21: A folder as it appears before Sharing (left), after Sharing (center) and when users are connected (right).

Unsharing

There are two ways to make shared items unavailable to network users: you can turn File Sharing off completely, or you can turn File Sharing off for individual folders and volumes.

To turn File Sharing off completely, open the Sharing Setup control panel and click the FILE SHARING STOP button, as described earlier. When File Sharing is turned off, the settings and access privileges set with the SHARING command are retained for all shared folders and volumes, and will go back into effect when File Sharing is again turned on.

To turn off the sharing of a particular folder or volume only, select the appropriate folder or volume icon, choose the SHARING command and deselect the "Share This Item And Its Contents" option. When you close the Sharing dialog box, the selected folder or volume will become unavailable for network access. (An Alert dialog box will appear if users are currently accessing the shared item, as shown in Figure 9.22.) Note that all access privilege settings are lost when sharing is turned off for a particular folder or volume; you'll have to reset them the next time the item is shared.

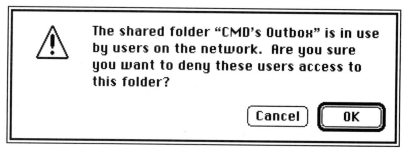

Figure 9.22: Unsharing with users.

As an alternative to turning off File Sharing either completely or for particular folders or volumes, you could also change the "Allow User To Connect" and "Allow Guest To Connect" options in the user icons found in the Users & Groups control panel. This method is not generally recommended, but it does allow access privilege settings to remain in force while temporarily making it impossible for some or all users to connect.

Access Privileges

Shared folders, volumes and folders enclosed within those shared folders and volumes are provided to other network users according to access privilege settings you apply in the Sharing dialog box. These privileges, along with users and groups designated in the Users & Groups control panel, are the key to controlling File Sharing.

As shown in Figure 9.23, the three access privilege options are assigned to three different users or groups. Option settings and combinations you apply determine how network users can access and modify your shared data and storage space. Let's look at these access privileges, the users and groups they can be assigned to, and the results of applying them in different combinations.

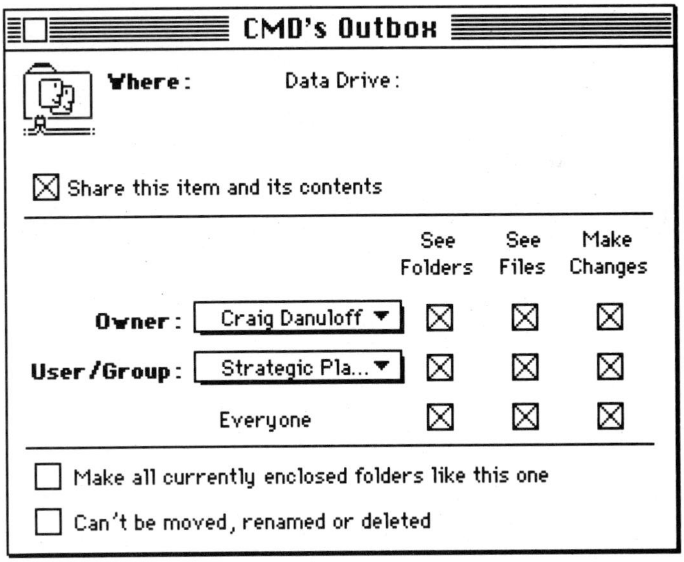

Figure 9.23: The access privilege options.

- **The See Folders option**. When this option is set, all folders within the selected folder or volume are shown to the specified user or group. Deselecting the "See Folders" option hides all folders from the specified user or group — users don't even know which folders exist in the selected folder or volume. When the "See Folders" option is deselected, an icon appears in all windows accessed via File Sharing, letting the user know that folders are not being displayed.

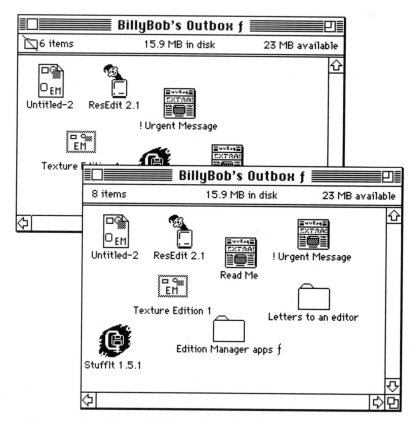

Figure 9.24: A shared folder with and without See Folders privilege.

- **The See Files option**. All files contained in the selected folder or volume appear normally to the specified user or group. Deselecting this option hides all files from the specified user or group—users don't know which folders exist in the selected folder or volume. When the "See Files" option is deselected, an icon appears in all windows accessed via File Sharing, letting the user know that files are not being displayed.

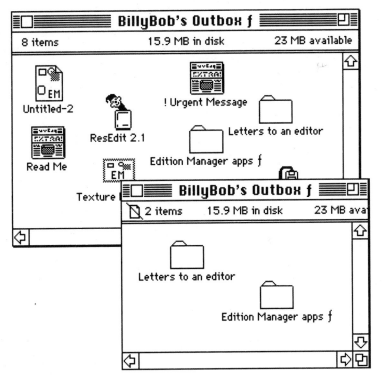

Figure 9.25: A shared folder with and without See Files privilege.

- **The Make Changes option**. When the "Make Changes" option is set, the user can save new files, change existing files and create new folders. When the "Make Changes" option is deselected, the folder or volume is *write protected*: no new files, folders and changed files can be written. When the "Make Changes" option is deselected, an icon appears in all windows accessed via File Sharing, letting the user know that the folder or volume is write protected.

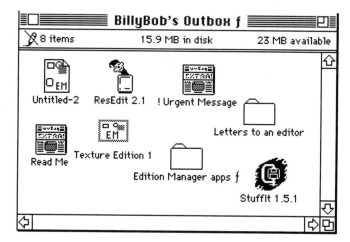

Figure 9.26: Shared folder without Make Changes privilege.

These three options are assigned individually to three user categories:

- **Owner.** The owner of a folder or volume is the person or group who can change the access privileges of that folder or volume while accessing it over the network. The person who creates a folder is automatically the owner of it; therefore, you are default owner of the folders and volumes on your Macintosh. When a user creates new folders in shared folders or volumes, however, that user becomes the owner of the new folders.

  Using the pop-up menu, the owner can be designated as any defined user or group. Or, selecting the <any user> option gives any guest who accesses the folder or volume full owner privileges (including the right to reassign access privileges.) When setting access privileges on remote volumes, the "Owner" pop-up menu does not appear and the Owner Name must be entered manually.

- **User/Group**. The User/Group category assigns access privileges to one specific user or group. When sharing folders or volumes, select the desired User/Group from the pop-up menu listing of all registered users and groups. When setting access privileges on remote volumes, the "User/Group" pop-up menu does not appear and the Owner Name must be entered manually.

- **Everyone**. The Everyone category assigns access privileges granted to all Guests who connect to the Macintosh that contains the selected folder or volume. Of course, in order for Guests to log on, the "Allow Guests To Connect" option must be set in the Users & Groups control panel.

Access Privilege Strategies

This elaborate matrix of categories and access privilege levels allows precise control over the way shared files can be used. Several common ways of using access privileges are described below:

- **Create an Out-box Folder**. The key aspect of an Out-box is that those who pick up the files can see them but not make changes to them. This is accomplished by providing "See Files" and "See Folders" privileges but withholding "Make Changes," as shown in Figure 9.27. Of course, those who should not have access to the files in the Out-box should not even be allowed to see files or folders.

```
┌─────────────────────────────────────────────────────────┐
│ ▤□▤▤▤▤▤▤▤▤▤  CMD's Outbox  ▤▤▤▤▤▤▤▤▤▤▤▤ │
├─────────────────────────────────────────────────────────┤
│  ┌────┐                                                  │
│  │ ▞▚ │   Where :         Data Drive :                   │
│  │▞▚ ▞│                                                  │
│  └────┘                                                  │
│  ─╨──                                                    │
│                                                          │
│  ☒ Share this item and its contents                     │
│  ─────────────────────────────────────────────────────  │
│                              See     See     Make        │
│                            Folders  Files  Changes       │
│                                                          │
│     Owner : ┌─────────────────┐                          │
│             │ Craig Danuloff ▼│   ☒      ☒      ☒        │
│             └─────────────────┘                          │
│ User/Group: ┌─────────────────┐                          │
│             │ Folks I Trust  ▼│   ☒      ☒      ☐        │
│             └─────────────────┘                          │
│                Everyone          ☒      ☒      ☐        │
│  ─────────────────────────────────────────────────────  │
│  ☐ Make all currently enclosed folders like this one    │
│  ☐ Can't be moved, renamed or deleted                   │
└─────────────────────────────────────────────────────────┘
```

Figure 9.27: A set of access privileges that define an Out- box.

- **Create an In-box Folder.** The opposite of an Out-box, an In-box allows users to add files, but not to see anything that's already there—it's like a mail slot. This is defined using the opposite set of access privileges, as shown in Figure 9.28.

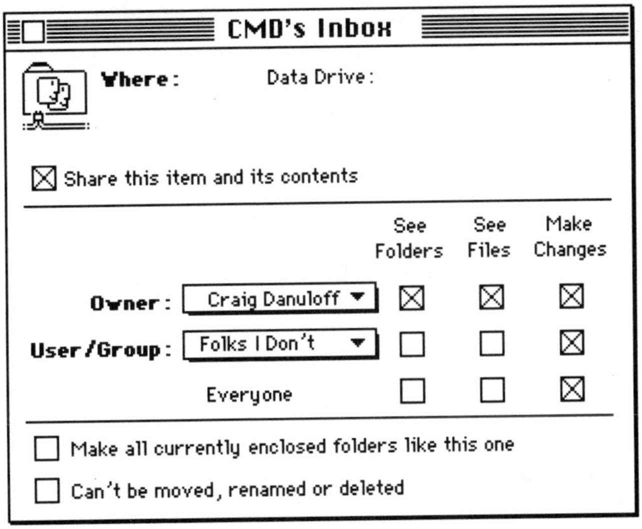

Figure 9.28: A set of access privileges that define an In- box.

- **Create a bulletin board.** Combining the attributes of Out-boxes and In-boxes in various folders and enclosed folders, you can create a place where people can read and retrieve some files and add and modify others, depending on who they are and which folder they're accessing. Figure 9.29 shows a set of enclosed folders and the privileges that provide such an arrangement.

Bulletin Board ƒ

Where: Test Drive:

☒ Share this item and its contents

	See Folders	See Files	Make Changes
Owner: Craig Danuloff ▼	☒	☒	☒
User/Group: <None> ▼	☒	☒	☒
Everyone	☒	☒	☒

☐ Make all currently enclosed folders like this
☐ Can't be moved, renamed or deleted

Mrktg InBox ƒ

Where: Test Drive: Bulletin Board ƒ:

Inside: Bulletin Board ƒ

☐ Same as enclosing folder

	See Folders	See Files	Make Changes
Craig Danuloff ▼	☒	☒	☒
Marketing Wi... ▼	☐	☐	☒
Everyone	☐	☐	☐

rrently enclosed folders like this one
ved, renamed or deleted

Financial Reports

Where: Test Drive: Bulletin Board ƒ:

Inside: Bulletin Board ƒ

☐ Same as enclosing folder

	See Folders	See Files	Make Changes
Owner: Craig Danuloff ▼	☒	☒	☒
User/Group: Financial Spe... ▼	☒	☒	☐
Everyone	☐	☐	☐

☐ Make all currently enclosed folders like this one
☐ Can't be moved, renamed or deleted

Figure 9.29: Provileges for several folders in a bulletin board.

- **Provide a group work area.** A simpler but more common way to use access privileges is to make a set of files available to specific users and groups. For example, you may have a folder to which the members of the "Engineers" Group have full privileges, while members of the "Sales Reps" team can see the files but not modify them.

Monitoring File Sharing

The File Sharing Monitor control panel gives you information about the items shared, the users connected to your computer, and the activities of these users. Open the File Sharing Monitor, and the control panel shown in Figure 9.30 appears.

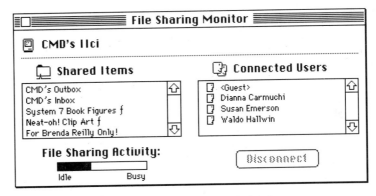

Figure 9.30: The File Sharing Monitor dialog box.

The scrolling window on the left side of this dialog box presents a list of the folders and volumes you've shared. The one on the right side lists network users currently connected to your Macintosh. You can disconnect any user by selecting the user's name from this list and clicking the DISCONNECT button. A dialog box lets you give the selected user warning by delaying disconnection for the number of minutes you select, or you can use the default 0 minutes and disconnect them immediately.

The last item in this control panel is the File Sharing Activity Monitor. This gauge fluctuates with the demands on your computer system as connected users access your Macintosh. When the demand is high, the

local operation of your Macintosh slows. If slowdowns caused by remote users are a persistent problem, you may need to limit the access
of Registered Users and Guests by reducing the amount of shared data
you make available. Or you can shift some shared data to dedicated
AppleShare file servers.

Moving On...

The power and possibility the File Sharing offers will undoubtedly
change the way you work on a Macintosh network. File Sharing removes almost all the barriers—physical and psychological—that
previously inhibited the flow of data between computers. With File
Sharing, you can

- Make any folder or volume on your computer available to
  anyone connected to your Macintosh network.

- Designate who can access the files and folders you share.

- Specify privileges extended to each regular user, and network
  guest.

In *Chapter 10, Working on a Network*, you'll see the other side of the
File Sharing coin—accessing data shared by other Macs, and by
centralized file servers. You'll also look at other aspects of network life,
such as coexistence with Macs running System Software 6.0x.

Chapter 10: Working on a Network

Macintosh users have long known the benefits of computer networking. Shared printers, and other peripheral Mac-to-Mac communications, and remote access to network file servers are commonplace on almost every Mac network. System 7 offers additional networking capabilities, such as File Sharing, support for aliasing, the Edition Manager and IAC.

This chapter focuses on using your Macintosh network to access AppleShare and File Sharing volumes; the effects of access privileges; and how you control files stored on remote volumes. We'll also look at IAC's Program Linking and networks that include Macs still running System Software 6.0x.

Accessing Network Volumes

As described in *Chapter 9, Introduction to File Sharing*, every System 7 Macintosh on your network can share up to 10 folders or volumes with other network users, based on user and group access privilege designations for each Macintosh that shares network data. In addition, dedicated AppleShare file servers can make any number of complete volumes available to all network users, according to specified access privileges.

Connecting to other System 7 Macs for File Sharing and AppleShare file server access is easy. This section describes how to do it and how to manage shared data.

Connecting With the Chooser

The first step in accessing network data is to open the Chooser (in the Apple Menu) and click on the AppleShare icon in the upper left corner as shown in Figure 10.1. The available network file servers appear on the right side of the window, and if your network is divided into zones, those zones are listed in the lower left corner of the Chooser.

If a zone list appears in your Chooser, select the zone in which that Macintosh is registered; available server volumes in that zone will appear.

These file server names include dedicated AppleShare file servers and System 7 Macs using File Sharing. There's no way to tell from the listing which are AppleShare servers and which are File Sharing

Macintoshes, except by matching them with the names of File Sharing Macs in the serving machine's Sharing Setup control panel. In any case, as a client accessing data over the network, it makes no difference to you whether you're accessing data from a dedicated AppleShare file server or from a File Sharing Macintosh.

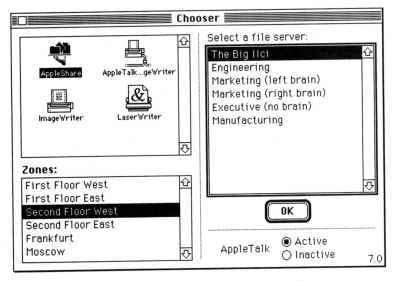

Figure 10.1: The Chooser with zone and file server listings.

When you've located the name of the file server you wish to access, double-click on the file name, or click the OK button below the file server list. The Connect dialog box appears (shown in Figure 10.2). This dialog box gives you the option of connecting to the selected file server as a Guest or as a Registered User.

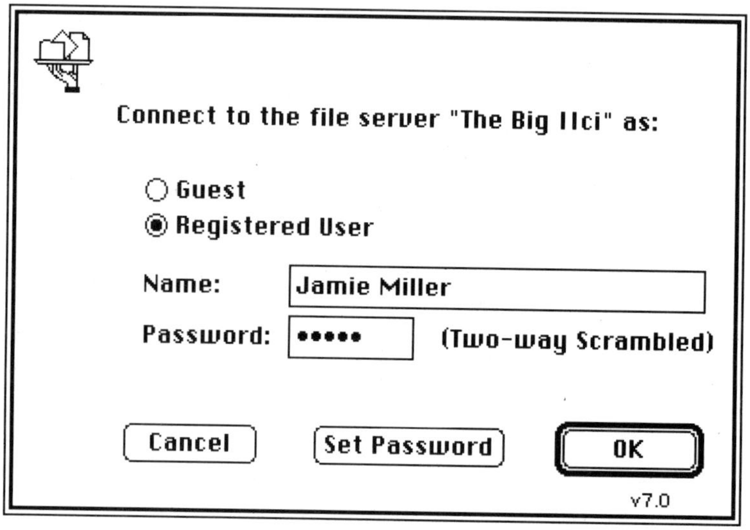

┌───┐
│ **Connect to the file server "The Big IIci" as:** │
│   │
│ ○ Guest   │
│ ◉ Registered User   │
│   │
│ Name: │ Jamie Miller   │   │
│ Password: │ ••••• │ (Two-way Scrambled)   │
│   │
│ (Cancel)   (Set Password)   (OK)   │
│   v7.0   │
└───┘

Figure 10.2: The Connect dialog box.

In order to connect as a Registered User, a user icon with your name and password must exist on the AppleShare server or File Sharing Macintosh. This shows that the system administrator or Macintosh owner has created and defined your Macintosh as a Registered User, as described in *Chapter 9, Introduction to File Sharing.*

You can now click the "Registered User" option. The Owner Name specified in your Sharing Setup control panel will appear as the default in the Name option box. If this is not the name under which you're registered, make required changes to the "Name" option. If a password has been assigned, enter it in the "Password" option. If none is needed, leave the option blank. Then click the OK button.

Connecting as a Guest is simpler but may restrict your access privileges. Of course, this is your only option if you're not a Registered User. To connect as a Guest, click the "Guest" option, then click the OK button. If the selected file server does not allow Guests to connect, the "Guest" option will be dimmed. In this case, the only way to connect is to contact the Macintosh owner or server administrator and ask to become a Registered User.

The final option in the Connect dialog box is the SET PASSWORD button which allows Registered Users with appropriate access privileges to reset their passwords for a particular file server. Changing your password will affect only the currently selected file server, not all servers on which you're a Registered User.

Selecting Specific Volumes

After identifying yourself as either Registered User or Guest, and clicking the OK button, a list of available volumes on the selected server appears, as shown in Figure 10.3. (If an incorrect name or password was entered, an Alert dialog box appears and you'll be returned to the Connect dialog box.)

This dialog box lists all volumes that the selected server is sharing with the network. (When accessing File Sharing volumes, it's not possible to differentiate between shared folders and shared volumes, so we'll use the term volumes generically.) The names of any volumes you're not allowed to access will be dimmed. You can mount any one non-dimmed volume by double-clicking on the volume name or selecting the volume name and clicking the OK button. To mount more than one volume, hold down the shift key while selecting volume names, then click the OK button.

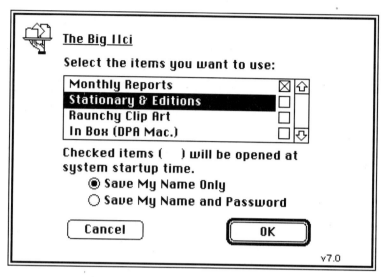

Figure 10.3: Available Server Listing.

You can also configure the volume to mount automatically each time you start up your Macintosh, by clicking on the check box next to a volume name. But you'll have to enter your password manually each time you start your Macintosh and the volume is mounted, since by default your password is not stored as part of this automatic-mount process. To simplify the automatic mount (but at the same time reduce security), click the "Save My Name and Password" option, then double-click the volume name or click the OK button.

After mounting a volume, you're returned to the Connect dialog box. To mount additional volumes from the selected file server, click the OK button again to return to the volume list, and repeat the mounting process for another volume.

Remote Volumes and Access Privileges

Any remote volumes you've mounted appear on your desktop using the AppleShare Volume icon, as shown in Figure 10.4. This icon also accompanies these volumes in Open or Save As dialog boxes. These volumes are used just like local volumes (those physically connected to your Mac) except for any restrictions imposed by your access privileges. When your Macintosh is communicating with remote volumes, arrows flash just to the left of your Apple Menu, as shown in Figure 10.4.

Monthly Reports

Figure 10.4: A volume icon on the desktop (left), and the activity arrows that flash while remote volumes are accessed (right).

As described in Chapter 9, access privileges determine whether you can See Folders, See Files and Make Changes to available volumes. The Finder windows for remotely accessed volumes indicate your access privileges by displaying small icons in the upper left corner, just below the title bar (shown in Figure 10.5). To see your assigned access privileges, choose the Sharing command from the File Menu while the folder is selected or open.

Figure 10.5: The Cannot Write, Cannot See Folders and Cannot See Files icons.

When you don't have Make Changes privileges, you can't save or copy
a file to a volume. In Save dialog boxes, the S<small>AVE</small> button is dimmed
when the correct volume is write protected in this way; and, at the
Finder, any attempt to copy or create files will bring up the dialog box
shown in Figure 10.6. This same dialog box will appear if you attempt
to create a new folder on a volume for which you don't have See
Folders privileges.

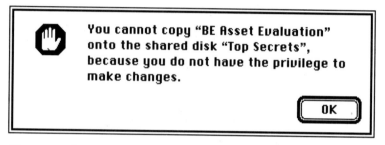

You cannot copy "BE Asset Evaluation"
onto the shared disk "Top Secrets",
because you do not have the privilege to
make changes.

OK

Figure 10.6: Not Enough Access Privileges dialog box.

Use the S<small>HARING</small> command to see the complete access privileges for any
volume you can mount. Select the volume icon and choose the S<small>HARING</small>
command from the File Menu. If you own the volume, you can change
these access privileges. If you create a folder on a shared volume,
you're automatically assigned as the folder's owner and allowed to use
the File Menu's S<small>HARING</small> command to reset the access privileges.

A Volume Access Shortcut

To avoid this lengthy process every time you mount a networked volume, you can create an alias of the volume icon that appears on your
desktop, and store that icon in a convenient spot on your hard drive. In

fact, you can create a folder full of network volume icons, as shown in
Figure 10.7.

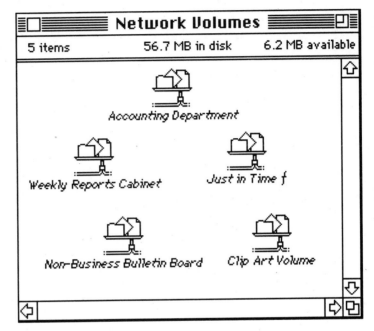

Figure 10.7: Folder of volume aliases.

Double-clicking on the network volume alias icon mounts the volume,
after you supply any necessary passwords. This shortcut can save lots of
time and effort.

Disconnecting From Remote Volumes

There are three ways to disconnect a mounted network volume:

- **Trash the volume.** Simply drag the volume icon into the trash can. Just as this action ejects removable disks, it releases mounted file server volumes.

- **Shut Down or Restart.** All mounted volumes are also released when you use the Shut Down or Restart command.

- Put Away. The File Menu's Put Away command, or its keyboard equivalent, Command-Y, dismounts any selected volumes.

Accessing Your Hard Drive Remotely

When File Sharing is running, you can access your entire hard drive and all volumes currently mounted from anywhere on your network—unless you've deselected the "Allow User To See Entire Volume" option in the Owner Preferences window of the Users & Groups control panel. This option, found in the Users & Groups control panel, is accessed by double-clicking on the user icon that displays your Owner name.

To reach your hard drive from another Mac on your network, select the Chooser just as you would to log into any network volume. Locate the name of your Macintosh in the scrolling file server list, and double-click on it. A new dialog box appears, listing the name of each hard drive connected to your Macintosh. These are not volumes you've shared with the Sharing command; they're complete hard drives as they appear on the Macintosh desktop. To mount your drive, double-click on the drive name, or select the drive name and click the OK button.

Your hard drive then appears on the desktop of the Macintosh you're using, with AppleShare volume icons. You now have complete access to your drive, including all files and folders, with no limitations based on access privileges. You can create files and folders, delete files, redefine Users & Groups, set File Sharing access privileges or do anything else you could do if you were sitting at your own Mac keyboard.

When you're finished using a remotely mounted hard drive, you can release it, just like you would any other volume, by dragging it to the trash, using the Put Away command, or shutting down and restarting.

Program Linking

As mentioned in *Chapter 7, The Edition Manager and IAC*, applications specifically programmed to support Apple Events can communicate with application programs residing on any AppleShare server or File Sharing volume on the network. If you want these programs to communicate with the applications on your hard drive, you must specifically enable Program Linking.

The master control for Program Linking is found in the Sharing Setup control panel, as shown in Figure 10.8. The message in the Status area will document the Program Linking start-up process. Once Program Linking is running, the Start button becomes the Stop button.

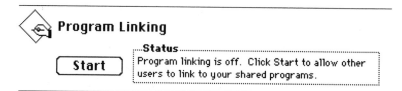

Figure 10.8: The Sharing Setup dialog box provides the master control for Program Linking.

Program Linking must also be enabled in the Macintosh owner icon found in the Users & Groups control panel. (The Macintosh owner icon has a dark border around it and displays the name entered in the Sharing Setup dialog box.) Double-clicking on this icon displays the dialog box shown in Figure 10.9. The "Program Linking" option, in the lower portion of this dialog box, enables Program Linking.

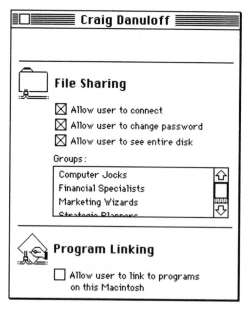

Figure 10.9: The User Options dialog box for the Macintosh owner.

Program Linking, turned on and enabled, can apply to any applications that support it. Only System 7-Friendly applications are capable of supporting Program Linking, but they don't all support this feature.

To initiate Program Linking, highlight the application you wish to use, then choose the Sharing command from the File Menu. A Sharing dialog box appears, as shown in Figure 10.10.

Figure 10.10: An application's Sharing dialog box.

If the application you selected supports Program Linking, the Allow Remote Program Linking check box is displayed. Otherwise, this option will be dimmed. Click the check box to allow Program Linking, then close the Sharing dialog.

Networks With Macs Running System 6.0x

If some of the Macintoshes on your network aren't upgraded to System 7, you can still run them on the network. It's no problem to run System Software 6.0x and System 7 on the same network, with one small exception. The exception is the LaserWriter driver file that's installed with System 7.

Updating LaserWriter Drivers

In order to allow everyone on your network to share the same laser printers without having to constantly restart them, you'll have to copy new LaserWriter driver version 7.0 into the System folder of all Macintoshes still using System Software 6.0x. There are three files you will need to copy; the LaserWriter driver, LaserPrep and Backgrounder. You can either manually copy these files from the System 7 Printing disk or from the System 7 CD-ROM, or run the Printer Update script which will use the Installer to add these files to any existing System folder.

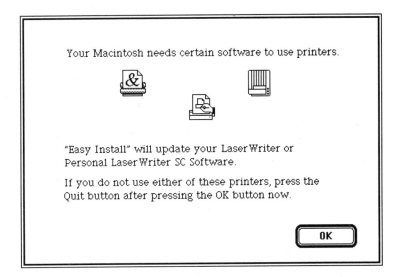

Figure 10.11: The Printer Update Installer screen.

Replacing existing LaserWriter drivers with the LaserWriter driver version 7.0 will work fine—they won't even notice the difference. It's easy to tell when the LaserWriter driver version 7.0 is being used because its icon is different from the one used by earlier versions. The icons for LaserWriter driver version 7.0 and version 5.2 (which is commonly used with System Software 6.0x) are shown in Figure 10.12.

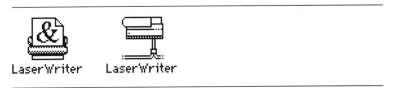

Figure 10.12: The LaserWriter 7.0 (left) and 5.2 (right) icons.

It's not impossible to use the older LaserWriter drivers with System 7, which you might be tempted to do if only a few people on your network have upgraded, but this can cause problems with background printing, and is generally not advised.

If you don't use the same versions of the LaserWriter drivers throughout your network, those who have the different version will be greeted by the Reinitialize Printer dialog box (shown in Figure 10.13) whenever they attempt to print. There's no technical problem with constantly reinitializing, but it wastes lots of time. It also causes any downloaded fonts to be removed from the printer's memory at each restart. So, upgrading all LaserWriter drivers to 7.0 is the practical solution.

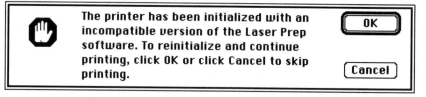

Figure 10.13: The Restart Printer dialog box.

Accessing File Sharing Volumes From System 6.0x

As explained in *Chapter 9, Introduction to File Sharing*, any System 7 Macintosh can share up to 10 folders or volumes with the Macintosh Network. These shared volumes are available to Macs running earlier System Software versions as well as those using System 7.

The only requirement is that the AppleShare init be installed in the System folder. The Access Privileges desk accessory should also be installed. Running any version of the System Software Installer and choosing the AppleShare (workstation software) option will install all the necessary files automatically.

Once these files are installed, File Share volumes, as well as AppleShare volumes, are accessed exactly as described earlier in this chapter, using the Chooser. There are no functional differences in accessing volumes from Macs running System Software 7.0 and those running earlier System Software versions.

Moving On...

Most Macintosh users are first interested in connecting to a network in order to share peripheral devices, such as laser printers, or perhaps network modems. But networks also make it possible for computers to communicate with each other, and for data to be shared either between computers or by accessing centralized file servers.

In this chapter you've seen how to make the most of these abilities:

- Using the Chooser to select an available File Sharing Macintosh or AppleShare server.

- Mounting volumes and setting up automatic mounting connections.

- Working with assigned access privileges.

Next, in *Chapter 11, Memory Management*, we focus on the important issue of effectively using the memory available in your Macintosh. We'll examine several System 7 tools that enhance your available memory, and ways you can control the memory used by your applications.

Chapter 11: Memory Management

When someone asks you about your Macintosh, you probably say something like, "I've got a IIci with 5 megs of memory and an 80-meg hard drive." It's no accident that the three variables you use to describe your computer are its model name, the amount of installed RAM and its hard disk size. These are the factors that determine what you can do—the speed and range of activities you can perform—with your computer.

With System 7, the amount of RAM installed in your Mac is still important, but it's no longer the total measure of memory or the only important memory issue. In this chapter, we look at the overall picture of Macintosh memory, including the new Memory control panel options, the About This Macintosh dialog box and ways you can configure applications to use memory most efficiently.

The Memory Control Panel

One of the realities Macintosh users have to confront is the finite amount of memory available in their computers. Today's software seems to have an insatiable appetite; new technologies, like multi-tasking, 24-bit color and sound, intensify the problem. The crusade for additional memory has traditionally encountered certain roadblocks: the operating system's limited ability to address the need for large amounts of memory, the computer's physical limitations and the high price of memory chips.

System 7 begins the process of breaking down these barriers, or at least temporarily pushing them back. The Memory control panel is one of System 7's new memory-related features. However, availability of Memory control panel options depends on the Macintosh model. As explained below, some models don't support virtual memory, and some don't support 32-bit addressing; therefore, these options are not presented on Macs that don't support them.

In addition to the two new memory-extending options, virtual memory and 32-bit addressing, the Memory control panel also offers the "Disk Cache" option (formerly part of the general cdev and known as the "RAM Cache" option in previous System Software versions).

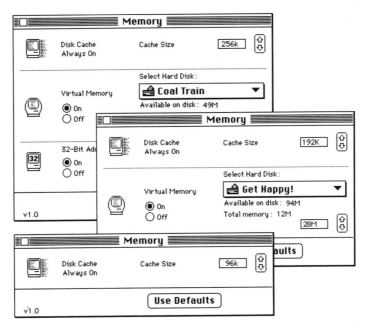

Figure 11.1: The three versions of the Memory control panel that appear on Macintoshes.

Disk Cache

A disk cache is a small section of Macintosh RAM set aside to store a copy of the most recent data read from disk (or volume) into memory. Storing this copy makes the data readily available when it's needed again. Reaccessing data via the RAM-based cache, rather than having to reread it from disk, saves considerable time.

By default, your Macintosh uses 32 KB of cache for every one megabyte of RAM installed in your Mac. If you have 4 megabytes of RAM, for example, 128 KB would be the default cache setting. Using the arrows, you can increase or decrease your disk cache size as required.

For most users, settings between 96 KB and 256 KB are sufficient. Unless you have specific memory limitations, you shouldn't reduce the cache below its default setting, since the small amount of memory the cache consumes significantly improves your Macintosh's performance.

Virtual Memory

Virtual memory is a software trick. It uses space on your hard drive to "fool" the Macintosh into thinking there's more available memory than there really is. Using virtual memory, a Macintosh with only 2 or 4 megabytes of actual RAM can act like it has 12 or more megabytes. In fact, in conjunction with 32-bit addressing (discussed later in this chapter), virtual memory can provide your Macintosh up to 1 gigabyte (1000 megabytes) of memory.

Virtual memory substitutes hard disk space for RAM. One benefit of using this device is that hard drive space is generally much less expensive than actual RAM. In addition, with 32-bit addressing, virtual memory can provide access to more memory than is possible with RAM chips alone. (The 32-Bit Addressing option is described later in this chapter.)

However, using virtual memory has two main drawbacks. First, performance is slower than with real RAM, since the mechanical actions required of your hard drive are no match for the electronic speed of RAM chips. Second, virtual memory appropriates hard disk space normally available for other activities.

In order to use virtual memory, your Macintosh must be equipped with a 68030 or better processor, such as the Macintosh SE/30, Macintosh IIci, IIsi or IIfx. Virtual memory can also be used with a 68020 Macintosh II, with a PMMU chip installed. Virtual memory cannot be used with the Macintosh Plus, Classic, SE, LC, or Portable.

Without 32-bit addressing, the "Virtual Memory" option provides the following amounts of memory to your Macintosh:

■ Macintosh Plus, Classic, SE, Portable, LC or II w/o PMMU	None
■ Mac IIx, IIcx, SE/30 or II w/PMMU	14 megs less 1 meg per NuBus card
■ Macintosh IIci, IIsi or IIfx	14 megs less 1 meg per NuBus card

With 32-bit addressing, the "Virtual Memory" option provides these amounts of memory:

■ Macintosh Plus, Classic, SE, Portable, LC or II w/o PMMU	None
■ Mac IIx, IIcx, SE/30 or II w/PMMU	14 megs less 1 meg per NuBus card
■ Macintosh IIci, IIsi or IIfx	1 Gigabyte

Enabling Virtual Memory

If your Macintosh can use virtual memory, choose the "Virtual Memory" option in the Memory control panel to turn virtual memory on. After clicking the Oɴ button, the "Select Hard Disk" option becomes available. From the pop-up menu, select the hard disk volume on which the virtual memory storage file will be created and stored.

The amount of available space on the selected hard disk is displayed below the hard disk pop-up menu. The amount of free space available determines the amount of virtual memory that can be configured. A VM Storage File, equal to the total amount of memory available while using virtual memory, will be placed on the selected disk. In other words, if your Macintosh has 4 megabytes of actual RAM, and you wish to reach 12 megabytes using virtual memory, a 12 megabyte VM Storage File must be created on the selected volume.

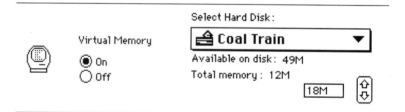

Figure 11.2: The "Virtual Memory" option determines the size and location of the virtual memory file.

Appearing below the "Available On Disk" option is the total amount of memory currently available. The "After Restart" option indicates the amount of memory specified, including actual RAM and virtual memory. Use the Up and Down Arrows to modify this specification. If the "After Restart" option is not visible, click the Up or Down Arrow until it appears.

The amount of memory you can specify depends on your hardware configuration and the "32-Bit Addressing" option setting. Without 32-bit addressing, you can specify up to 14 megabytes of memory *minus* one megabyte for each NuBus card installed in your Macintosh. If 32-bit addressing is turned on, up to 1 gigabyte of memory can be specified, depending on the free space available on the selected hard disk.

Any changes made to the "Virtual Memory" option will not take effect until your Macintosh is restarted. When you finish setting the Memory control panel options, close the control panel and use the Special Menu RESTART command. To verify that virtual memory is on, choose the ABOUT THIS MACINTOSH command to display the current memory status. (More information on the About This Macintosh dialog box later in this chapter.)

Virtual Memory Performance

Virtual memory works by moving information between a disk-based swap file and the RAM inside the computer; even when virtual memory is being used, the Macintosh communicates only with the real RAM. This movement of data between hard disk and RAM, technically known as *paging*, causes the Macintosh to perform slower than it does when using actual RAM alone.

The amount of paging slowdown depends on how much actual RAM is available and how virtual memory is being used. The more available RAM, the less paging interference. The type of activity called for also affects paging; working on multi-megabyte data files and frequent switching between open applications are examples of activities that usually require more paging and therefore decrease performance.

A good rule of thumb in determining your own RAM/virtual memory mix: You should have enough actual RAM to cover your normal memory needs and enough supplemental virtual memory to handle occasional abnormally large requirements. If you find that approximately 4 mb of RAM let you work comfortably in the three or four open applications you use regularly, but you occasionally need 8 mb to open additional applications or work with large data files, then 4 mb of real RAM and 10 mb of virtual memory would probably be appropriate. Trying to get by with just 2 mb of real RAM and 10 mb of virtual memory would result in prohibitively slow performance and the potential for crashes caused by the heavy paging.

Disabling Virtual Memory

Virtual Memory can be turned off by selecting the Memory control panel "Off" option and restarting your Macintosh. After disabling virtual memory, the VM Storage File is usually deleted from your hard drive automatically. If it isn't, you can remove it by dragging it to the Trash Can.

32-Bit Addressing

In the past, 8 megabytes was the maximum amount of RAM that could be installed, or used, on the Macintosh. This limitation was posed by the way the available memory chips were addressed by the Macintosh System Software, including those parts that reside on the ROM chips on the computer's logic board. When used on Macintosh computers containing newer versions of the ROM chips, System 7 breaks the 8-megabyte barrier, allowing up to 1 gigabyte of RAM (a gigabyte equals 1000 megabytes!).

This extended ability to use memory is called *32-bit addressing*, referring to the number of digits used in the new memory-addressing scheme. The Mac's older memory scheme is *24-bit addressing*, since only 24 digits are used. 24-bit addressing is still used on most Macintosh models, and is also supported by System 7.

The ROM chips required for 32-bit addressing are *32-bit clean ROMs*, and are currently included in the Macintosh IIci, IIsi and IIfx *only*. The other Macintosh models (Plus, Classic, SE, SE/30, Portable, II, IIx, IIcx and II LC) do not have 32-bit clean ROMs, and therefore can't use 32-bit addressing. At the time of this writing, Apple had not announced plans to offer owners of older Macintosh models 32-bit clean ROM upgrades. It's reasonable to expect that most future Macintosh models will also provide 32-bit clean ROMs.

For 32-bit clean ROMs, the Memory control panel includes the "32-Bit Addressing" option, as shown in Figure 11.3. When the option is set to "Off," the Macintosh uses 24-bit addressing. When set to "On," the Mac uses 32-bit addressing. Changes to this option take effect only after restarting the Macintosh. Macs with older ROMs will not display this option in the Memory control panel.

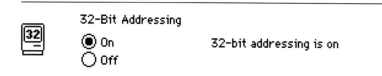

Figure 11.3: The "32-Bit Addressing" option.

When 32-bit addressing is turned on, the Macintosh can utilize up to 128 megabytes of real RAM memory and up to 1 gigabyte of virtual memory (with the "Virtual Memory" option described earlier in this chapter). Unfortunately, not all software applications are compatible with 32-bit addressing; so 32-bit addressing will have to be turned off when you're using an incompatible application. 32-bit addressing compatibility is one of the requirements for System 7-Friendly applications, so most new and upgraded applications should present no compatibility problems.

Running an application that's not compatible with 32-bit addressing will cause a dialog box to appear, warning you that you must restart your Macintosh with 32-bit addressing turned off. In some cases, however, this dialog box will not appear and you'll have to find this out the hard way, by experiencing a system crash or unpredictable behavior.

The "32-Bit Addressing" option should be turned on only if you're using more than 8 megabytes of RAM or more than 16 mb of virtual memory. Otherwise, 32-bit addressing is unnecessary and may lead to a crash.

Memory Control Panel Tips

- **Use at least the minimum recommended Disk Cache.** The Disk Cache speeds up operation, so you should leave it set to at least 32K for every 1 megabyte of RAM installed in your Mac. (That means 64K for 2 megabytes, 128K for 4 megabytes and 256K for 8 megabytes.)

- **Install enough real RAM in your Macintosh.** Real RAM chips should provide enough memory to cover your normal daily memory needs—at least 4 megabytes and in some cases up to 8 megabytes. Although virtual memory can provide inexpensive additional memory, 80 percent of your memory needs should be covered by real RAM. The performance drawbacks of relying too heavily on virtual memory don't justify the relatively small amount of money saved.

- **Extend your available memory with virtual memory.** Once you've installed enough RAM to satisfy your everyday needs, use the "Virtual Memory" option to give yourself extra memory to cover special occasional situations, such as working with large color images, animation or more than the usual number of simultaneously open programs.

  If you have 4 or 8 megabytes of real RAM in your Mac, 10 to 12 megabytes of supplemental virtual memory is recommended. IIci, IIsi and IIfx users can go beyond the 14-meg limit up to 1 gigabyte, although amounts of 20 to 30 megabytes will usually suffice.

■ **Use 32-bit addressing carefully.** Many existing programs will not be compatible with 32-bit addressing until they're replaced or upgraded to be System 7-Friendly. When using a program for the first time after turning on 32-bit addressing, save your data frequently until you're sure the program is working properly. Leave the "32-Bit Addressing" option turned off if you don't need to use it.

Controlling Memory

Once you've determined how much memory you need and made it available to System 7 (by installing RAM chips and using the "Virtual Memory" and "32-Bit Addressing" options), you'll want to manage that memory wisely and use it economically. Managing your Mac's memory allows you to make sure that each application has enough memory to operate properly, and that enough total memory is available to open as many different applications as necessary.

System 7 provides two excellent tools for memory management—the About This Macintosh dialog box and the Get Info dialog box. We'll look at both of these tools in this section.

About This Macintosh

In Finder 7, the familiar ABOUT THE FINDER command has been renamed and is now called ABOUT THIS MACINTOSH; also, the dialog box associated with it has been improved. As shown in Figure 11.4, the About This Macintosh dialog box provides information about the Macintosh being used, your System Software version, installed and available memory, and the amount of memory used by each open application.

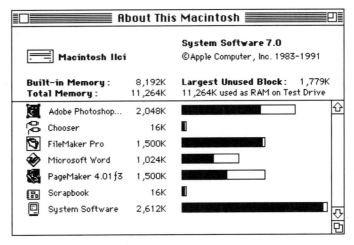

Figure 11.4: The About This Macintosh dialog box.

The upper section of the dialog box gives the icon and name for your Macintosh, the System Software version currently in use, and the following data related to the memory available in your Mac:

- **Built-in Memory.** The amount of actual RAM installed in your Macintosh, not including virtual memory. This listing does not appear on Macintoshes that don't support virtual memory, such as the Macintosh Plus, Classic, Portable and Macintosh II LC.

■ **Total Memory**. Documents the total memory available in your Macintosh, including installed RAM plus available virtual memory. If virtual memory is being used, the name of the hard disk storing that file and the amount of hard drive space being used are listed to the right of the Total Memory listing.

Virtual memory and hard drive designations are set via the Memory control panel, as described earlier in this chapter.

■ **Largest Unused Block**. The largest contiguous section of memory currently not being used by open software applications. This number is important because it determines both the number and size of additional software applications you can open.

In some cases, the Largest Unused Block will not equal the amount of total memory available, less the size of all open applications. That's because as applications are launched and quit, memory becomes fragmented—gaps are created between sections of memory that are used and those that are available. To defragment your memory and create larger unused blocks, quit all open applications and then relaunch them. As they're relaunched, applications will use available memory sequentially, leaving the largest possible unused block.

Each software application requires a particular amount of memory in order to be opened successfully. When a program is launched, if its memory requirement is larger than the Largest Unused Block, it can't be opened. So you need to know approximately how much memory an application needs.

The lower portion of the About This Macintosh dialog box displays
information about each open application, including its name, icon
and amount of memory allocated and used.

■ **Application name and icon**. Each open application is listed
   in alphabetical order along with a small version of its icon.

■ **Amount of memory allocated**. Just to the right of the application name, the total amount of memory allocated to that
   program, along with a bar graph showing this amount in
   relation to amounts used by other open applications. The
   total bar represents total allocated memory; the filled portion
   of the bar represents the portion of that allocated memory
   currently in use.

■ **Amount of memory used**. In most cases when an application is opened, only a portion of its total allocated memory is
   used immediately. Usually, some of the memory is used by the
   application itself, some is used to hold open document files,
   and some is left over for use by the software's commands and
   features. Only the memory currently being used appears as the
   filled-in percentage of the memory allocation bar.

If you leave the About This Macintosh dialog box open and
visible while you work in your applications, you can watch the
memory percentage change as you open files and perform
different software tasks.

An About This Macintosh Tip

- **A secret dialog box.** Holding down the option key changes the ABOUT THIS MACINTOSH command into the ABOUT THE FINDER command, which brings up a copyright screen (shown in Figure 11.5), that first appeared in Finder 1.0 in 1984.

Macintosh Finder © Apple Computer, Inc. 1983-1991

Figure 11.5: The About The Finder dialog box.

Applications and Memory

Using the information provided in the About This Macintosh dialog box, you can take charge of your Macintosh memory. You can adjust memory allocations and take some control over the way the applications use this memory when you find you're running short of memory, or when applications are working improperly due to a shortage of memory.

You set an application's memory allocation in the Get Info dialog box's "Memory" option, as shown in Figure 11.6. The default value for this option is set by the application developer; but often you'll need to reset this option to improve performance of or reduce memory requirements.

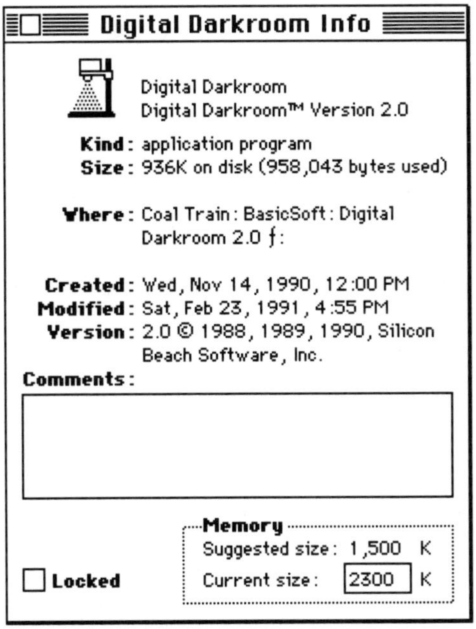

Figure 11.6: The Get Info dialog box for an application.

The "Memory" option has two parts: "Suggested Memory Size" and "Application Memory Size."

- **Suggested Memory Size.** The amount of RAM memory the developer recommends to properly run the application. You can't change this option, but it's very valuable as a reminder of the original "Application Memory Size" setting.

- **Application Memory Size**. Specifies the actual amount of RAM memory that the application will request when it's launched. (By default, the "Application Memory Size" is equal to the "Suggested Memory Size.") You can change the amount of memory that will be allocated by entering a new value in this option, then closing the Get Info dialog box.

When an application is launched, the program requests the amount of memory specified in the "Application Memory Size" option. If this amount is available in an unused block, the memory is allocated and the program is opened. You can check the size of the largest available block in the About This Macintosh dialog box, as described earlier.

If the amount of memory requested is larger than the largest available unused block, a dialog box will appear, either stating that not enough memory is available (shown in Figure 11.7) or asking if you want to try to run the application using less memory (shown in Figure 11.8).

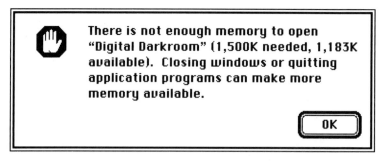

Figure 11.7: The Not Enough Memory dialog box.

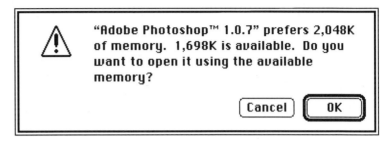

Figure 11.8: The Almost Enough Memory dialog box.

When the application is open, its name appears in the About This Macintosh dialog box—along with the amount of memory allocated and a bar graph displaying total allocated RAM (marked in white) and portion of memory actually being used (marked in black). Watching this bar graph as you work allows you to monitor the application's memory status and anticipate potential problems.

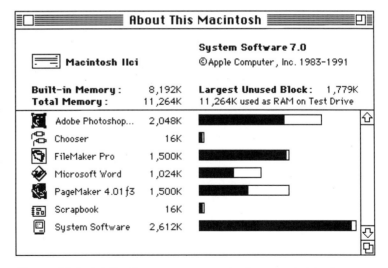

Figure 11.9: Application memory use is documented in the About This Macintosh dialog box.

Optimally, 15 to 25 percent of the space in the memory allocation bar should remain open, or unused. Most applications will not use all their allocated memory at all times—usage will vary as commands and features are used. When an application runs out of memory (the bar is totally black) the potential for crashing increases dramatically. So you usually want each application to have access to slightly more RAM than it needs.

There are actually two reasons for modifying the "Application Memory Size" option: to increase the allocation to improve performance and avoid program crashes; and to *decrease* the requested allocation in order to run the program using less memory.

Increasing Application Memory

Making the Application Memory Size larger than the Suggested Memory Size provides additional memory that can in many cases improve application performance, allow larger and more complete document files to be opened and reduce or eliminate the possibility of memory-related crashes.

These effects are hardly surprising, when you consider how an application uses its allocated memory: it must control and manage its own code, data from any open document files, and all data manipulations performed by its commands and features. And it must do all this with an allocated memory that's less than the total size of the application program and its data files, let alone what it needs to manipulate its data. As a result, software must constantly shift parts of its own code and data from open documents back and forth between disk-storage memory and real memory. Providing additional memory minimizes this activity and allows the program to concentrate on operating efficiently.

For most programs, increasing the Application Memory Size by 20 to 25 percent is optimal, but if you experience frequent "out of memory" errors in any software application, continue increasing the Application Memory Size until these errors are eliminated. (As described above, most programs should display approximately 15 to 25 percent free space in the memory allocation bar in the Get Info dialog box.)

Decreasing Application Memory

Setting the Application Memory Size below the Suggested Memory Size usually lets you successfully launch the application with less memory. This is not generally a recommended practice, but in many cases software will operate successfully using less RAM than the developer suggested.

Don't be afraid to try it—just be sure to test the application in this configuration before working on important data, and save frequently once you begin working. Start by reducing the Application Memory Size only 5 to 10 percent; if you find the About This Macintosh dialog box shows large amounts of unused space, you may be able to reduce the allocation even more.

With the advent of virtual memory support, the need for most Macintosh users to reduce the Application Memory Size should become less common. Even if you have only 2 megabytes of RAM installed, using virtual memory is preferable to reducing the Application Memory Size.

You're less likely to experience crashes or loss of data using virtual memory than with Application Memory Sizes reduced. (See the complete discussion of virtual memory earlier in this chapter.)

Of course, the best long-range solution is to add enough RAM to your Macintosh so you won't have to depend on either virtual memory or Application Memory Size reductions.

Conclusion...

The amount of memory available on your Macintosh determines, in large measure, what you can do with your computer. As we've seen in this chapter, System 7 gives you much more control over memory availability and how that memory is utilized.

- Virtual memory lets you "create" memory by using space on your hard drive.

- 32-bit addressing makes it possible to access a vast amount of memory.

- The Get Info dialog box helps you control the amount of memory an application uses.

- The About This Macintosh dialog box provides constant feedback about what's happening with your Mac's memory.

And so we conclude our look at System 7. Over the past 11 chapters, we've examined nearly every aspect of the System Software, and, we hope, provided the explanations, information, tips, tricks and suggestions you were looking for when you first grabbed this book off the bookstore shelf.

Remember, as System 7 continues to evolve, and new tips and tricks are discovered, we'll keep you informed with *The System 7 News*, the free newsletter you're entitled to with the purchase of this book. (See the ordering coupon in the back of the book for details.) And until then, we welcome your comments, suggestions and discoveries; see the *Foreword* for information on how to reach us.

Appendix A: Installing System 7

Installing System 7 requires three steps: preparing your hard drive, running the System 7 Installer and arranging the files on your hard disk so that you can use your system comfortably and efficiently.

Preparing your hard drive includes backing up your data and arranging the fonts, desk accessories, Fkeys, sounds and inits so that they can be ready for System 7. The System 7 Installer can be run from a System 7 CD-ROM; from the System 7 Installation floppy disk set; or from an AppleShare file server on your network. Like past System Software installers, it allows you to customize the files and utilities it provides. Post-installation tasks include installing fonts, desk accessories, Fkeys, sounds and inits that you work with during the pre-installation, and customizing your Mac using the tools described earlier in this book.

This appendix takes you step-by-step through the installation process, and provides all the information you need to get started with System 7.

Hardware Requirements

You can install System 7 on any Macintosh model, as long as it has at least 2 megs of installed memory and a hard disk drive. You'll need 3 to 5 megabytes of free hard drive space (depending on the installation options you choose) to hold System 7 and all its related files.

If you have a Macintosh Plus, Classic, SE, II, LC or Portable, you can't use System 7's "Virtual Memory" or "32-Bit Addressing" options. If you have a Macintosh IIx, IIcx, a Mac II with an optional PMMU installed, or an SE/30, you can use the "Virtual Memory" but not the "32-Bit Addressing" option. Users of the Macintosh IIci, IIsi and IIfx can use all System 7 features.

System 7 is compatible with all existing Macintosh SCSI peripherals, although some of the inits or control panels these peripherals use may be incompatible. In most cases, you'll be able to get new System 7-compatible software from hardware vendors. Most third-party video monitors and display adaptors should also be compatible, although software driver updates may be required for these, too. Any printers you currently use with your Macintosh will continue to be compatible.

Preparing to Install

Before running the System 7 Installer application, it's important to back up your existing data and prepare your hard drive. There are several different ways to prepare your hard drive, involving varying degrees of effort, complexity and security:

- The simplest and most common way is to verify the compatibility of the software on your hard drive, then run the System 7 Installer.

- The second, more complex method assumes that installing a completely new System folder is a better way to start. This requires completely removing the existing inits, DA's and cdevs from your System folder then reinstalling them after the installation.

- The third method adds reinitializing, or reformatting, of the hard drive to the second step. This method is used mostly by Mac fanatics, who take advantage of the upgrading "event" to improve hard drive performance.

Back Up Your Hard Drive

No matter which path you take to prepare for the installation of System 7, your first step should be a complete backup of all data on your hard drive. There's always the remote possibility that the installation process could leave your hard drive inaccessible. It would be foolish to install System 7 without first backing up your data!

In fact, you should always back up your data before performing any
major modification to your hard drive or System Software. If you have
a regular backup scheme in place, the effort required to do a backup
should be minimal. If you don't have a regular backup scheme in
place, then the effort required will be worth it, and if you're smart
you'll use this opportunity to start a new habit of complete and regular
backups.

If your hard drive is partitioned, be sure to back up each partition.
Although the System 7 installation will be targeted as a single partition
only, it will affect the hard drive in ways that could put all your data at
risk. Again, this is highly unlikely but worth the effort of taking pre-
cautions.

So, have you backed up your data yet? DO NOT CONTINUE until
you've done a complete backup!

Run the Compatibility Checker

To help you discover which inits, cdevs, utilities and applications
you're currently using are compatible with System 7, Apple developed
the Compatibility Checker HyperCard stack, which provides a very
good, although not comprehensive, survey of the files on your hard
drive and a summary of the way these files will react once System 7 is
installed.

The stack also provides a handy tool for moving all your System folder
files known to be incompatible, or untested by Apple for compatibility,
to a special System folder subfolder, where they will not conflict with
System 7. You can then test each of these files individually, or replace
them with newer System 7-Friendly versions.

In order to use the Compatibility Checker, you must have HyperCard Version 1.2.2 if you're using System Software 6.05 or earlier, and HyperCard Version 2.1 if you're using System Software 6.05 or later. You can launch the Compatibility Checker stack directly, or it can be accessed through the Before You Install System 7 Stack.

After launching the Compatibility Checker, you move to the Set Up card, as shown in Figure A.1. You can use this card when you want to select volumes to check their applications and utilities for System 7 compatibility. In most cases, you should select all of the volumes you'll use on your new system. Click the START CHECKING button to initiate the verification process.

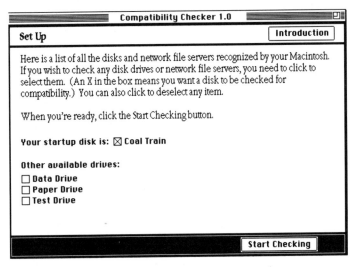

Figure A.1: The Compatibility Checker's Set Up card.

As the Compatibility Checker examines your volumes, a progress bar documents percentage of completion. When all volumes and the current System folder have been checked, an incompatibility warning card, like the one shown in Figure A.2, will appear on-screen if a problem or a suspected incompatible file has been found in the System folder. This card lists files known to be incompatible with System 7 and those not checked for compatibility.

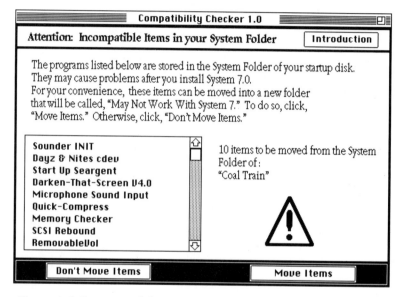

Figure A.2: Incompatibility Warning card.

The Compatibility Checker can move these files to a safe location, the May Not Work With System 7 folder, where they can't cause problems. This is done by clicking the Move Items button. You can later replace those that are incompatible with newer System 7-compatible versions, and test those that Apple has not tested.

The next card that appears is the complete Compatibility Report (shown in Figure A.3), which lists each executable file found on the selected volumes, plus each init or cdev, and documents its status as identified by Apple.

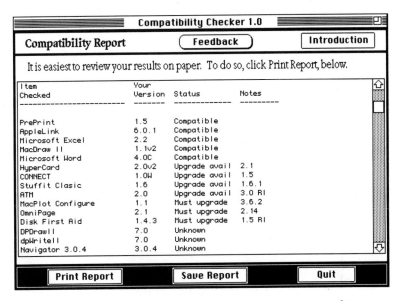

Figure A.3: Compatibility Report as it appears on-screen. (Note: Data shown may not be accurate. See your Compatibility Checker for specific information.)

There are four main status categories in this report:

- **Compatible**. An application is either System 7-compatible, or System 7-Friendly and you'll have no problems using it with System 7.

- **Upgrade available**. Although your version is System 7-compatible, the software developer recommends using a more recent version with System 7.

- **Must upgrade**. The software is incompatible with System 7. You must use a newer version with your new System Software.

- **Unknown**. The software has not been tested for compatibility. Most of these items will prove compatible with System 7, but you'll have to make that determination yourself, as described later in this chapter.

Other codes also appear next to some status names. They're explained in the lower portion of the Compatibility Report.

It's a good idea to print the entire Compatibility Report, by clicking the PRINT REPORT button, since you'll probably need this information later. You can also use the Save REPORT button to write the report to disk, which lets you view the report in your favorite word processor.

Choose the Quit command to exit HyperCard.

Preparation Scheme 1: Quick and Dirty

The most common and most straightforward method of preparing to install System 7 involves nothing more than running the Compatibility Checker.

- **Run the Compatibility Checker.** Use the MOVE ITEMS button to place all incompatible and untested items in the May Not Work With System 7 folder. Print a copy of your Compatibility Report using the PRINT REPORT button.

Then, using the System 7 Installer, System 7 will be placed into your existing System folder, replacing the current System Software files. Fonts, desk accessories and the inits and cdevs that were not moved by the Compatibility Checker will be automatically positioned.

Complete details on the System 7 Installer are provided later in this chapter.

Preparation Scheme 2: Safe and Sure

Rather than installing System 7 over your existing System Software, you can manually remove all fonts, DA's, Fkeys and non-System files from your System folder, delete that System folder and install System 7. This allows the System 7 Installer to create a new System folder without having to move any existing resources or files.

This installation strategy has two possible benefits. First, since the software installation is "fresh," there's no chance that incompatible files will appear in your System folder, or that the installation will have trouble removing your existing System Software. Second, by manually moving all your fonts, DA's, inits, cdevs and other files, you get the chance to reconsider each before adding them to your System 7 System folder. This allows you to remove some items you really don't need, and makes a more efficiently organized System folder.

1) **Run the Compatibility Checker.** Use the MOVE ITEMS button to place all incompatible and untested items in the May Not Work With System 7 folder. Print a copy of your Compatibility Report using the PRINT REPORT button.

2) **Remove existing fonts.** Use the Font/DA Mover to copy all fonts except Chicago, Geneva, New York, Monaco, Times, Helvetica, Courier and Symbol out of the System file and into a new Suitcase file. (If you have complete families of Times, Helvetica and Courier fonts in your System folder, rather than the Apple-supplied versions, you should include these in your new font Suitcase. If you have full families, you'll see font version listings such as "B Times Bold"; or the font names appear in their respective bold and italic type in the Font/DA Mover listing.)

This suitcase file should be saved out of the System folder, and you should place a backup copy on a floppy disk or other backup volume.

3) **Remove existing DA's**: Use the Font/DA Mover to copy all DA's except Puzzle, control panel, Alarm Clock, Chooser and Keycaps to a new Suitcase file.

This Suitcase file should be saved out of the System folder, and you should place a backup copy on a floppy disk or other backup volume.

4) **Remove existing Fkeys**: If Fkeys were ever installed into your System file, move them out into a separate file.

5) **Remove other non-System Software files**. Copy all files in your System folder that aren't part of the Apple System Software into a new folder, including all inits, cdevs, dictionaries, preferences files, help files and others. If possible, sort these files into separate folders according to type. Copy the May Not Be Compatible With System 7 Folder created by the Compatibility Checker into this new folder as well. Back up all these files onto floppy disks or other backup volume.

6) **Delete the existing System folder.** To do this, restart your Macintosh with a floppy boot disk. Drag the System folder to the Trash Can, and choose the EMPTY TRASH command from the Special Menu. (Be sure you've backed up your entire hard disk and all the fonts, DA's and other System folder files before taking these steps.)

You're now ready to use the System 7 Installer to install System 7. A new System folder will be created on your hard disk. (Complete details on using the System 7 Installer, how to reinstall the fonts, DA's and other files you removed from your old System folder are included in the "Configuring System 7" section later in this appendix.)

Preparation Scheme 3: Safer and Surer

As you can see from the length of this appendix, installing new System Software is a major effort. Many people take advantage of this remodeling process to reinitialize or reformat the hard drive. This step is not required, but it's a good idea, especially if your hard drive has not been reformatted in some time (or since it was brand new). It can increase the overall safety of your data and improve your hard drive performance.

Reformatting your hard drive is not really difficult. However, reformatting removes all data currently stored on the drive, and can cause or uncover problems that were "waiting to happen." Therefore, you should not proceed unless you

A) have a few hours to kill.

B) have made two backup copies of all the data on your hard drive (yes TWO!).

C) have the formatting software originally used to format your hard drive or a commercially available package like SilverLining (I recommend using SilverLining instead of the software included with your hard drive, in most cases).

D) are comfortable with the idea of formatting your hard drive, or can get assistance from someone with experience in this type of operation.

If all of these are true, then

1) **Perform Steps 1-5 as described in Preparation Scheme 2.** Back up all fonts, DA's and other files that were removed from the System folder to floppy disks or another backup volume.

2) **Format your hard drive.** Take the time to let the formatting software test all the blocks on your hard drive. Any "soft spots" identified can be remapped so they're not used to store any of your data.

You're now ready to use the System 7 Installer to install System 7.

After the installation,

3) **Configure the System folder.** Following the steps described in the "Configuring System 7" section of this appendix, add the fonts, inits, control panels and other files to your System folder.

4) **Restore your software and utilities.** From your backup, add all your software applications then your utility programs to your hard disk. Adding these files before restoring any of your data writes them sequentially in your hard drive's foremost blocks. This helps to keep your hard drive defragmented and improves performance.

5) **Restore all your data files.** From your backup, copy all data back onto your hard drive.

Using the Installer

The System 7 Installer application can be run from the System 7 CD-ROM, from floppy disk or from a mounted AppleShare file server. Unlike earlier versions of the Installer, you can actually install System 7 onto the hard drive that's your current Startup Disk (the one containing the System Software the Mac is currently using).

Before running the Installer, you should disable any virus-checking utilities you regularly use, since these would likely be triggered repeatedly by the actions of the Installer, making it difficult or impossible for the Installer to complete its tasks successfully.

If you are going to install from an AppleShare volume containing the System 7 installer, mount that volume normally, using the Chooser. If you're installing from a System 7 CD-ROM, insert the CD so it appears on your Finder desktop. To install from the System 7 floppy disk set, insert Install Disk 1.

Launch the installer application by double-clicking on its icon. You're now ready to install System 7.

Setting Installer Options

The first screen of the Installer is the Easy Install dialog box, shown in Figure A.4, which includes a recommended set of installation options. It also displays the name of the drive the System Software will be installed on. If the selected disk is not the one on want, click the SWITCH DISK button until the name of the desired hard drive appears.

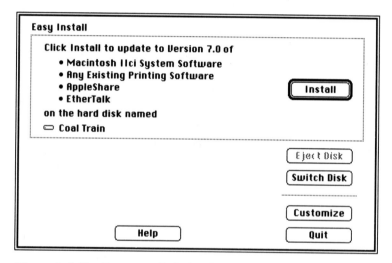

Figure A.4: The Easy Install dialog box.

There are three ways to proceed from the Easy Install dialog box:

- **Install**. Click the INSTALL button to install the listed software onto the named hard disk or volume. Use this option if you're sure you want the recommended options, or you're not sure which options you want installed. (The discussion later in this chapter should help you avoid that situation.)

- **Customize**. Clicking the "Customize" option lets you select the specific options you want installed along with your System Software. The Customize dialog box is shown in Figure A.5, and details on all customization options follow.

- **Quit**. Forget this whole thing, let's go back to System Software 6.0x!

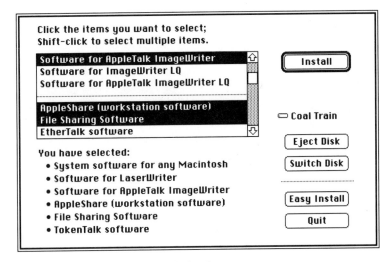

Figure A.5: The Customize dialog box.

The scrolling window in the Customize dialog box provides options covering the System Software, printing software, File Sharing software and network driver software. Click on the options you want, holding down the shift key to select multiple items.

Summary of Customize dialog box options:

- **System Software**. These options include System Software For Any Macintosh, System Software For <Specific Macintosh>, Minimal System Software For Any Macintosh and Minimal

System Software For <Specific Macintosh>. Choose only one option that includes the words System Software.

Choose System Software For Any Macintosh if the hard drive you're installing System 7 on will be connected to different Macintosh computers at different times. If you were to choose one of the System Software options specific to one Macintosh model, that hard disk would not be able to start up some Macintosh models. This option might add a few more files than you really need for your Macintosh, but these files consume only a few K of disk space and will cause no problems for you.

Choose System Software For <Specific Macintosh> if you're sure the hard drive you're installing on will be used with one specific Macintosh model only.

Choose Minimal System Software For Any Macintosh if you're installing on a hard drive that will be used on more than one Macintosh model, but you have limited free space on that hard drive.

The "Minimal" option can also be used to create a 1.44mb floppy disk of System 7.

Choose Minimal System Software For <Specific Macintosh> if you're sure that the hard drive you're installing on will be used with one specific Macintosh model only, and there's limited free space on that hard drive.

- **Printer drivers**. The options for printer drivers include Software For All Apple Printers, Software For LaserWriter, Software For Personal LaserWriter SC, Software For ImageWriter and

Software For AppleTalk ImageWriter. Choose according to the printers you'll use with your Macintosh. There's no limit to how many of these options you can select.

- **File Sharing software**. If you will be operating System 7 on a network and want to share folders or volumes with other Macintoshes or access your hard drive from another network Macintosh, select this option.

- **Network drivers**. If an Ethertalk or Tokentalk network card is installed in your Macintosh, select the appropriate network driver option. You can install both of these drivers, but you'll likely need only one of them at most. If you're using an AppleTalk network, you don't have to select either option.

After selecting the appropriate options, click the INSTALL button to begin the installation. You can also use the EASY INSTALL button to return to the previous dialog box, or the QUIT button to cancel the entire installation.

Once the installation begins, its progress is displayed. If you're installing from floppy disks, you'll be prompted for disks as required. When the installation is complete, the Installation Successful dialog box, appears. Click the CONTINUE button if you need to return to the Easy Install dialog box, or the QUIT button, to return to the Finder.

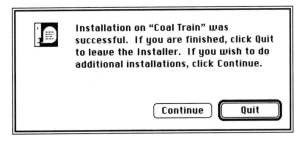

Figure A.6: Installation Successful dialog box.

After quitting the Installer, you should restart your Macintosh to confirm that installation was successful and that System 7 will launch properly. Welcome to System 7!

Configuring System 7

Now you can customize your System Software by adding fonts to the System file and adding additional extensions, control panels and other files to the System folder. You can then convert your desk accessories, and start taking advantage of new System 7 features by configuring the Label Menu and customizing the Apple Menu.

Installing Fonts

Fonts are installed into the System file in System 7 by simply opening the font Suitcase (double-click on it) and dragging the font icons onto the System folder icon, the System file icon, or into the open System file window. PostScript screen fonts and TrueType fonts are installed this way. (See "Configuring Your System" in Chapter 8 for details on the font installation process.)

You can also use fonts without installing them into the System file via utilities like Suitcase II or MasterJuggler. These utilities are still very useful with System 7 because they allow you to attach and detach fonts more quickly than you could add or remove them from the System file.

For your PostScript fonts, you can drag printer font files into the open System file window, but don't drag them onto the System folder icon; if you do, they'll be placed in the Extensions folder and as of this writing they won't work properly there.

Installing Extensions and Control Panels

Extensions (inits) and control panels are installed into the System folder by dragging their icons onto the System folder icon. The Macintosh will then automatically place them in the Extensions or Control Panels folder. Alternatively, you can manually drag them into the Extensions or Control Panels folder yourself. (See "Adding Files to the System Folder" in Chapter 4 for more information on installing extensions and control panels.)

Since extensions and control panels can contain init code—executed at startup—that modifies the System file as it's loaded into memory, it's important to avoid those that are incompatible with System 7. The report you created with the Compatibility Checker will identify extensions and control panels that are compatible and those that require an upgrade before they can be used with System 7.

Copy all files the Compatibility Checker listed as compatible to the System folder. Don't install those requiring an upgrade; contact the software developer at the address listed in the Compatibility Report to obtain a compatible version.

Many of your files will be listed by the Compatibility Checker as "Unknown," which leaves it up to you to test their compatibility. The only way to do this is to add these files one at a time to your System folder, then restart your Macintosh and test for compatibility.

It's easy to tell that a file is incompatible—your Mac crashes on startup. If this happens, press the reset switch on your Macintosh or turn its power off and on, then hold down the shift key during startup. This will disable all extensions, allowing you to open the System folder and remove the incompatible file.

If the Macintosh starts up without incident, test the init or extension by using it in one or two different situations. In most cases, if incompatibilities didn't show up during startup, they'll become apparent as soon as the extension or control panel is used. If you find an incompatible file, remove it from your System folder.

Continue this testing process for each new init and extension until all the ones you want to use have been added.

To make this task easier, check Macintosh-related magazines and your local user group for extended compatibility lists. If your inits or control panels are listed as compatible, you won't need to do your own testing.

Installing Other Files

If you removed other files from your previous System folder, such as dictionaries, help files, preferences files or even entire folders, reinstall those by copying them into the System folder. Most of these files should go into the System folder itself, although some preferences files may operate properly if installed into the Preferences folder.

One hopes that in future software applications upgrades all these ancillary files will be placed into the Preferences folder, allowing the System folder itself to remain uncluttered.

Converting Desk Accessories

If you installed System 7 over your existing System Software, the desk accessories in your System folder were automatically removed from their DA Suitcases and placed into the Apple Menu folder found inside the System folder.

If you moved desk accessories into a DA Suitcase before installing System 7, or you want to use DA's that were not in your old System file, you must remove them from their DA Suitcases. Double-click on any DA Suitcase, and all enclosed DA's will appear with individual application icons. Dragging them out of the DA window and into any other folder or volume converts them into double-clickable applications. (A more complete discussion of converting DA's is found in the "Desk Accessories" section of Chapter 5.)

Once a DA has been converted into an application, it can be used just like any application. You can store the converted DA in any folder; you can usually launch it by double-clicking on its icon; and you can install the DA or its alias in the Apple Menu folder so it can be launched from the Apple Menu.

Configuring the Label Menu and the Apple Menu

Now that your System folder is fully configured, you're ready to start using System 7. Although this entire book is dedicated to the new System 7 features, two particularly notable sections are those on customizing the Label Menu, found in *Chapter 3, Managing Your Hard Drive*, and customizing the Apple Menu, in *Chapter 4, The System Folder*.

Briefly, the Label Menu is customized with the Labels control panel, accessed via the Control Panels folder from the Apple Menu. The Apple Menu is customized by adding the aliases of applications, folders, files and volumes to the Apple Menu folder inside the System folder.

Appendix B: Beyond 7.0

Since its initial release, System 7 has been enhanced with several new extensions and a new update—System 7.0.1. The first Apple extension, called MODE32, allows the Macintosh IIx, IIcx, SE/30 and Mac II and LC (with the optional PMMU chip) to use 32-bit addressing, making their ROMs "32-bit clean," as mentioned in Chapter 11. The MODE32 extension is available free from Apple dealers, user groups and on-line bulletin boards.

System 7.0.1 was released to support the new Mac Classic II, Quadra 700, Quadra 900 and the Powerbooks. While it can be used on any Macintosh, Apple has recommended that existing System 7.0 users not upgrade to Version 7.0.1 because it's only needed for the new CPUs. Independent tests, however, have found improvements in the ROM-based Standard Apple Numeric Environment (SANE) on the Mac IIci, IIfx and IIsi if the machines have either a built-in or optional math co-processor.

Tune-Up, another recent Apple release, installs an extension called System 7 Tuner, as well as new versions of the Chooser, File Sharing Extension, LaserWriter and StyleWriter files. Installing the Tune-Up files improves the performance of System 7.0 or 7.0.1, fixes a number of bugs in the first two releases of System 7, allows the Finder to copy files faster, improves printing speeds, enhances memory management (especially in low-memory situations) and corrects several file-sharing problems. The System 7 Tune-Up disk is also free and is available from Apple, Apple dealers, user groups and on-line bulletin boards.

The most recent enhancement to System 7 (as of early 1992) is the QuickTime extension. QuickTime gives System 7 the ability to create and display moving images, as described in Appendix C.

Appendix C: QuickTime

The Macintosh has led the way for personal computers in typography, graphics, sound and high-resolution color. With the introduction of QuickTime, the Mac is the first personal computer to offer video, animation and high-quality sound to all its applications as an integrated part of its system software.

What Is QuickTime?

QuickTime is an extension—enabled when placed into your System Folder's Extensions Folder—that gives your Macintosh the ability to play and record moving video images, animation and sound in ways never before possible. It makes moving images and sounds a basic type of Macintosh data. All types of applications—word processors, databases, presentation graphics packages, spreadsheets, page-layout programs, etc.—will be able to incorporate these moving images as easily as they now do still-motion graphics.

QuickTime can be used on any Macintosh model containing a 68020 or later processor that uses System 6.07, System 7.0 or later.

Although QuickTime was officially released in January 1992 (seven months after the initial release of System 7), Macintosh users could get it from Apple for a small fee prior to that. It was also available at no charge from user groups and bulletin boards. Since January 1992, however, QuickTime is now included as part of the System 7 Personal Upgrade Kit and the System 7 Network Upgrade Kit.

The QuickTime Movie

The QuickTime extension adds support to your Macintosh for a new file format, called Movie, that uses the file type MooV. Like other file formats (Text, Pict, EPS, TIFF, etc.), the Movie file format saves a certain kind of data—in this case moving video, animation or sound (or all of these media)—in a way that will play at a specified rate and quality. By defining this new file format at the system software level, Apple makes it easy for application developers to take advantage of it and create sophisticated uses for moving images on the Macintosh.

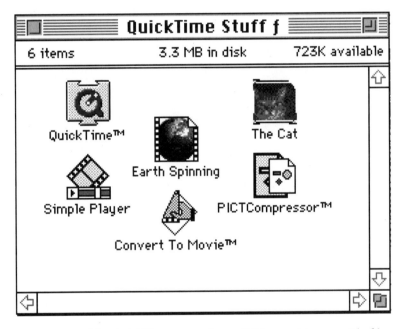

Figure C-1: The QuickTime extension, utilities and two sample files.

A QuickTime movie acts much like any other text or graphic element. You can select a movie, cut, copy or paste it either within or between QuickTime-savvy applications, and store it in the Scrapbook. In most cases, you can't tell that an object is a movie until you select it; before that it looks just like any other graphic element. When selected, however, a movie displays a set of controls that identifies it.

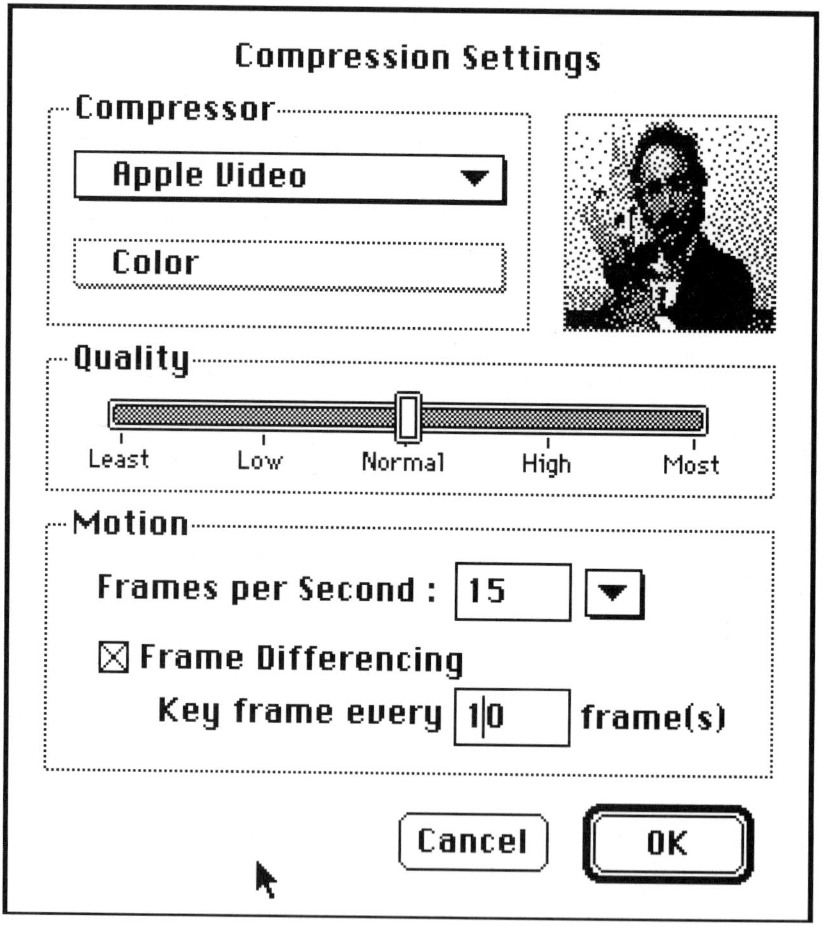

Figure C-2: A standard movie window with controls.

These controls allow you to adjust the volume and play the movie, as well as fast-forward, reverse or randomly adjust the movie. In some applications, these basic controls can be enhanced, but the minimum set of controls are always available.

The image you see in a movie element when the movie isn't playing is called its *poster*. The poster is a selected image from the movie. Because it's often not the first frame of the movie, you'll see the image of the poster jump to another image when the movie begins.

If the poster is a still-frame from the movie, a *preview* is a moving representative of the movie. Not all movies have previews, but most longer ones do. A preview gives you a quick look at the movie highlights. Many standard file dialog boxes let you see the poster or a preview, before opening a movie file.

QuickTime & Data Compression

One of QuickTime's most important technological breakthroughs is the real-time compression and decompression it provides video, animation, photographs and other graphics. Currently, QuickTime supports a number of different compression schemes, including MPEG, JPEG and Group 3 Fax, but it can easily support others as necessary. Initially provided as a software-only solution, compression can achieve ratios as great as 25:1 without any visible loss in image quality. (With specialized hardware, compression ratios as high as 160:1 are possible.) If the appropriate hardware is installed, QuickTime supports hardware compression/decompression.

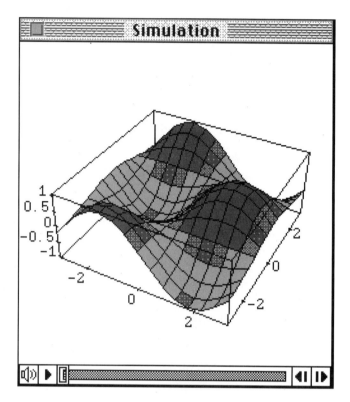

Figure C-3: A QuickTime Compression Options dialog box.

Compression is particularly important because of all the data needed
to generate moving images and accompanying sounds. A good rule of
thumb for estimating movie size is that every minute of motion consumes 10 MB of disk space. As another example, a seven-minute,
full-size, full-resolution video movie could consume 200 MB in its
uncompressed form. Compressed, that same movie might need only
45 MB. Of course, most movies are significantly shorter (lasting between 5 and 30 seconds), so files in the 200K to 1 MB range will be
common.

The actual size of a QuickTime movie depends on the following:

■ Image size. Measured in horizontal and vertical pixels, determines how large the movie will appear on-screen. The larger the image, the larger the movie file.

■ Resolution. QuickTime supports all the Mac's resolutions, including 1, 2, 4, 8, 16, 24 and 32-bit. The higher the resolution, the larger the movie file.

■ Frames per second. Most QuickTime movies are recorded using 10, 12 or 15 frames per second (fps), compared to 30 fps for commercial-quality video. Higher fps rates result in larger movie files.

■ Audio sampling rate. This can be thought of as the "resolution" of the sound. The Macintosh supports 8, 11, 22 or 44 Khz audio sampling. The higher the sampling rate, the larger the sound portion of a movie file.

■ Compression. As mentioned earlier, QuickTime supports a number of compression schemes; and for each you can select the degree of compression used. Increasing compression reduces movie size but will usually also affect quality.

■ Content. Beyond the above-mentioned technical factors, the actual set of sounds and images contained in a movie determines its size.

QuickTime Utilities

With the QuickTime extension, Apple has provided three small utilities to help you get started.

- Simple Player. This utility allows you to open, view and play any type of QuickTime movie.

- Convert To Movie. This program converts many older video and animation formats, including the popular PICS format, to the QuickTime movie format.

- PICTCompressor. With the Movie format, QuickTime offers some extensions to the PICT format. This program lets you compress PICT files to save space on Macs running QuickTime.

Movies & Your Software

Although Apple has provided QuickTime support for movies at the system-software level, not all of your existing applications will immediately support QuickTime movies. In most cases, support for movies will be added to your software in future upgrades. Many Macintosh applications have already been upgraded; other upgrades are scheduled. For specific details, check with your application developers.

To get movie compatibility before your application is upgraded, Apple has released another extension called Wild Magic. This lets most applications that support the PICT file format work with QuickTime movies. Although Wild Magic isn't part of Apple's official QuickTime package, it can be easily obtained from most user groups or on-line bulletin board services. Because it "tricks" older applications into doing something they weren't designed to do, you should be careful when first experimenting with movies in a new application. In many cases, this method works quite well.

Glossary

Alias
: An alias is a duplicate icon created for any file, folder, or volume. The alias icon is linked to the original icon used to create it, and opening the alias opens the original file. Even if an alias is moved or renamed, the link to the original file remains.

Apple Menu folder
: A folder inside the System folder used to hold all applications, documents, folders, volumes and desk accessories that you want to appear in the Apple Menu. Up to 50 files or aliases can be stored in this folder.

Comments

Short descriptive notes attached to any file, folder, or volume. Comments are entered into the Get Info dialog box by choosing the Get Info command. To display comments in Finder windows, use the Views control panel to select the "Show Comments" option. You can search for a file by text contained in its comment using the FIND command.

Control Panels
folder

A folder inside the System folder which contains all control panel files used on a Macintosh. Control panels must reside in this folder so that they are properly loaded at startup, although you can create aliases of them and store those aliases in other locations.

Desktop (level):

The top of the Mac's disk and file hierarchy, equivalent to the display seen at the Finder desktop. The desktop level includes all mounted hard disks and volumes, mounted floppy disks and any files or folders that have been placed on the Finder desktop.

Edition files

Edition files are normal Macintosh files that contain text or graphic elements saved by the CREATE PUBLISHER command. Edition files are imported into other documents using the SUBSCRIBE TO command.

Edition Manager

A feature that allows software applications to exchange data using the PUBLISH and SUBSCRIBE commands. This umbrella term covers both the specific commands associated with data exchange and the underlying technology that manages edition files after they have been created.

Extensions

A small program that modifies or extends the capabilities of the System Software. These include startup programs (inits), printer drivers, network drivers and other types of files. All extensions must be kept in the Extensions folder inside the System folder in order to load properly at startup.

Font Scaler

A small program that is automatically sent to PostScript printers when documents containing TrueType fonts are printed.

File Sharing   A feature that allows any Macintosh running System 7 to make folders and volumes available to other network users, and to access shared data from other File Sharing Macs, or from AppleShare file servers.

Help Balloons   Small information windows that pop-up to provide simple explanations of commands, dialog box options and on-screen icons. Help Balloons only appear when the SHOW BALLOONS command is selected, and can be removed by choosing the HIDE BALLOONS command.

Hiding   Removing the windows of an open application from the screen without quitting the application. This is done with the HIDE commands found in the Applications Menu. To see windows after they are hidden, the SHOW commands are used.

Hierarchical view   The ability of a Finder window to display a folder and the files inside that folder in a single window.

IAC   An abbreviation for Inter-Application Communication. This is a set of protocols that make it possible for Macintosh applications to communicate and control each other. IAC is used by Apple Events, which are commands issued and understood by some software applications that have been specifically upgraded for System 7.

Inits   See Extensions.

Labels   A set of user-defined categories that can be applied to any file, folder, or volume as a means of classification. Labels are defined with a title and color using the Labels control panel, and applied by selecting an icon, or group of icons, and choosing the appropriate label from the Labels menu.

Publish/Subscribe   See the Edition Manager.

Startup folder   A folder inside the System folder used to store applications, folders or documents that you want opened automatically at startup.

Stationery Pads   Any document in System 7 can be designated a Stationery Pad, or template. Stationery Pads are automatically duplicated when opened, providing their content as the starting elements that make it easier to create other documents.

System 7-Friendly   Software applications that pass Apple's checklist for compatibility and compliance with System 7. This checklist includes support for MultiFinder, the Edition Manager, IAC, Balloon help, File Sharing, 32-bit addressing, Stationery Pads, and more. An application that works well under System 7 but fails in one or more of these areas will not be deemed System 7-Friendly by Apple.

System 7-Savvy   Another name for System 7-Friendly, as described above.

32-bit addressing   A method of addressing memory which makes it possible for users of the Mac IIci, IIsi, and IIfx to use up to 128 megabytes of actual memory, and up to 1 gigabyte of virtual memory. Some software is incompatible with 32-bit addressing. The current standard is 24-bit addressing, which is still used on all other Macs, and with software that is not compatible with 32-bit addressing.

TrueType   An outline font format created by Apple for System 7. TrueType fonts are scaled on-screen to provide smooth high resolution display, and print at the resolution of the output device on either PostScript, TrueImage or QuickDraw printers.

TrueImage   A PostScript clone interpreter language, created by Microsoft, and used in some new printers. TrueImage can print PostScript files and supports both PostScript and TrueType fonts.

Virtual memory   A scheme which allows hard drive space to act like RAM, providing applications with additional memory. Because it uses hard drive space in place of SIMMs, virtual memory comes as close to providing something for nothing as anything you're likely to find on the Macintosh.

Index

the Ventana Press

Desktop Design Series

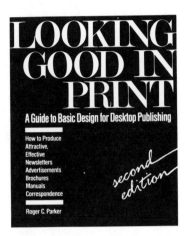

Newsletters from the Desktop
$23.95
306 pages, Illustrated
ISBN: 0-940087-40-5

Now the millions of desktop publishers who produce newsletters can learn how to improve the design of their publications.

The Makeover Book: 101 Design Solutions for Desktop Publishing
$17.95
282 pages, Illustrated
ISBN: 0-940087-20-0

"Before-and-after" desktop publishing examples demonstrate how basic design revisions can dramatically improve a document.

Type from the Desktop
$23.95
290 pages, Illustrated
ISBN: 0-940087-45-6

Learn the basics of designing with type from a desktop publisher's perspective.

Looking Good in Print, Second Edition
$23.95
410 pages, Illustrated
ISBN: 0-940087-32-4

With over 100,000 in print, **Looking Good in Print** is looking even better. More makeovers, a new section on designing newsletters and a wealth of new design tips and techniques to broaden the design skills of the ever-growing number of desktop publishers.

The Presentation Design Book
$24.95
258 pages, Illustrated
ISBN: 0-940087-37-5

How to design effective, attractive slides, overheads, graphs, diagrams, handouts and screen shows with your desktop computer.

PageMaker Design Companion
$21.95
300 pages, Illustrated
ISBN: 0-940087-79-0

A complete, fact-filled guide which illustrates PageMaker's powerful graphics capabilities and teaches users to create a wide range of appealing documents.

Available Fall 1991

TO ORDER additional copies of *The System 7 Book* or any other Ventana Press books, please fill out this order form and return it to us for quick shipment.

	Quantity	Price	Total
The System 7 Book	_____	x $22.95 =	$_____
Looking Good in Print	_____	x $23.95 =	$_____
The Gray Book	_____	x $22.95 =	$_____
The Makeover Book	_____	x $17.95 =	$_____
Type From the Desktop	_____	x $23.95 =	$_____
The Presentation Design Book	_____	x $24.95 =	$_____
Newsletters From the Desktop	_____	x $23.95 =	$_____
The PageMaker Design Companion	_____	x $23.95 =	$_____

Shipping: Please add $4.50/first book for standard UPS, $1.35/book thereafter; $8.00/book UPS "two-day air," $2.25/book thereafter. For Canada, add $8.10/book.

= $_____

Send C.O.D. (add $4.20 to shipping charges) = $_____

North Carolina residents add 6% sales tax = $_____

Total = $_____

Name _____

Company _____

Address (No P.O. Box) _____

City _____ State _____ Zip _____

Daytime Phone _____

_____ Payment enclosed (check or money order; no cash, please)

_____ VISA _____ MC Acc't # _____

Expiration Date _____ Signature _____

Please mail or fax to:

Ventana Press, P.O. Box 2468, Chapel Hill, NC 27515

919/942-0220, FAX: 800/877-7955

T O ORDER additional copies of *The System 7 Book* or any other Ventana Press books, please fill out this order form and return it to us for quick shipment.

	Quantity	Price	Total
The System 7 Book	_____ x	$22.95 =	$_____
Looking Good in Print	_____ x	$23.95 =	$_____
The Gray Book	_____ x	$22.95 =	$_____
The Makeover Book	_____ x	$17.95 =	$_____
Type From the Desktop	_____ x	$23.95 =	$_____
The Presentation Design Book	_____ x	$24.95 =	$_____
Newsletters From the Desktop	_____ x	$23.95 =	$_____
The PageMaker Design Companion	_____ x	$23.95 =	$_____

Shipping: Please add $4.50/first book for standard UPS, $1.35/book thereafter; $8.00/book UPS "two-day air," $2.25/book thereafter. For Canada, add $8.10/book.

= $_____

Send C.O.D. (add $4.20 to shipping charges)   = $_____

North Carolina residents add 6% sales tax   = $_____

Total = $_____

Name _____

Company _____

Address (No P.O. Box) _____

City _____ State _____ Zip _____

Daytime Phone _____

_____ Payment enclosed (check or money order; no cash, please)

_____ VISA   _____ MC   Acc't # _____

Expiration Date _____ Signature _____

Please mail or fax to:

Ventana Press, P.O. Box 2468, Chapel Hill, NC 27515

919/942-0220, FAX: 800/877-7955

To ORDER additional copies of *The System 7 Book* or any other Ventana Press books, please fill out this order form and return it to us for quick shipment.

	Quantity	Price	Total
The System 7 Book	_____ x	$22.95 =	$_____
Looking Good in Print	_____ x	$23.95 =	$_____
The Gray Book	_____ x	$22.95 =	$_____
The Makeover Book	_____ x	$17.95 =	$_____
Type From the Desktop	_____ x	$23.95 =	$_____
The Presentation Design Book	_____ x	$24.95 =	$_____
Newsletters From the Desktop	_____ x	$23.95 =	$_____
The PageMaker Design Companion	_____ x	$23.95 =	$_____

Shipping: Please add $4.50/first book for standard UPS, $1.35/book thereafter; $8.00/book UPS "two-day air," $2.25/book thereafter. For Canada, add $8.10/book.   = $_____

Send C.O.D. (add $4.20 to shipping charges)   = $_____

North Carolina residents add 6% sales tax   = $_____

                                             Total = $_____

Name _____

Company_____

Address (No P.O. Box) _____

City_____ State _____ Zip _____

Daytime Phone _____

_____ Payment enclosed (check or money order; no cash, please)

_____VISA _____ MC   Acc't # _____

Expiration Date _____ Signature _____

Please mail or fax to:

Ventana Press, P.O. Box 2468, Chapel Hill, NC 27515

919/942-0220, FAX: 800/877-7955

A Good Way to Stay Ahead of the System

Two Free Issues of System 7 News

As System 7 evolves, you'll want to stay up-to-date on everything from bug fixes to new features. Twice a year, *The System 7 Book* author Craig Danuloff will provide the news you need to stay abreast of any changes in Apple's new operating environment.

You'll learn new tips, tricks and shortcuts to streamline your work; you'll also get the latest on new System 7 utilities, shareware and hot third-party applications.

If you purchased *The System 7 Book* directly from Ventana Press, you'll receive *System 7 News* automatically. If you purchased the book elsewhere, please complete the form below and return it.

Order card for *System 7 News*, two free updates on the Mac's System Software:

Name _____

Company _____

Address_____

City_____ State _____ Zip _____

Telephone: _____

A Good Way to Stay Ahead of the System

Two Free Issues of System 7 News

As System 7 evolves, you'll want to stay up-to-date on everything from bug fixes to new features. Twice a year, *The System 7 Book* author Craig Danuloff will provide the news you need to stay abreast of any changes in Apple's new operating environment.

You'll learn new tips, tricks and shortcuts to streamline your work; you'll also get the latest on new System 7 utilities, shareware and hot third-party applications.

If you purchased *The System 7 Book* directly from Ventana Press, you'll receive *System 7 News* automatically. If you purchased the book elsewhere, please complete the form below and return it.